D1476937

American Cooking: The Melting Pot

LIFE WORLD LIBRARY
LIFE NATURE LIBRARY
TIME READING PROGRAM
THE LIFE HISTORY OF THE UNITED STATES
LIFE SCIENCE LIBRARY
GREAT AGES OF MAN
TIME-LIFE LIBRARY OF ART
TIME-LIFE LIBRARY OF AMERICA
FOODS OF THE WORLD
THIS FABULOUS CENTURY
LIFE LIBRARY OF PHOTOGRAPHY
THE TIME-LIFE ENCYCLOPEDIA OF GARDENING
THE AMERICAN WILDERNESS
FAMILY LIBRARY
    THE TIME-LIFE BOOK OF FAMILY FINANCE
    THE TIME-LIFE FAMILY LEGAL GUIDE

American Cooking:
The Melting Pot

by

James P. Shenton, Angelo M. Pellegrini,

Dale Brown, Israel Shenker

and Peter Wood

and the Editors of

TIME-LIFE BOOKS

photographed by Richard Meek

TIME-LIFE BOOKS, NEW YORK

THE CONSULTANT: James A. Beard *(above, left)* is the leading authority on regional American foods. His many books include *How to Eat Better for Less Money, Delights and Prejudices* and *The James Beard Cook Book.*

THE CONSULTING EDITOR: The late Michael Field *(above, right)* was one of America's best-known culinary experts and cooking teachers. His books include *Michael Field's Cooking School, Michael Field's Culinary Classics and Improvisations* and *All Manner of Food.*

THE PHOTOGRAPHER: Richard Meek *(above, left)* did most of the photography for this book. His work also appears in four other FOODS OF THE WORLD volumes: *The Cooking of Scandinavia, The Cooking of the Caribbean Islands, American Cooking: The Northwest* and *American Cooking: The Great West.* Still-life materials for his pictures were chosen by Yvonne McHarg.

THE CHEF: John Clancy *(above, right)* heads the kitchen staff that tested the recipes for this book and the other volumes in the FOODS OF THE WORLD library. He also teaches cooking classes in Manhattan and on Long Island.

THE AUTHORS: Several contributed to the text material in this volume. Pictures of five of them appear on page 208, and brief biographies appear on the opening pages of their chapters.

THE COVER: Many peoples have brought many soups to America, and some have become vital parts of the national cuisine. Among the most popular or potentially popular are *(clockwise, starting with the Oriental spoon)* Chinese cellophane-noodle soup with meatballs; Italian minestrone; Jewish chicken soup with matzo balls; creamy Romanian leek *ciorba,* sprinkled with parsley and chives; Hungarian goulash soup; and Puerto Rican *sopa de fideos,* a puréed vegetable soup with vermicelli and rounds of corn.

Contents

The Recipe Booklet that accompanies this volume has been designed for use in the kitchen. It contains more than 145 recipes, including all of those printed here. It also has a wipe-clean cover and a spiral binding so that it can either stand up or lie flat when open.

The place: New York Harbor; the year: 1905. About to disembark, an immigrant Italian family gets its first close look at the country where it has cast its lot. Another Italian family's experience with the Melting Pot is told in Chapter 2.

Introduction:

Finis to the Biggest Library in the Food World

After five and a half years of staff work, after 27 volumes and 27 Recipe Booklets, after the testing and tasting of some 3,000 recipes, and after translations into seven languages for more than 25 countries, the FOODS OF THE WORLD library is at last complete. This book, called *The Melting Pot,* offers a sampling of cuisines brought to America and naturalized by millions of families like the expectant group about to disembark at left. And it is the final volume in the library.

The library has been a success, with an average of two million copies sold each year, and a minimum of complaints about soufflés that failed to rise. So many things in this world refuse to go according to plan that it is a pleasure for the editors to look back over this undertaking and say, "It's done, it worked and we planned it that way."

Planning it and sticking to the plan was a good part of the pleasure. Food is one of the most subjective of all subjects, and "the food field" is one of the most temperament-ridden of all establishments. We decided to embrace that problem, and accordingly we planned to have the books in the library written not by conference committees and not by Milquetoasts, but by authors who knew their minds and could speak their minds; and for illustrations we looked for photographers with their own definite points of view. We also wanted the best consultants anywhere, to help create authentic and workable recipes. That called for some marvelous manhunts to seek such people out and sign them up, in places like Tiberio's in London; the Château Mercuès and Vienne and Plascassier, all in France; and restaurants in Tangier, Morocco, and St. Helena, California. We did not get everybody we hoped to enlist but we got some we had not counted on, such as one notoriously cantankerous food authority who began by sniffing in public at our maiden effort (on the cooking of provincial France) and wound up writing one of our books (on classic French cooking). And to avoid any armchair editing, we made sure that no matter what country or region we were to deal with, somebody went there specifically in behalf of FOODS OF THE WORLD.

The combined experiences and contributions of all those who worked on the library—several hundred people in all—amount to a major exercise in group journalism. As the one whose responsibility has been to orchestrate the group, I'd like to thank, and congratulate, them all.

—*Richard L. Williams, Editor*
FOODS OF THE WORLD

I

by JAMES P. SHENTON

A professor of American history at Columbia University, James Shenton has specialized in the study of immigrants in the United States. He has lectured on television and written, among other books, *An Historian's History of the United States*.

The Infinite Variety of the Melting Pot

Ingredients from all over the world, each important in the Melting Pot cuisines, have found their way into American markets. 1. Coriander leaves *(cilantro)*; 2. Cross sections of lotus root; 3. Cellophane noodles; 4. Garlic heads; 5. Green (unripe) plantain; 6. Papaya; 7. Jumbo pasta shells; 8. Plum tomatoes; 9. Hot dried red peppers; 10. Hot pickled red peppers; 11. *Kolbász;* 12. Sweet red bell peppers; 13. Matzos; 14. Red cabbage. (For information on some of these ingredients, see Glossary.)

In 20th Century America a single family can be a Melting Pot in miniature. I know this as a historian—but I also know it more directly, as a member of just such a family. When my mother brings her four children and 12 grandchildren together at her table, she presides over a complex ethnic medley—English, Irish, Slovak, Polish, Italian, Dutch, Scottish and French Canadian. This American mini-League of Nations, assembled over a span of three generations, represents an equally complex variety of the world's cuisines, all now somewhat Americanized and all good.

The story of the mixture really begins with my grandparents. In 1919 my paternal grandparents brought my father and his three brothers from Macclesfield, England, to Paterson, New Jersey. They were Protestants, convinced of the eternal superiority of all things English. Five years later, my father complicated the family heritage by marrying the youngest daughter of immigrants who had set out in 1879 from a mountain village north of Presov, in what is now Czechoslovakia. No one quite remembers why they left their homeland (my mother vaguely recalls that it had something to do with hard times under the Hungarians who then ruled over Slovakia). Whatever the reason, it gave my brother, my two sisters and me a heritage that was peculiarly American. We were English and Slovak, Protestant and Roman Catholic, seven eighths Caucasian and one eighth Oriental (my maternal grandfather was half Tartar). And in my own generation, this exotic inheritance was further widened by intermarriage to include all the other ethnic strains I have listed.

At home I entered upon my culinary inheritance through Slovak cook-

ing. My mother and her family never gave up their customs and traditions —and it is the woman of the house, after all, who cooks the meals. But my mother's Slovak cuisine had an amazingly wide range, for its roots went back to the cosmopolitan Austro-Hungarian Empire of pre-World War I days. In her goulash, her stuffed cabbage or peppers, her jam- or cheese-filled pancakes, there were influences from every part of that vast empire—from Slovakia, Romania, Croatia, Serbia, Slovenia, Hungary and Austria. It was a constant delight to explore the cultural and culinary connections between these regions of Central and Southeastern Europe.

Long before my explorations began, I had come to know the food of Central Europe. My earliest memories are of my grandmother's clapboard house in Passaic, New Jersey, a house surrounded by flowers in summer, with a vegetable garden and a chicken run in the backyard. There I watched in dismay as Grandma Julia poured milk-soaked corn through a funnel into the throat of a struggling goose. (The result, I was told, would be a fat goose, and a goose liver that would weigh more than a pound—the correct ingredient for liver sausage.) I remember my Uncle Bill donning white socks for the ritual of pressing down a barrel of newly made sauerkraut with his feet, and no apples have ever tasted better to me than the ones that were pickled with that sauerkraut. Best of all, though, I remember the foods of the Christmas and Easter holidays.

Two nights before Christmas, Mother started baking nut and poppyseed rolls and her special poppy-seed cake *(Recipe Index).* (When the cake was sliced, the children yearned for a tiny silver pellet hidden in it, for Uncle Bill always made that pellet turn magically into a silver dollar.) More impressive in their variety were the strudels: the traditional apple, sour-cherry and cheese strudels; the less well-known nut and poppy-seed strudels; and, odd but delicious, the sweet cabbage strudel.

On Christmas Eve, for the final meal of the meatless Advent fast, dinner began after a toast in kümmel. First everyone received two *oplatky,* small waferlike breads baked by nuns from the same dough that is used for Communion wafers. Each spread his *oplatky* with honey and joyously consumed them. Then we had a wild-mushroom soup; my mother still speaks nostalgically of mushroom hunts in the fields and woods of New Jersey. Next came two simple casserole dishes, one of cabbage and small potato dumplings, the other of mashed potato dumplings covered with butter and cheese. A festive sweet, and one that the children especially loved, was *bobalky:* rolled pipes of bread that were cut into pieces and scalded, drained and rolled in ground poppy seeds and sugar or honey.

The preparations for Easter were even more elaborate. I remember Grandma hurrying away on Holy Saturday to have her basket of Easter food blessed at the church. In the basket, covered by a hand-embroidered linen cloth especially made for the occasion, were ham, sausage, freshly ground horseradish, Easter cheese called *syrek,* an Easter bread called *paska* and decorated eggs. Nowadays our *paska* is made by a local baker. It is still rich and buttery and chock-full of white raisins, and its shiny brown top bears a cross, but Grandma's elaborate decorations are gone. I still remember my awe at her ingenuity in placing a chicken of dough at one corner of her *paska,* a nest of dough eggs at the other. Nor have I forgotten her dazzlingly decorated Easter eggs, on which she lavished an otherwise repressed artistic talent.

Holidays were not the whole of life, and through the year there have always been the never-ending pleasures of fine foods. My mother still greets the fall with jars of pickled beets and red cabbage. In winter she makes steaming beef or chicken broth served with boiled beef or chicken that flakes at the touch of a fork; or pea and bean soups based on long-simmered ham-bone stock; or a vegetable soup so rich that a spoon will nearly stand on end in it. There are tiny dumplings for the broths—and also more elaborate dumplings called *pirohy,* filled with cottage cheese, sweet cabbage, mashed potatoes or *lekvar* (prune or apricot butter). For main courses, my mother's repertoire includes stuffed veal, chicken paprika, breaded veal and pork cutlets, potted beef and—best of all, perhaps—crisp roast duck. My 10-year-old nephew Guy insists that no one can roast a duck better than his Grandma. She knows better, though, and explains: "It isn't just me, Slovaks and Czechs have a way with duck."

Though I grew up with Slavic home cooking, some of my closest friends were Italian, Jewish or Greek, and I began early to explore their styles of cooking too. When my brother married into a family of both northern Italian and Polish origins, I came to know the delights of the rich rice dish called *risotto.* As prepared by his mother-in-law Mrs. Varetoni (who learned it from *her* Italian mother-in-law), it begins with a whole chicken simmered in water to make a stock. The rice is browned in olive oil in a separate skillet, and chopped vegetables, chicken livers, ground pork, veal and beef and button mushrooms are all browned separately in butter. All this and more is combined in a big pot, covered with chicken broth and simmered. The whole is a meal unto itself, well worth the patience and time it demands.

From our Italian butcher—who happens to be Mr. Varetoni—my family learned the virtues of "nature-fed" veal, a pale pink meat obtained from calves that have fed solely on their mothers' milk. Pounded thin, such veal makes superb *scaloppine,* and our own schnitzels took on a new dimension when we learned to combine them with Parmesan cheese and prosciutto. Mr. Varetoni also introduced us to his magnificent rolled veal, enclosing Genoa salami and grated Parmesan, and lightly seasoned with thyme, sage, garlic and parsley. In the home of a friend called Dino, I learned to enjoy the cornmeal mush called *polenta,* and wondered whether Columbus ever realized that in opening the New World he was also opening his own homeland to the pleasures of Indian corn.

Italians introduced espresso coffee into the United States—and I still remember my delight in discovering that coffee and anisette liqueur are natural companions. The Italian neighbors who revealed that delight to me also fostered my taste in the wines of local vintage. (In our neighborhood we knew that when the sidewalk in front of Cisternino's vegetable store was piled high with boxes of grapes the vintage would soon be tested.) And there were afternoons helping Dino run his family's still, where we supervised the conversion of raisins, sugar and water into our version of *grappa*—which we called "Italian white lightning," and which compared favorably with Grandma's homemade kümmel. I never needed a

Red Lodge, Montana (population 1,800), has been a microcosm of the Melting Pot ever since the 1880s, when the discovery of a rich coal field brought miners from a dozen nations to the town. A "Festival of Nations" is held there every August, and on each of its nine days, cooks of a different national origin display their skills. Above, women of Scottish descent offer scones and other baked goods on their day.

history text to explain why Prohibition was a total failure among immigrant Americans, who simply could not believe that the wines of the gods were wicked. They gave too much pleasure.

As I grew older, Mike Curzan, a Jewish friend, unveiled for me the pleasures of the Jewish table, and once again I met a mixture of the half-familiar and the completely new. I enjoyed the familiar stuffed cabbage, mushroom-and-barley soup and poppy-seed "Danish"—and encountered the one-upmanship of gefilte fish (no Jewish cook worth her salt has ever admitted that her gefilte fish has its match anywhere). *Verenikas* and *pirogen,* two names for basically similar dumplings, were old friends with a somewhat different look. And the solemn yet joyous setting of the Seder, or Passover feast, recalled the profoundly religious meaning of our own most memorable family feasts. It was all different, yet familiar.

At the home of my friend George Frangos, I plunged into the Greek cuisine, and realized once and for all that the cooking styles of Eastern and Central Europe are closely interrelated. George's parents had come from Imbros, an island off the Dardanelles, and Mrs. Frangos had mastered the secrets of both Greek and Turkish cooking. At my first meal at her table, I was astonished to see stuffed peppers, filled with a delicate mixture of ground meat, onions, rice, raisins, pine nuts, mint and cinnamon; by my Slavic standards they were exotic, but good. The *dolmades* that followed disclosed that stuffed grape leaves, for all their unfamiliarity, were delicious. At home and among our Italian friends I had learned to enjoy lamb; with the help of the Frangos family I extended my expertise to the

myriad kabobs. When I indicated that I enjoyed the resinated wine called *retsina* and the powerful brandy called Metaxa, I was immediately dubbed a true "son of Hellas." The desserts completed my surrender: *baklava* and *galaktobouriko* were obviously cousins of my familiar strudel.

In the years since I met the Frangos family I have become accustomed to spending Easter Eve with them at St. Basil's Academy in Garrison, New York, and in the tiny chapel at midnight have been struck again and again by the proud endurance of immigrant traditions. A couple of Easters ago another thought struck me: for almost all the immigrants I knew, the Easter season was the gastronomic high point of the year. I asked Mrs. Frangos why this was so, and she thought for a moment, then replied: "Well, of course, it was then that God gave us His Son for our salvation. But also, it is the season when life begins again. Easter reminds us that if we treat God's earth well, we will know abundance."

Experiences and memories like mine can be matched in every part of America. They reflect the diversity of American origins, but they also reflect a particular aspect of our diversity, because they are drawn from immigrants who arrived here within the last century.

Until the 1880s, most American immigrants came from Northern and Western Europe. For the most part, the cuisines of these immigrants have been absorbed in the mainstream of American cooking. Indeed, it would be more correct to say that they have created American cooking. From New England down along the Atlantic seaboard, British settlers established great styles of cooking—among the oldest American styles we

Visitors gather outside a hotel called Old Post Office to study and copy down recipes for dishes they have tasted at Red Lodge's Festival of Nations. Each day, recipes are posted on the hotel window by the cooks who prepared them.

ORIENTAL PIZZA

539
539

SALE

Middle Eastern PASTRIES 7up

PASTRY

LAHMAJIN PIZZA

PASTRIE PAKLAVA

The Originators of KOSHER CHINESE FOODS

BERNSTEIN-ON-ESSEX ST.

MOZZARELLA

BEST QUALITY

公司 HUN HING, INC.

GOLD PASAJES SEGUROS 13

OLD DENMARK

135

LA·SEGUNDA·PERLA
···107···
RESTAURANT & CUCHIFRITO

HUNGARIAN PACKING HOUSE

A photographic medley of food stores and restaurants, all in New York City, suggests that, in matters of food, no guarantee of excellence is more attractive to Americans than a bold statement of a distinctive ethnic origin—unless, perhaps, it is an even bolder statement of *two* ethnic origins *(above, left).*

TRY OUR DELICIOUS
Sauerbraten
READY TO COOK

歡迎外賣

Mee Sum Mee Tea House & Pastry
餅画啡咖・桌美茶若

ITALIAN SPECIALTIES
555   TODARO BROS. DELICATESSEN

FORMAGGIO FRINLANO

TODARO BROS delica 555

Andrea Affronti   ITALIAN & FRENCH   CAKES
PASTRY   *For All Occasions*
38 · ANDREA AFFRONTI PASTRY SHOP · 538

GREEK BAKERY
BAKLAVA
629

HELINIKON
ZAHAROPLASTEION

ORIGINAL
YONA SHIMMEL'S
KNISH BAKERY
PARTY SNACKS
COCKTAIL KNISHES

know today. The French contributed to the Creole cooking of Louisiana; the Spaniards to the cooking of the Southwest. Germans developed Pennsylvania Dutch cooking, one of the glories of the Eastern Heartland. In the Northwest, Scandinavians adapted their cooking styles to American ways and raw materials; their cooking, too, has been largely assimilated by other Americans living among them. All of these diverse culinary styles are discussed in the volumes of FOODS OF THE WORLD devoted to regional American cooking.

Beginning in the early 1880s, however, the picture changed. A "new immigration," as the historians call it, began to pour into America from Southern, Central and Eastern Europe. By 1925 some 14 million of these immigrants had come to the New World. Most had only recently broken out of semifeudal ways of life, yet their muscles and sweat stoked the engine of American industrialization. Their bodies filled city tenements, and many American streets throbbed with foreign ways of life: Chicago's Noble Street became as Polish as Warsaw's Krakowskie Przedmieście; Mulberry Street, in lower Manhattan, echoed with the sounds of Naples.

From the beginning, the newcomers adapted as best they could to American ways. Eager to establish themselves as "real Americans," they often suppressed or blurred their native language and customs. In the kitchen they learned to make use of American foodstuffs, and produced a variety of hyphenated cuisines that are discussed in detail in this book—Italian-American, Hungarian-American, Polish-American and the rest. The very term "Melting Pot," first used in a play by Israel Zangwill in 1908, was coined to describe the absorption of the new immigrants in the crucible of American life.

But the newcomers stubbornly clung to their old ways, too. After their first exposure to American life, they were often less ready to concede the automatic superiority of everything American. They began to look at their new world with a more critical eye, and they came to realize that they, too, had much to contribute to their adopted nation. One of them, the Romanian-American author Konrad Bercovici, described their state of mind in 1925 this way: "You will hear them say that there are sentiments inexpressible in English. That the meat at home tastes better. That it gives more vigor and is sweeter. That the vegetables and fruit taste better in their country. The American table has been enriched with tens of dishes unknown here a few generations ago."

As the numbers of new immigrants grew, and as their sense of pride and identity deepened, new institutions developed to meet their needs. For example, the Roman Catholic Church—that master of historical adjustment—continued to create ethnic parishes in the teeming centers of immigration. In turn, these parishes mounted fund-raising drives that often came to their climax in a grand dinner or picnic. Ethnic restaurants multiplied in the urban ghettos. And as the immigrants were thrown together in factories, mines and churches they came to recognize certain fascinating similarities in their culinary backgrounds.

Many of them had come from Austria-Hungary, a vast Central European empire that included within its boundaries northern Italians, Germans, Czechs, Poles, Ukrainians, Jews, Hungarians, Romanians, Slovaks,

Slovenes, Croats and Serbs. These peoples included Roman and Greek Catholics, Orthodox Christians, Protestants, Jews and Moslems. Austria-Hungary was an empire without a nationality—but it was also a mélange of cuisines. The Italian *gnocchi* (dumplings) had migrated across the Alps to become the Czech *noky* and the Austro-Hungarian *Nockerln.* Various veal dishes had found their way from Italy into Central European cuisines as one kind of schnitzel or another. What were called *pierogi* in Poland were called *pirohy* in Slovakia. Hungarian paprika had turned up in the cooking of the Slovaks, Czechs and southern Slavs.

A similar intermixture had taken place in the old Ottoman Empire. Turkish shish kabob had become Greek *souvlaki,* Serbian *ražnjići* and the *shashlyk* of the Caucasus. As I learned at the Frangoses' home, the stuffed peppers of the Austro-Hungarians had their counterparts among the peoples of the Ottoman Empire. The Ottomans themselves had always applied the old adage that good food knows no boundaries, and had annexed, mixed, modified and spread the diverse cuisines they had encountered along their paths of conquest.

Within these great empires, however, different styles of cooking had also been used to proclaim an ethnic and even a national identity. The oppressed peoples of the Russan Empire had jealously preserved their distinctive national cuisines. Divided among three empires—Russian, German and Austro-Hungarian—the Poles had discovered that their common religion, language and cuisine all gave them a single identity, well worth preserving. And, in the New World, the new immigrant continued to follow this pattern. As always, he was ready to incorporate new foods and new recipes; he was ready to share his cooking, as well as add to it, but not ready or willing to renounce it.

The best way to translate these generalizations into reality is to consider a specific case in point. Take, for instance, the Poles who settled in the great industrial belt that stretches from Pennsylvania to the Great Lakes. In South Bend, Indiana, the Polish-American community increased tenfold in the quarter century before 1900, and supported a number of churches and social organizations. In a count taken a decade later, South Bend—with a total population of 53,684—proved to have 31 Polish-American groceries, 18 meat markets, nine bakeries and eight confectioneries to serve this community. To the east, in the coal towns of Pennsylvania, Polish-American homes could be identified by their vegetable gardens, chicken runs and an occasional milk cow. With these, the practical Poles supplemented their wages and ensured against hunger in periods of unemployment and strike. But for the most part, American bounty enabled them to enjoy foods that had been holiday fare in the Old Country. Their days of rest, particularly, took on a holiday tone. A generation later a historical researcher, writing of a bleak mining town in Luzerne County, Pennsylvania, sketched a picture of those days:

> *On Sundays and holidays the entire Polish neighborhood or individual families with boarders gathered in a nearby grove or on the lawn. Large tables set under the trees groaned beneath the weight of food which was washed down by draughts of beer from the keg. After the "przekąska" [a big spread of*

*cold foods], the men played cards or exhibited feats of en-
durance and strength in wrestling matches, while the youth
danced folk dances to the tune of the accordion or violin . . .
When twilight fell, the men, tranquilly puffing on their pipes
and smoking cigarettes, began their political sessions, a veri-
table town hall meeting on the village green. Political issues
were threshed out, kings were made and unmade, grievances
against bosses, wages, discriminations were denounced vigorously. With the toning down of exuberant activity, the talk
turned to the home they left behind—the home in Poland.*

Throughout America millions of people still keep such ancient traditions alive. Our holiday seasons are often mixtures of many foreign traditions, and our kitchens are still redolent of dishes that originated across
the sea; even when only the barest fragments of the old languages sur-
vive in America, they are likely to include the names of these dishes. And
no matter how long we have been here, we Americans still take pride in
our descent from immigrants, and in the fateful experience that brought
our ancestors to these shores.

It is an experience that continues to repeat itself. Since World War II
some 700,000 Puerto Ricans—about a fourth of the present home-island
population—have journeyed to the American mainland, bringing with

18

For all their diversity, the peoples of the Melting Pot are united in an appreciation of fine baked breads and coffeecakes. A sampler of international favorites includes *(from left to right):* Polish rum-glazed *babka;* Armenian sesame-sprinkled *peda;* German Texas *Stollen;* Lithuanian potato bread, usually served with sweet butter; Italian sesame sticks; and Puerto Rican *almojábanas.* (See the Recipe Index for all but the sesame sticks.)

them a foreign language and an alien culture. To be sure, there are differences between this migration and earlier ones. This time the newcomer travels by airplane rather than steerage (the accommodations are tighter than ever, but the flight is mercifully brief). The Puerto Rican comes from a tropical island, but one that is well supplied with American-style supermarkets, and he is already familiar with many mainland foods. On the other hand, his mainland compatriots are only now beginning to learn the pleasures of Puerto Rican specialties. Among New York connoisseurs, the *pastelillo* is beginning to find a place on the hors d'oeuvre table. In the Puerto Rican ghettos (usually the same ghettos that once sheltered the masses of the new immigration), greengrocers offer plantains and yuca. And just as the German introduced us to the delicatessen, the Puerto Rican has brought us the *bodega,* that strange combination of an everyday American grocery and a Caribbean market.

The pattern is familiar: once again, the American experience is shaping a new man, the mainland Puerto Rican-American. When the process is completed, a new piece will be fitted into the mosaic of American life —and nowhere is the change more likely to be marked than at the dinner table. As we Americans have worked to create a single nationality out of our diversity, we have learned that as men break bread together, they are made one. In the joy of sharing food and drink, they are reminded that they are not strangers, but brothers.

To serve 4

1 large green plantain (about ½ pound)
1 quart cold water
Salt
Vegetable oil or lard for deep frying

Tostones *(Puerto Rican)*
FRIED PLANTAIN CHIPS

To peel the green plantain, slice off the ends with a sharp knife and cut the plantain in half crosswise. Make four evenly spaced lengthwise slits in the skin of each half, cutting through to the flesh. Then, starting at the corner edge of one slit, use the knife and your thumb to work the skin away from the meat a strip at a time, pulling it off crosswise rather than lengthwise. Slice the plantain diagonally into ¾-inch-thick slices.

Combine the water and 2 tablespoons of salt in a deep mixing bowl and drop in the plantain slices. Soak at room temperature for 30 minutes.

Fill a deep fryer or large heavy saucepan with the oil or lard to a depth of 2 or 3 inches and heat to 300° on a deep-frying thermometer. Remove the plantain slices from the water (do not discard the water) and spread them out on paper towels. Pat them dry with additional paper towels and drop them into the oil. Fry for about 5 minutes, or until the plantain slices are a pale gold; do not let them get brown. With a slotted spoon, transfer them to paper towels and with a metal spatula or the heel of your hand, press down on the slices until they are only ⅓ inch thick.

Reheat the oil to 350°. Put the chips back in the salted water for about 2 minutes, then drain them in a sieve. Deep-fry the chips for 3 to 4 minutes, being careful to stand away from the pan when you drop them in, for the fat will splutter. As they become crisp and golden, transfer them to paper towels to drain.

Sprinkle the chips with salt and serve warm or at room temperature as an hors d'oeuvre, or as an accompaniment to meat or fish.

To make two 11-inch round loaves

½ cup lukewarm water (110° to 115°)
2 packages active dry yeast
2 teaspoons plus 2 tablespoons sugar
6 cups all-purpose flour
1 tablespoon salt
1¾ cups lukewarm milk (110° to 115°)
4 to 5 tablespoons olive oil
2 tablespoons unsalted butter, softened
1 egg yolk, beaten with 1 tablespoon water
4 tablespoons white sesame seeds

Peda *(Armenian)*
WHITE BREAD WITH SESAME SEEDS

A peda, which looks rather like an oversized doughnut with the dough from the hole put back in, can be spread with butter and served like any other white bread. In Fresno, California, however, it provides the foundation for a "Fresno sandwich," an Armenian version of an Italian hero, in which the loaf is cut horizontally through the middle and filled with kufta *(Recipe Index), broiled skewered lamb or hamburger.*

Pour the lukewarm water into a small bowl and sprinkle in the yeast and 2 teaspoons of the sugar. Let the mixture rest for 2 or 3 minutes, then stir to dissolve the yeast. Set the bowl in a warm, draft-free place (such as an unlighted oven) for 5 to 8 minutes, or until the yeast bubbles and the mixture almost doubles in volume.

Place 5½ cups of the flour in a deep mixing bowl and add the remaining 2 tablespoons of sugar and the salt. Make a well in the center and pour in the yeast mixture, lukewarm milk and 3 tablespoons of the olive oil. With a large wooden spoon, gradually incorporate the dry ingredients into the liquid. Stir until the dough can be gathered into a ball. Place the dough on a surface sprinkled with some of the remaining ½ cup of flour. Add only enough flour to keep it from sticking to your hands. Knead for about 10 minutes, pushing the dough down with the heels of your hands, pressing it forward and folding it back on itself. When the dough is smooth and elastic, cut it in half.

With a pastry brush, spread the butter on two baking sheets. With your hands, flatten the dough into round cakes, each 1½ inches thick and about 8 inches in diameter. Place them on the baking sheets. With a 3-inch cookie cutter, remove a circle from the center of each round of dough, then put the circle back into the hole. Brush the loaves with the remaining olive oil, cover lightly with a towel and set aside in the draft-free place for about 1 hour, or until the dough has doubled in volume.

Preheat the oven to 350°. With a pastry brush, coat the surface of the loaves with the beaten egg-yolk-and-water mixture, and sprinkle with the sesame seeds. Bake in the center of the oven for 30 minutes, then transfer the loaves to wire racks to cool before serving.

Caraway Rye Bread *(Czech)*

To make two 13-inch loaves

½ cup lukewarm water (110° to 115°)
1 package active dry yeast
1 teaspoon sugar
2 to 2½ cups white all-purpose flour
2 to 2½ cups rye flour
1 tablespoon salt
1 cup lukewarm milk (110° to 115°)
¼ cup distilled white vinegar
1 tablespoon unsalted butter, softened
½ cup white or yellow cornmeal
1 egg white, beaten to a froth
3 tablespoons caraway seeds

Pour ¼ cup of the water into a small bowl and sprinkle in the yeast and sugar. Let it rest for 2 or 3 minutes, then stir. Set the bowl in a warm, draft-free place (such as an unlighted oven) for 5 to 8 minutes, or until the yeast bubbles and the mixture almost doubles in volume.

Place 2 cups of white flour, 2 cups of rye flour and the salt in a deep mixing bowl and make a well in the center. Pour in the yeast mixture, the remaining ¼ cup of lukewarm water, the milk and vinegar and, with a large wooden spoon, gradually incorporate the dry ingredients into the liquid. Stir until the mixture is smooth, then beat until the dough can be gathered into a ball. Place on a lightly floured surface and knead, pushing the dough down with the heels of your hands, pressing it forward and folding it back on itself. Sprinkle equal amounts of rye and white flour over the ball by the tablespoonful, adding up to ½ cup more of each if necessary to keep the dough from sticking to your hands. Knead for about 10 minutes, or until the dough is smooth and elastic.

With a pastry brush, spread the softened butter evenly over the inside of a large bowl. Place the dough in the bowl and turn it about to butter the entire surface. Drape the bowl with a kitchen towel and set it aside in the draft-free place for about 1½ hours, or until the dough doubles in volume. Punch the dough down with your fist and set it in the draft-free place to rise again for 45 minutes, or until it has doubled in volume.

Scatter the cornmeal on a large baking sheet and set aside. Cut the dough in half and shape each half into a tapering loaf about 12 inches long and 2½ inches wide in the center. Place the loaves 2 inches apart on the baking sheet and, with a large knife, make ½-inch-deep diagonal slashes at 2-inch intervals on the top of each loaf. Set the loaves in the draft-free place to rise for about 30 minutes.

Preheat the oven to 400°. Brush the egg white over the tops of the loaves. Sprinkle the loaves with the caraway seeds and place them in the center of the oven for 15 minutes. Reduce the oven temperature to 375° and bake for 30 to 35 minutes longer, until the loaves are golden brown. Transfer to wire racks and let them cool before serving.

To make about 3 cups

CHICKEN FAT
½ pound (1 cup) fresh pieces of
    chicken fat, finely diced
¼ cup finely chopped onions

CHOPPED LIVER
1 pound fresh chicken livers
2 cups finely chopped onions
3 hard-cooked eggs, finely chopped
2 teaspoons salt
¼ teaspoon freshly ground black
    pepper

GARNISHES (optional)
1 hard-cooked egg, finely chopped
½ to 1 cup *grebenes (see recipe)*

Gehakte Leber (Jewish)
CHOPPED CHICKEN LIVER

CHICKEN FAT: Combine the chicken fat and ¼ cup of onions in a
large, heavy skillet and, mashing the fat with the back of a spoon, cook
over low heat for 30 minutes, or until the dice have rendered most of
their liquid and they are crisp and brown. With a slotted spoon, transfer
the browned bits of fat and onion (called *grebenes*) to paper towels to
drain; save them as a garnish for the liver or for *kasha varnishkes (Recipe
Index)*. Strain the fat through a fine sieve set over a bowl. Return 8 tablespoons of the rendered fat to the skillet and set the rest aside.

CHOPPED LIVER: Preheat the broiler. Broil the livers on a rack 4 inches
from the heat for 4 to 5 minutes on each side, until the livers are firm
with no trace of pink inside them. Chop them fine.

Heat the chicken fat in the skillet over moderate heat. Add 2 cups of onions and, stirring frequently, cook for 5 minutes, or until they are soft
and translucent. Stir in the chopped livers and chopped eggs, transfer to
a deep bowl, and beat with a large spoon until the ingredients are well
combined. Beat in the salt and pepper, and taste for seasoning. If the mixture seems too dry, add 1 or 2 tablespoons of the reserved rendered chick-
en fat. Spoon the chopped liver into a small bowl or 3-cup crock and
refrigerate, tightly sealed, for at least 2 hours, or until chilled. To serve,

An American cocktail party or buffet might include any or all of these exotic hors d'oeuvre, brought to the U.S. by immigrants. Clockwise from the white basket at right, which contains *pyriszhky,* mushroom-filled pasties from the Ukraine, the hors d'oeuvre are: mushrooms stuffed with ricotta and prosciutto, from Italy; Puerto Rican deep-fried plantain chips; cubes of beef grilled with a Japanese *teriyaki* glaze; Jewish chopped chicken liver, to be served on slices of Czech caraway-seed rye bread. See the Recipe Index for directions.

mound the chopped liver on a chilled platter, or over lettuce leaves on individual serving plates. It may also be served with cocktails, accompanied by bread or crackers. Garnish if you wish with chopped egg or *grebenes.*

Funghi Ripieni (Italian)
CHEESE-STUFFED MUSHROOM CAPS

Preheat the oven to 400°. Place the ricotta in a large mixing bowl and, with a wooden spoon, beat in the parsley, prosciutto, salt, a few grindings of black pepper and the lemon juice. Beat vigorously until the ingredients are well combined and the mixture is smooth. Set aside.

In a 10- to 12-inch stainless-steel or enameled skillet, heat the oil until a light haze forms above it. Drop in the mushroom caps and fry over moderate heat for about 2 minutes, then turn them over and fry for another minute or two until they are lightly browned. Remove from the heat.

Fill the mushroom caps with the ricotta mixture and top each cap with bits of mozzarella. Arrange the caps side by side in a shallow baking dish or jelly-roll pan and bake in the center of the oven for 8 minutes, or until the filling begins to bubble. Slide the caps under a hot broiler for 30 seconds to brown the mozzarella topping. Serve at once as an accompaniment to drinks or as part of an antipasto.

To make 18

1 cup ricotta cheese
¼ cup finely chopped parsley
¼ pound prosciutto (thinly sliced Italian cured ham), finely chopped
2 teaspoons salt
Freshly ground black pepper
1 tablespoon strained fresh lemon juice
4 tablespoons olive oil
18 medium-sized mushroom caps
2½ ounces mozzarella cheese, cut into ¼-inch bits (½ cup)

23

To make about 4 dozen

DOUGH

¾ cup lukewarm water (110° to
   115°)
1 package active dry yeast
½ teaspoon sugar
3 to 3½ cups all-purpose sifted
   flour
1 teaspoon salt
3 tablespoons unsalted butter,
   softened
3 eggs, lightly beaten

MUSHROOM FILLING

8 tablespoons (1 quarter-pound
   stick) unsalted butter
½ cup finely chopped onions
1 pound mushrooms, finely chopped
2 hard-cooked eggs, peeled and
   finely chopped
⅓ cup boiled rice
1½ teaspoons salt
¼ teaspoon freshly ground black
   pepper
4 tablespoons finely chopped parsley

CABBAGE FILLING

3 tablespoons unsalted butter
1 cup finely chopped onions
1½ pounds cabbage, coarsely
   chopped
1 teaspoon sugar
1½ teaspoons salt
¼ teaspoon freshly ground black
   pepper
½ cup water

1 egg, lightly beaten with
   2 tablespoons milk

Pyriszhky (Ukrainian)
SMALL BREADS WITH MUSHROOM OR CABBAGE FILLING

In a small bowl, sprinkle the ¾ cup of lukewarm water with the yeast and the ½ teaspoon of sugar, and let the mixture rest for 2 or 3 minutes. Stir to dissolve the yeast, then set the bowl aside in a warm, draft-free place (such as an unlighted oven) for 10 to 15 minutes, or until the yeast bubbles and the mixture almost doubles in volume.

Place 3 cups of flour and 1 teaspoon of salt in a large mixing bowl and make a well in the center. Drop in the yeast mixture, 2 tablespoons of the butter and the eggs and, with a large spoon, gradually incorporate the flour into the liquid ingredients. Stir until the ingredients can be gathered into a ball, then transfer the ball to a lightly floured surface. Knead the dough, pressing it down, pushing it forward with the heel of your hand and folding it back on itself, until you have a smooth, medium-soft dough. Add up to ½ cup flour by the tablespoonful if the dough sticks to your hands or the board.

Coat the bottom and sides of a large mixing bowl with the remaining tablespoon of softened butter and place the dough in the bowl. Drape the bowl with a kitchen towel and set it aside in the warm, draft-free place for 45 minutes, or until the dough almost doubles in volume. Punch it down with a blow of your fist and set it aside to double again in volume.

MUSHROOM FILLING: Melt 8 tablespoons of butter in a 10- to 12-inch skillet over moderate heat. When the foam begins to subside, stir in ½ cup of onions and the mushrooms and, stirring frequently, cook for 4 to 6 minutes, or until the onions are soft and translucent. Remove the pan from the heat and transfer the onions and mushrooms to a large bowl. Add the chopped eggs, rice, 1½ teaspoons of salt, ¼ teaspoon of black pepper and the parsley, and toss together lightly but thoroughly with a wooden spoon. Taste for seasoning, and set the filling aside to cool to room temperature.

CABBAGE FILLING: Melt 3 tablespoons of butter in a 10- to 12-inch skillet over moderate heat. Stir in 1 cup of onions and, stirring frequently, cook for 4 to 6 minutes, or until they are soft and translucent. Add the cabbage, 1 teaspoon of sugar, 1½ teaspoons of salt and ¼ teaspoon of black pepper, then pour in the ½ cup of water. Bring to a boil over high heat, then reduce the heat, cover the skillet and simmer for 45 minutes. Uncover the pan, raise the heat to high and boil briskly until the liquid in the pan has evaporated. Put the contents of the skillet through the finest blade of a meat grinder, or chop them as fine as possible with a large heavy knife. Taste for seasoning, and cool to room temperature.

TO ASSEMBLE AND COOK: Preheat the oven to 325°. Place the dough on a large surface and pull off pieces equal to about 2 tablespoons. Flatten the pieces, one at a time, into oval shapes about ¼ inch thick. Place 2 teaspoons of filling in the center of each dough oval and pull one side of the dough over the filling. Press the edges together.

Set the *pyriszhky* an inch apart on a cookie sheet and, with a pastry brush, coat them with the egg-and-milk mixture. Bake in the center of the oven for 10 to 12 minutes, or until they are golden brown.

Serve the *pyriszhky* hot, either as an accompaniment to clear chicken or beef soup, as an hors d'oeuvre or as a first course.

Bulvinis Ragaisis *(Lithuanian)*
POTATO BREAD

In a small bowl, sprinkle the water with the yeast and sugar. Let it stand for 2 or 3 minutes, then stir to dissolve the yeast. Set the bowl in a warm, draft-free place (such as an unlighted oven) for 5 to 8 minutes, or until the yeast has doubled in volume. Pour the milk into a small bowl and grate the potato into it.

In a deep mixing bowl, combine 3 cups of flour and the salt. Make a well in the center and pour in the yeast and the milk mixtures. Add the egg and sour cream and stir the dry ingredients into the liquid. Beat vigorously until the dough can be gathered into a ball. Transfer the dough to a lightly floured surface and knead, adding up to ½ cup more flour if necessary to make a smooth, medium-firm dough. Place in a buttered bowl and drape with a kitchen towel. Set aside in the warm, draft-free place for 1 hour, or until the dough doubles in volume.

With the tablespoon of softened butter, coat a 9-by-5-by-3-inch loaf pan. Place the dough in the pan, drape with the towel and set aside in the warm, draft-free place again until the dough doubles in volume. Preheat the oven to 375°. Brush the loaf with the egg-and-milk mixture and bake in the center of the oven for 35 to 40 minutes. Then cool on a wire rack.

To make one 9-by-5-by-3-inch loaf

¼ cup lukewarm water (110° to 115°)
1 package active dry yeast
½ teaspoon sugar
¾ cup lukewarm milk (110° to 115°)
1 medium-sized baking potato, peeled
3 to 3½ cups all-purpose flour
2 teaspoons salt
1 egg
2 tablespoons sour cream
1 tablespoon butter, softened

1 egg, lightly beaten with 1 tablespoon milk

Rum Babka *(Polish)*

CAKE: With a pastry brush, coat a 2-quart *Gugelhupf* pan or Turk's-head mold with 1 tablespoon of the butter. In a small bowl, sprinkle ¼ cup of the lukewarm milk with ½ teaspoon of sugar and the yeast. Let the mixture stand for 2 or 3 minutes, then stir to dissolve the yeast. Set the bowl aside in a warm, draft-free place (such as an unlighted oven) for 6 to 8 minutes, or until the mixture almost doubles in volume.

Preheat the oven to 350°. Combine the flour, salt and 1 cup of sugar in a large bowl, and make a well in the center. Pour in the yeast mixture, the remaining milk, the egg yolks and eggs, and 8 tablespoons of butter. With a large spoon, stir the ingredients together. Knead the dough on a lightly floured surface—pushing it down with the heel of your hand, pressing it forward and folding it back on itself—for about 10 minutes, until smooth and elastic. Place the dough in a buttered bowl, drape with a kitchen towel, and set aside in the draft-free place for 1½ hours, or until the dough has doubled in volume. Punch the dough down with your fist and knead in the raisins and orange rind. Place the dough in the prepared pan, drape with a towel, and set aside in the draft-free place until it almost fills the pan. Bake in the center of the oven for 30 minutes, then reduce the oven temperature to 325° and bake for 20 minutes longer. Transfer the cake to a deep platter.

SYRUP: In a 1½- to 2-quart enameled or stainless-steel saucepan, combine 1 cup of sugar, the apricot juice, lemon juice and rum. Bring to a boil over moderate heat, stirring constantly until the sugar has dissolved. Reduce the heat and simmer uncovered and undisturbed for 5 minutes.

Puncture the hot cake at 1-inch intervals with the tines of a fork. Pour half of the syrup over the cake and let it soak in, then turn the cake over, puncture the bottom and soak with the remaining syrup.

To make 1 large cake

CAKE
1 tablespoon butter, softened, plus 8 tablespoons (1 quarter-pound stick) unsalted butter, softened
2 cups lukewarm milk (110° to 115°)
½ teaspoon plus 1 cup sugar
1 package active dry yeast
5½ cups all-purpose flour
1 teaspoon salt
4 egg yolks
2 whole eggs
1 cup seedless white raisins
1 tablespoon grated orange rind

SYRUP
1 cup sugar
1½ cups apricot juice
2 teaspoons strained fresh lemon juice
8 tablespoons dark rum

by ANGELO M. PELLEGRINI

Born in Casabianca, Italy, Professor Pellegrini came to America at the age of 10. He has taught English at the University of Washington in Seattle since 1930. Among his books are *Wine and the Good Life* and *The Food Lover's Garden*.

An Italian Odyssey: from Famine to Feast

I remember it as the "last supper," the last time we supped on misery before moving 8,000 miles westward to the land of plenty. We were in Casabianca, a Tuscan farming village west of Florence. The time was a day in late July, 1913. Tired and hungry after long hours hoeing and weeding corn, we—five children and mother—sat down to supper. When Mother had served us, she told us to join her in prayer. In simple yet authoritative words, commanding rather than imploring, she asked Holy Mary to send Father back to us, "immediately, alive, and in good health."

We had always done our praying in church, never at the dinner table, so this departure from custom, and the nature of Mother's request, spoken with tears flowing down her cheeks, filled us with fear. We understood now that her usual cheerfulness had been a pretense for our sake; finally she could no longer conceal her worry. Father had gone to America a year and a half earlier. At first there had been a letter every six weeks, but for the past five months there had been none. His last letter had said that the railroad section gang he was working with was moving west. Had he deserted us? Had he been in a fatal accident? We feared the worst. As the eldest son—I had just completed the third grade in school —I was now the man of the family, as Father had told me I would be if anything happened to him. Apparently the hour of my investiture had arrived. The occasion was heavy with doom. It burned so into my consciousness that I can still summon up its terror.

So we ate in tears. At the time we were desperately poor; not only had Father's letters stopped coming, but also the money he had regularly sent

Known variously as a grinder, submarine, torpedo or hero (reputedly from the saying, "You've got to be a hero to eat one"), the variations of the Italian-American sandwich are endless. Stuffed between halves of Italian bread *(top)* are slices of bologna, salami, provolone, green peppers and lettuce. The sesame bread *(center)* is smothered with *mortadella,* prosciutto and tomatoes, and a hot version *(bottom)* features veal and peppers *(Recipe Index).*

with them. We could no longer afford the occasional meat we had formerly enjoyed. Our supper that night consisted of soupy cooked cabbage
poured over stale bread, and since we baked infrequently in order to save
fuel, the bread was moldy as well as stale. The wine was thin, stretched
with water to make it go further. Such was our meal.

But I remember it as the "last" supper for a happy reason: it was the
last time that we ate in such gloom. Our prayer was quickly, if not literally, answered: a letter did come from Father, and gaiety dispelled the de-
spair. He was not only alive and in good health, he was full of love for
his family. From a place called Chicago, his gang had moved out to a
small town on the Pacific Coast; and from there he had gone to another village nearby, where he was now working. "It is a little paradise," he
wrote, "our future home. Sell everything and come on the next boat out
of Genova. I am sending you the money for the journey." Before we
could go to join him, there would be more suppers of bad bread and
greens with scant condiment; but we no longer ate in sadness.

There was little to sell, and that was quickly done; so we were soon at
sea. It did not matter that we were crowded in the steerage of a rotten
ship, suffering fits of seasickness, in constant fear of going under; always
we kept a firm grip, finding strength to endure in the awareness that each
day brought us closer to that "little paradise." On the 18th day we were
in New York, where we were detained in what appeared to be a prison.
After two days of anxious waiting we were examined, declared free of dis-
ease and sent along to the railway station.

We were going to the state of Washington, to a town called McCleary.
The best we could pronounce it was "Meech Clearg." Railway officials in
impressive uniforms scanned maps. Then they simply announced that in
America there was neither a McCleary nor a Meech Clearg. Thinking
now on paradise lost, we wept. The dignitaries conferred once more, pon-
dered our plight and found a solution. An interpreter told us we would
be sent to the largest city near the center of Washington State. The sta-
tionmaster there, it was hoped, would help us find Meech Clearg. Accordingly, tagged like so much baggage, we were each given a small bag
of food—yellow cheese, a sandwich and fruit—and shipped to Yakima.

So once more we moved westward, on land now, on a train that
screeched and lurched and stopped and started with a caprice of a mule.
We were by turns unbearably hot and insufferably cold. The little bags of
food were soon devoured. At some of the stations someone would come
aboard with fruit, sweets and sandwiches for sale; but most of the time
we had nothing. Unable to speak the language, we could not make our
needs known, and for fear of being left behind we did not dare get off
the train when it stopped. So we endured hunger and hoped, with all the
fervency our exhaustion permitted, that Meech Clearg did in fact exist.

We arrived in Yakima on the seventh day. We were motioned off the
train, and Mother went immediately to the ticket agent brandishing a
paper on which was written "McCleary, Wash." in Father's meticulously
clear hand. The agent called an associate. They conferred; they consulted
timetables and maps. Then came the chilling verdict, delivered by signs
and gestures: there was no such place. Hoping to conjure what did not

exist, Mother repeated "Meech Clearg" three times in loud clear tones. The dignitaries smiled and shook their heads. From this verdict there was no appeal; hope was no longer possible. Seeking consolation in each other, we filled the station with our wailing.

Then came the miracle. Addressing Mother, a young man asked in faultless Italian, "Why do you weep?" His name was Carlo and, incredibly, he worked with Father on the railroad for the Henry McCleary Timber Company. He had come to Yakima to see a sick friend and was about to return to Meech Clearg. He explained that the village was a lumber camp recently established, unincorporated and 10 miles from the nearest railroad station, Elma. That was the reason it "did not exist" for stationmasters. To reach it one took the train to Elma, and from there passengers were taken to the camp in a freight car powered by a gasoline motor. It was now 11 o'clock. The train for Elma would leave at 1:30. Were we hungry? Would we like something to eat? . . .

What a sudden reversal of fortune! The next two hours, in the care of that heavenly guide, were so happy that we could not believe them real. Carlo took us to a modest little restaurant where we were fed beefsteak, fried potatoes, green beans, and apple pie with ice cream. He explained that the cream, the sugar, the coffee on the table—all luxuries that we had seldom seen in Italy—were free; that we might use as much as we pleased. He also told us that in saloons in America anyone who bought a glass of beer was given free food—bread, sausage, salami, cheese; and that butchers gave away liver, kidneys, tripe, tongue and hearts to any good customers who might want them. We listened in humble amazement as he told us that in Washington cattle, pigs and sheep roamed the countryside as if no one owned them; that in America everything was big, as witness the huge steaks we were served, one of which in Italy would have been enough for an entire family.

Thus, as we were about to enter it, we were introduced to the "little paradise" Father had found for us, and we soon learned that neither he nor Carlo had exaggerated its virtues. It is a pleasure, even after so many years, to recall what that "little paradise" meant. Here is what we found in Meech Clearg, in the heart of the prodigal Northwest: a seven-room house with electric lights, hot and cold water, comfortable beds, a Monarch wood range, and a huge potbellied wood stove for heating; acres of virgin land that we might cultivate without charge; free fuel for an eternity in the forest at the back door; fish so plentiful that at certain seasons we might take them from the streams with our bare hands; hills and meadows alive with game; employment in the mill and on the railroad. And at the edge of town, on the brow of a gentle rise, a school.

These were the blessings we found; and I write about them in the happy awareness that they were substantially what was found not by just a few, but by many of the three and a half million people of Italian origin who were in America by 1920. They came from all parts of Italy, though the majority emigrated from the poorer regions south of Florence. They were poor and provincial; most had never traveled farther than their legs could carry them in a day. Thus they were innocent of cuisines beyond their own regions, and it was in the Little Italy of the American metropolis

Homage to the Italian Butcher

An observer can get carried away watching an Italian-American butcher prepare veal, simply because the man's artistry is so exquisite.

Take Dominic, a young third-generation Italian-American with black curly hair and the hands of a surgeon. He works in New York, at his family's shop on Second Avenue, near where he grew up in one of the city's shrinking but fiercely partisan Italian neighborhoods. Reared on roller skates and stickball, he had no closer contact with raw nature as a kid than swimming off the sea wall along the East River. But as he sculpts and picks at a chunk of veal with his razor-sharp knife, eliminating every last scrap of membrane, gristle or vein, he exhibits the influence of his Milanese forebears. It is as much a part of him as his love of the New York Yankees.

In Lombardy—and throughout most of Italy, for that matter—most farms did not have the pasturage to raise cattle; when it was time to wean a calf, it was time also to butcher it. The objective of the butcher was the fine texture and tenderness of veal, rather than the robust flavor of mature beef.

Of all the cuts from this milk-fed animal, none was more esteemed than the slices that so agreeably absorbed the Italian cook's palette of sauces in such classic dishes as scaloppine al marsala, scaloppine al limone and saltimbocca.

It is this skill that Dominic practices as he takes a solid pale-pink morsel of veal the size of a baby's fist, slices and unfolds it, pounds it to a cardboard thinness —and proudly presents it to his customer, like a jewel on a bed of brown wrapping paper.

As night falls on the busy Feast of San Gennaro, carnival crowds spill over into Grand Street under a canopy of lighted arches.

For the Feast of San Gennaro, Naples Comes to the Sidewalks of New York

For most of the year there is little about Mulberry Street to distinguish it from any of the other tenement-lined streets of Little Italy in lower Manhattan. But as September 19 (the Feast Day of San Gennaro, patron saint of Naples) nears, a six-block stretch of Mulberry Street erupts in a gay, gaudy, crowded, pungent fair that lasts for 10 days and 9 nights. For nearly half a century this Vesuvius of southern-Italian merrymaking has provided New York's Italian community with an outlet for pent-up nostalgia and for expressing its essentially village-oriented heritage. Each evening during the festival, beginning before dusk and lasting long into the night, third- and fourth-generation Italian-Americans from elsewhere in the city and from the suburbs come to the Mulberry Street area as if attracted to a shrine. Thousands of tourists and New Yorkers of other ethnic backgrounds add to the throng, which surges along a solid wall of carnival stalls and food carts.

The Feast of San Gennaro has a religious background, but it is the carnival atmosphere and the Italian food that draw the crowds. A popular item on the six-block-long "table" is the Italian sausage, either hot or sweet (in the picture above, a skewer of sausages is held aloft by Dominic Paolicelli). Broiled over charcoal with red and green peppers, the sausage is eaten in a crusty segment of Italian bread. At left, Filomina Sorrento, outside the Mulberry Street pastry shop she and her husband have run for 40 years, displays her wares—*cannoli* on top, *pasticiotti* and *sfogliatelle* below.

that the southern Italian ultimately learned about *osso buco* and veal *scaloppine,* and his neighbor who came from the north met up with pizza and eggplant Parmesan. Here was a melting pot within the Melting Pot: first in their homes and then in restaurants patronized almost entirely by fellow immigrants, they expanded, perfected and "naturalized" their regional dishes and put together what became the Italian-American cuisine —a combination utterly new under the sun.

Unlike the Lithuanians, Ukrainians and Romanians, who hoarded their culinary knowledge in tight little communities that even today seem like enclaves transplanted from abroad, the Italians generously shared the fragrant riches of their table. They introduced America to the wondrously varied world of pasta; they wrote into the American menu now-familiar dishes such as *lasagna* and *manicotti,* antipasto and minestrone, chicken *cacciatora* and *pasta e fagioli.* They gave the American larder new vegetables, from broccoli to fennel; new herbs, from rosemary to oregano; new cured meats, from salami to *mortadella;* new cheeses, from Parmesan to *pecorino romano.* It was they, too, who taught America the virtue that is in crisp-crusted bread; even in a city such as San Francisco, where so much of it (French as well as Italian) is so widely appreciated, it is baked by Italians. And wine: it is more thanks to "Dago red" than to the *château* vintages of Bordeaux and Burgundy that America at long last accepted wine as a dinner beverage. The millions from Italy made it in their basements from grapes shipped to them by fellow immigrants in California. Their hearty enjoyment of it, and their persistent offer of the friendly glass, tempered the American's aversion and persuaded him that wine should at least be drunk with Italian food in the newly discovered Italian restaurant. It was as good a start as any.

Such, in summary, are the elements of the Italian immigrant's cuisine in the U.S.A. America itself, suspicious at first and even scornful of the swart Italian and his strange foods, came eventually to accept, respect and admire both him and his cooking. And now, only 70 years after Italians began coming to the New World in large numbers, both the immigrant and his food are integrated into the American community.

As for my own family, half a century ago, we settled down to the happy challenge with joy in our hearts, skill in our hands, strength in our backs and a touch of ancestral gluttony to urge us on. Carlo had told us that in America one worked hard, 10 hours a day in fair weather or foul, for the good things one enjoyed. Well, that did not frighten us in the least; labor had been our way of life. We dug a cellar, planted a garden, built a barn for two cows, had pigs, chickens and rabbits. In that first garden we raised the basic vegetables: potatoes, peas, beans, three kinds of cabbage, turnips, parsley, celery, zucchini, chard, lettuce. On the adjacent acres that we were free to cultivate we raised food for our animals. In the streams we caught trout and salmon. We hunted grouse, quail, rabbit, never failing to get as much as we needed. And every day we sat down to a dinner that our masters in Italy, the *padroni,* could never surpass. We had the materials now, and the money to buy what we could not produce. We also had solid Mediterranean expertise in the kitchen: both Father and Mother were good cooks. Father had read Pellegrino Artusi's classic work on *l'arte di mangiare bene,* the art of good eating. Mother had worked for a time for a French family in Marseilles, where she had added to her skill at the stove.

Every good food that we had rarely had in the Old Country we could now command every day in the week. Steaks and chops and roasts, cut with a lavish hand by Charlie, the butcher, from gigantic carcasses that hung in his shop, were in our kitchen whenever we wanted them; when we bought our meat from him, there was always that gratuity of liver, or beef shank, or heart or other viscera, just as Carlo had said.

We brought our own Italian touch to these American riches. In the hog-butchering season we made prosciutto, ham Italian style, not smoked but salted and air-dried for a year. Also *pancetta,* the mild Italian bacon, cured the same way; and quantities of *fegatelli,* or chunks of pork liver, with cubes of tenderloin dipped in salt, pepper and spices, wrapped in caul fat (the membrane enclosing the pig's stomach), speared with a sprig of fennel and deep-fried in rendered pork fat. All these delights could be kept indefinitely in congealed lard and stored in the cellar.

We were fortunate that Father and Mother worked so well together. On Sundays and holidays, or when bad weather kept Father from work on the land, they always collaborated in the kitchen. I remember those special mornings—dinner was served promptly at 1 o'clock—when Mother prepared her chicken soup and Father his Italian-American version of sautéed rabbit. They had come to believe that the height of well-being was to have the means necessary to begin every dinner with a dish of chicken-and-beef broth. Accordingly, toward midmorning, Mother would put into the huge soup kettle an old hen or a surplus rooster, and cuts of beef shank or meaty soup bones. Then she would put wood to the fire in the stove and go about her other tasks.

Father would now appear, to continue where she had left off. In a white shirt open at the throat and sleeves rolled to the elbow, he would tackle the brace or more of rabbits he had killed and skinned and eviscerated the night before. First, he would cut them into small pieces, working slowly, every move deliberate and certain, like some artist guided by a clear vision of what he sought to create. Next he would brown the pieces in olive oil. (Back in our native Tuscany, oil pressed from olives is the cooking oil of choice, even though, in the dairy country in northern Italy, butter is preferred. Naturally, Father doted on olive oil, loving the flavor and aroma it imparted to food.) He would then add minced onion, then garlic, then parsley and thyme and rosemary and a fistful of boletus mushrooms that we had gathered and dried. A dash of allspice, a touch of red pepper, a glass of dry white wine, salt and pepper, and all the ingredients were in. He would now stir and sniff and move the huge skillet away from the intense heat on the broad surface of the wood range. Then, looking pleased and self-satisfied, he would light his pipe and pour himself a glass of wine.

Mother would now return hurriedly to the stove from whatever she had been doing. The soup kettle would be boiling. She would maneuver it to one side, skim away the foam and the fat, add salt, peppercorns, tomato paste and the necessary aromatics—onion, parsley, celery, carrot,

---

As International as Pasta

Along with their spiritual contributions to American life, Italian-Americans gave one very solid substance to the American table—pasta. Thomas Jefferson, that man of genius, loved the stuff, and after a trip to Italy he ordered and eventually acquired the first pasta machine to reach the United States. But the approach to pasta was less enlightened then than it is today; a recipe for spaghetti published in 1792 called for boiling it in water for three hours, then boiling it 10 minutes more in a broth, and finally mixing it with bread in a soup tureen.

By the end of the 19th Century, a number of Americans had followed Jefferson abroad and learned to enjoy pasta as it should be cooked and served. Ultimately, pasta came to rank with potatoes and rice as an American staple. But, in crossing the ocean, the national food of Italy came to be treated in new, inventive ways. The peculiarly American dish called spaghetti and meatballs is an example. Though it appears on the menu of nearly every Italian restaurant in the country, the combination does not exist in Italy; it is no more Italian than the fortune cookie is Chinese. If native Italians eat meat with their spaghetti, it is in a ragù, or sauce, containing ground meat—but some Italian-Americans accept the meatball-spaghetti combination as a delightful dividend of American opulence (though they accept true pasta dishes with greater delight). There is, however, one American invention that turns Italian gills green. That (Oh, ye Gods of Rome, hide your eyes!) is the use of macaroni in salads—cold, mind you, and dressed with mayonnaise. Basta to such a pasta!

Italian-style Farming on a Grand Scale

Ankle-deep in a field of chives that seems to stretch to the distant hills of California's Santa Clara Valley, 74-year-old Guglielmo Armanino *(left)* examines samples of the crop on which he has built a multi-million-dollar family business. Armanino came to America from Genoa in 1921, and soon followed the route of thousands of his compatriots to California. The state's combination of fertile soil and a climate reminiscent of the Mediterranean area seemed heaven-sent to these immigrants from the exhausted lands of northwestern Italy; within six months of his arrival Armanino himself was a truck farmer, raising the bell peppers, artichokes, eggplants and broccoli that are the particular favorites of Italian-Americans in the vegetable cornucopia of their adopted land. He also grew small crops of chives for his own table and a few local markets. But as American cooks became more sophisticated, the demand for the delicate oniony herb grew, and Armanino began to specialize. Today, with over 100 acres of chives in cultivation *(right)* and his own freeze-drying plant, Armanino is now the world's largest producer of the "orchid of the lily family," so called for its lovely blossoms.

Big Dividends
from Red Ink

It is a strange fact that, though the vast majority of Italian immigrants to America never ate in a restaurant in their native land, they were largely responsible for teaching the mass of Americans the pleasures of dining out. It happened like this:

As with most immigrant groups, Italian men generally came to America first, and sent for their families only after they had found work and a place to live. Gravitating to the growing Italian neighborhoods, these single men ate their first meals with already-established families—families of cousins, uncles or simply fellow townsmen from the old country. Some inevitably stayed on as paying guests. Mamma simply threw a little more pasta in the pot and stretched the sauce. Thus a number of Italian immigrant families discovered that there was money to be made in feeding others.

But what was it that transformed these informal Italian kitchens into the hundreds of little Gino's or Tony's or "mamma" restaurants complete with white tablecloths and bread sticks? First, there was the food itself. Most Americans were accustomed to a plate of meat, potatoes and vegetables within the parentheses of a bland soup and a heavy dessert. By contrast, there was a certain grace and form in the Italian meal as it became naturalized in America. It began with antipasto, to titillate but not satiate the diner. Next, perhaps, a bowl of minestrone. Then came steaming pasta in one of its variety of forms. The pasta was not intended to fill the void either; it left room for a small (and economical) portion of meat or chicken, with a vegetable on the side, followed by a crisp salad and dessert: spumoni or tortoni and cheese or fresh fruit if one wished.

(Continued on opposite page)

bay leaf. This done, she would get the kettle to boil briskly once more, then move it over moderate heat for a final hour of simmering. As dinnertime approached, the aroma of the rabbit mingled with the vapors of the aromatics and the rich chicken-and-beef broth to produce a symphony of culinary odors such as must permeate that nook reserved in eternity for the most reverent gastronomes.

There was a touch of madness in our celebration of the joy of merely eating well. The best of our life was lived at the table. We approached it with sniffs of happy anticipation. Any occasion, sacred or otherwise, was excuse for a dinner, a picnic, a banquet. Indeed, a full-dress banquet, or *pranzo,* often exalted such ordinary events as a son's graduation from high school. The cooking had an Italian accent; the eating was in the manner prescribed by that English gourmand, Dr. Samuel Johnson—with concentrated attention. Giovanni and Antonio would sniff the roast chicken that Maria had laved with a marinade of garlic, sage, parsley, onion, vinegar and olive oil in preparing it for the oven, and with impish play of flushed features they would congratulate each other: "America is good."

For a man such as Marco Spinoli, in 1928, that was an understatement. Our families had been neighbors in Tuscany, where our cuisine—in "the land of beef, beans and Chianti"—had seldom transcended tired bread, *polenta* with fish or onions, diluted soups and scantily seasoned greens. Marco and Father had come to America at the same time, and both had gone to work on the railroad; but Marco had proved to be one of the shrewd ones. He started his own business, selling groceries to the immigrants. Later he became a restaurateur and a landlord. He invested in A. P. Giannini's banking empire and became relatively wealthy.

I remember a *pranzo Luculliano* that Marco hosted to celebrate the marriage of one of his associates in 1928, when I was in law school. It began with a shot of whiskey, an American touch. Platters of antipasto constituted the first course. Each was a medley of thinly sliced prosciutto, salami and *mortadella;* fillets of anchovies, hearts of celery, radishes; black and green olives, mushrooms and hearts of artichokes in oil; green onions, *peperoncini* and a variety of pickled vegetables. These platters were on the table when we were called to dinner. Marco wished everyone *buon appetito,* the guests toasted each other, and the feast was under way. The crusts of the homemade bread crunched in strong peasant jaws; glasses clinked and voices exploded in good cheer. It was all wonderful to hear.

After the antipasto there was a bowl of clear broth, a dish that the Italian peasant all but reveres. It is nourishing, of course, when made with abundant beef or chicken; but because he loves it so and can afford it so seldom, he has ascribed therapeutic virtues to it. He also considers it the food of the aristocracy. Whoever can afford to have clear broth even once a week, on Sunday, has definitely arrived; and when anyone is indisposed with whatever ailment, the expressed wish is that there might be a dish of broth for him. The broth served by Signora Spinoli was made with both chicken and beef, boiled together and sprinkled with grated Parmesan and finely minced parsley. "It would resuscitate the dead," said one of the guests. "Have another bowl," said Marco, "there is plenty."

There was plenty indeed. Boiled beef and chicken were the next course.

These were served with a *pinzimonio,* a sauce made of olive oil, salt, pepper, minced garlic and parsley, a touch of vinegar. At the head of the table, arms upraised like a priest blessing his flock, Marco again urged everyone to do his utmost. "Eat, you sons of misery! Don't stand on ceremony. Take more!" And when a guest intimated that he was approaching his limit, Marco had the appropriate advice. "Take your time. The whistle no longer blows for us. And remember: he who goes slowly, goes sanely and far." Pleased with his own wisdom, and while we were waiting for the pasta—no *pranzo* was complete for Marco without pasta—he proposed that we all join him in a toast:

Bevevan i nostri padri,	Our fathers drank,
Bevevan le nostre madri,	Our mothers drank,
E noi che figli siamo,	And we who are their children,
Beviam, beviam, beviamo!	Let us drink, drink, drink!

Then came the spaghetti, steaming hot. Two large platters were passed around the table. The aroma of the sauce swirled above them, tantalizing even those who had delved too lustily into the preceding courses. Everyone ate heartily of it and praised the Signora who had made it. Being an accomplished cook from Tuscany, she had prepared the classic sauce, made with minced lean beef, chicken livers, a blend of aromatics, certain spices, wine and tomato paste discreetly used. Signora Spinoli laughed away the praise with a brush of her hand, insisting that she had used too much allspice, and waddled off to the kitchen. Twenty years of America had broadened the hips, monumentalized the bosom and brought a glow of well-being to her full round face.

The climactic course was a Signora Spinoli original inspired by American abundance: thin slices of veal (a meat the Italians taught the Americans to appreciate), lightly spread with herbs and sausage meat, rolled, dusted with flour, sautéed in olive oil and sprinkled with Marsala. It was accompanied by zucchini and artichoke hearts, sliced thin, rolled in flour, dipped in egg and fried in olive oil. When all these blessings were on the table, Marco's partner exclaimed, "I never dreamed there would be so much misery in the home of Marco Spinoli!" There were groans of exasperated contentment: appetites were now blunted.

When the nuts and *biscotti* and sweet wine arrived, paunches bulged, belts were loosened and the breathing was heavy. Cigars were passed around and Marco made his ultimate gesture, lighting them with a flaming dollar bill. "Viva l'America!" he cried. Coffee and bottles of *grappa* were put on the table and we turned to self-congratulatory rhetoric.

As the only university man the guests knew among the five or six thousand Italians who then lived in Seattle—we called it the "Italian Colony" —I was expected to say what those early immigrants loved to hear: "We are children of the oldest civilization in the Western world . . . We came to America to earn our bread with the pick and shovel . . . But we can hold our heads high . . . We are of the breed of Dante, da Vinci and Michelangelo." That sort of talk made their hearts swell with pride. Mussolini was in the headlines of world press. Giannini was the financial genius of the century. And they themselves, having struck it so rich, felt that they were constructed on the Caesar principle.

For a finish, there was the bitter foaming demitasse that Americans learned to call espresso. All prix fixe and—even more important—prix small. When the now-famous Mamma Leone's opened in New York in 1906 with room for 20 diners (it now seats 1,500), the price of a five-course meal was 50 cents— high for the time.

If the price of the food was reasonable, the spirit behind it was infectiously extravagant. In "Papa's Table d'Hôte," Maria Sermolino wrote of Italians like her father, who helped run one of New York's pioneer good Italian restaurants. "To them," she said, "life was not all hard and earnest. Life was an adventure to be enjoyed. A succulent capretto [kid] . . . was not nourishment you ate to keep alive, but for the joy in the taste of it. The translucent red Chianti was not a quick means to a stupor, but a tangy potion pleasing to the palate and stimulating to the gastric juices." The domestic counterpart of this last item, which gave small Italian restaurants a universal nickname, was the ubiquitous "red ink" that came to the tables of the "red-ink joints" in unlabeled bottles and was included in the price of the meal.

In short, what the Italians taught Americans was that eating out could and should be fun. It became even more fun during Prohibition, when the red ink was poured from gingerale bottles, the cocktail was served in a coffee cup and the local basement restaurant became the local, dimly lit speakeasy. By 1933, when the 18th Amendment was repealed, the red-ink joint was indelibly stamped on the American scene, and the habit of going out to dinner had become something Americans enjoyed not only when far from home, but also whenever they sought the sheer pleasure of sharing good food over a bountiful table and a bottle of wine. And if the lights were low and the company attractive, so much the better.

The star performer of "steelhead Pellegrini," a fresh five-pound steelhead trout, reposes on a bed of home-grown chard in author Angelo Pellegrini's patio in Seattle. Fronting it are ingredients for an Italian-inspired sauce—from left to right, salted capers, garlic and shallots, lemon, butter, parsley, flour, creamed morel mushrooms, pennyroyal and cream. Behind the fish, olive oil, fish stock and vermouth flank a bunch of Pellegrini-grown Oregon grapes.

Such was the grand cuisine of the Italian immigrants in the roaring '20s. By this time many had enlarged their cooking by incorporating into it certain American dishes and culinary practices; and the Italian cuisine itself, through the neighborly exchange between native and immigrant, was becoming increasingly appreciated in the American community.

The more skillful cooks among the immigrants further enlarged their cuisine by applying the Italianate elements of their art to the food resources of the region in which they now lived—an art that consists mainly in the use of fresh culinary herbs. If the French cuisine is distinguished by its sophisticated sauces, that of the Italian—more simple, more balanced in taste, less rich—owes its excellence to the wise use of garlic, shallots and such herbs as rosemary, sage, oregano, parsley, basil, thyme, marjoram, bay leaf. The preparation of fish dishes at my own home in the Puget Sound country is an example of this. In place of the traditional antipasto, we sometimes serve a Dungeness crab and Puget Sound shrimp cocktail—but instead of cocktail sauce we use olive oil, lemon juice and a fine mince of parsley, celery leaves, shallots, garlic and tarragon.

For the main course we may choose fillets of sole, not simply fried but rolled and cooked in a sauce made with shallots, parsley, garlic, capers, lemon juice, dry vermouth, cream and seasonings. Or king salmon, poached in white wine and finished under the broiler, spread with a simple sauce made with butter, parsley, garlic, lemon juice, white wine and seasonings. Or salmon steaks cooked in a fluid sauce made with olive oil, shallots, parsley, English pennyroyal, capers, dry vermouth, lemon juice, a touch of tomato sauce and seasonings. Or crabmeat, simmered briefly in an herb-tomato sauce that contains chopped spinach or chard.

To complement many of the above we may serve mashed potatoes —not plain, but blended with sour cream, grated Parmesan, a mince of parsley and green onions, and baked to a light-brown surface crispness in the oven. Or instead we may even Italianize Southern spoon bread, making it with the coarsely ground yellow cornmeal Italians use for *polenta*, and rendering it fluffy by folding beaten egg white into it.

With fish, and especially the crab-shrimp first course, we usually serve Folle Blanche, a white wine grown and brought to perfection by an Italian immigrant and his son in California, Louis M. and Louis P. Martini. Light, fruity and pleasantly tart, it is one of the better white wines that nicely complement seafood. The Italian immigrant of peasant stock does not traditionally discriminate between wines that do or do not "go with" a given food. Proverbializing that *tutte le uve fanno vino*—all grapes make wine—he drinks whatever wine he has on hand with the entire meal. But we are no longer peasants; we have acquired the means and the sophistication to perceive that there is merit in sensible discrimination; so we have "naturalized" some of our attitudes toward wine.

Nowhere in the world can one find better pork, beef and lamb than we have found in the U.S.A.; and when these meats are cooked in the Italian immigrant's kitchen, with his skill in the use of herbs and spices, the roasts and cutlets and stews are raised to the highest rank in anybody's *grande cuisine*. Try putting lamb chops in a marinade of olive oil, lemon juice, rosemary and garlic pressed or minced, before you put them under the broiler. Then let your palate judge. With chops, steaks and roasts, especially, we now prefer the robust red wines; and when we have their Pinot Noir or Gamay on hand, we drink the health of another immigrant winegrowing family in California, the family of the late Cesare Mondavi, whose widow Rosa and her sons, Robert and Peter, are respected vintners in the Napa Valley.

On such occasions I remember with affection and respect especially the mother, Rosa, in whose home I have had some of the most superb examples of the naturalized cuisine of the Italian immigrant in America. I often think of that noble lady—now in her late seventies and cooking for the sheer joy of it. For it was her cooking, and the cooking of other Italian housewives of her generation, that non-Italian Americans began to sniff with salivating curiosity years ago, and that eventually led to the immense popularity of the "Italian dinner" all across the country. It was what these ladies learned to do in their kitchens with American abundance that compounded the Italian immigrant's enthusiasm for the pleasures of eating. And this Latin enthusiasm itself contributed significantly to America's increasing interest in the culinary arts as a whole. In a country where the Puritan ethic had demanded an austere posture at the dinner table, people needed the Italian's unabashed Dionysian camaraderie to urge them on to the joyous realization that man ought to mind his belly very carefully and very studiously at least once a day.

Homemade Wine: a Matter of Grapes and Time

Millions of Italian-Americans can still remember a father or grandfather crushing grapes for his own red table wine. The idea may seem exotic and remote, but you need nothing more than grapes and patience to make wine in your home today—and there are now laborsaving devices (pictured on the following pages) to help.

The best grapes for making red wine are two varieties from California—zinfandel and alicante. Forget the legends of barefoot stomping: you need only crush the grapes with your hands or a potato masher to release their juice, called the "must." Good grapes have enough of their own yeast cells and sugar to ferment—that is, for the yeast to transform the sugar into alcohol—without outside help. (To make sure, however, use a saccharometer to test the sugar content of the must to see if more sugar should be added.)

The grapes and must begin their fermentation in well-scrubbed wooden tubs; after three days, the must is strained into large jugs, the jugs are sealed with a double-ball air trap that allows carbon dioxide to escape but prevents bacteria and dust from entering, and the wine is set aside for at least three months to bubble and ferment in peace.

Wine that is ready for bottling must be handled carefully, so as not to disturb the sediment on the bottom. Use a plastic or rubber siphon to transfer it to bottles, and a hand corker to seal the bottles tightly. The wine is now drinkable, but it will improve if you have the fortitude to let it age for another six months. (See the Recipe Booklet for detailed instructions, and page 199 for wine-equipment stores.)

Angelo Pellegrini *(left)*, author of this chapter and an experienced amateur wine maker, uses a "wine thief"—a glass tube—to test the quality of his 1969 Cabernet, aging in a 50-gallon oak barrel. Professor Pellegrini inserts the tube into the cask to withdraw a sample, then lets the wine run into a glass for tasting. The wine cellar in his Seattle home contains hundreds of bottles of homemade wine, supplemented each fall by new wine made from California's Napa Valley grapes.

Tools of Science for the Art of Wine Making

Modern aids to wine making include a saccharometer in a hydrometer jar *(left)*, which measures the sugar content of the grape juice; a double-ball air trap *(below)*, half-filled with water, which permits carbon dioxide to escape; a plastic tube *(right)*, used to siphon the wine from a barrel or jug to a bottle; and a hand corker *(far right)* to pound in the cork.

Brightly colored foil seals go over the corks, and a personal label identifies the maker, type of wine and year it was bottled.

To make two 11-by-16-inch pizzas (to serve 10 to 12)

DOUGH

3 cups lukewarm water (110° to 115°)
2 packages active dry yeast
½ teaspoon sugar
8 to 10 cups all-purpose flour
1 tablespoon salt
4 tablespoons vegetable oil
1 tablespoon unsalted butter, softened

TOMATO SAUCE

4 tablespoons olive oil
1 cup finely chopped onions
1½ teaspoons finely chopped garlic
3 one-pound cans solid-packed tomatoes, and their liquid
1 tablespoon basil
1 tablespoon oregano
½ teaspoon sugar
½ teaspoon freshly ground black pepper
1½ teaspoons salt
A 6-ounce can tomato paste

GARNISH

1 pound mozzarella cheese, coarsely grated
½ cup finely grated Parmesan cheese
¼ pound thinly sliced mushrooms (1 cup)
1 large green bell pepper, seeded, deribbed and thinly sliced
1 large red bell pepper, seeded, deribbed and thinly sliced
½ cup finely chopped onions
¼ cup olive oil

Pizza Siciliana *(Italian)*
SICILIAN PIZZA WITH PEPPERS AND MUSHROOMS

Unlike the familiar round, thin Neapolitan pizza, Sicilian pizza is a relative newcomer to pizza-loving America. Its soft, breadlike crust and rectangular shape actually make it a more practical recipe for the home. The ingredients for the garnish are flexible; you can substitute such items as sliced cooked sausages, black olives or anchovies for the mushrooms and peppers—or add any or all of them to the recipe given here.

Pour ½ cup of the lukewarm water into a cup and sprinkle with the yeast and ½ teaspoon of sugar. Let the mixture rest for 2 or 3 minutes, then stir. Place the cup in a warm, draft-free place (such as an unlighted oven) for 5 to 8 minutes, until the yeast bubbles and the mixture almost doubles in volume.

Place 8 cups of flour and the 1 tablespoon of salt in a large mixing bowl and make a well in the center. Pour in the yeast mixture, the remaining lukewarm water and the vegetable oil and, with a large wooden spoon, gradually incorporate the dry ingredients into the liquid. Continue to stir until the ingredients are well combined and can be shaped into a ball. Transfer the ball to a floured surface and knead, pushing the dough down with the heel of your hand, pressing it forward and folding it back on itself. Continue to knead, incorporating up to 2 more cups of flour if necessary to make a smooth, elastic medium-firm dough.

With a pastry brush, coat the bottom and sides of a large bowl with the tablespoon of softened butter. Place the dough in the bowl, drape it with a kitchen towel and place in the warm, draft-free place for 1 to 1½ hours, or until the dough doubles in volume. Punch it down with a blow of your fist and replace it in the bowl to rise until it again doubles.

Meanwhile, prepare the tomato sauce: In a 10- to 12-inch heavy skillet, heat the olive oil until a light haze forms above it. Add 1 cup of chopped onions and the garlic and, stirring frequently, cook over moderate heat until the onions are soft and translucent. Stir in the tomatoes and their liquid, the basil, oregano, ½ teaspoon of sugar, black pepper, 1½ teaspoons of salt and tomato paste. Bring to a boil over high heat, then lower the heat, partially cover the pan and simmer for 1 hour.

When the dough has risen the second time, punch it down with a blow of your fist and cut it in half. Roll out each half to fit into an 11-by-16-inch jelly-roll pan. Place the dough in the pans and stretch it with your fingers so that it fills the edges and corners. Drape with a towel and set aside again in the warm, draft-free place until the dough has risen almost to the top of the pans.

Preheat the oven to 500°. Divide the sauce in half and spread it over the top of the dough. Bake in the center of the oven for 30 minutes, then sprinkle the pizzas with the mozzarella and Parmesan, mushrooms, green and red pepper slices, and ½ cup of chopped onions. Dribble the ¼ cup of olive oil over the surface and bake for 10 minutes longer. Cut the pizzas into squares or rectangles and serve at once.

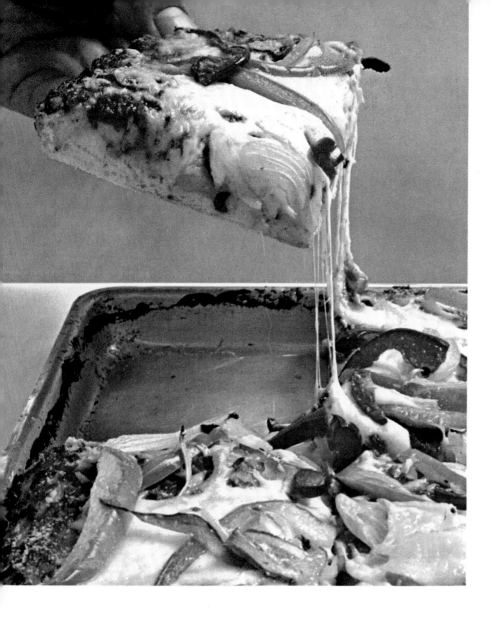

Dripping cheese and calories, a sizzling-hot square of juicy Sicilian pizza is lifted from its baking dish. The breadlike crust of the Sicilian version provides an unexpected touch for most American pizza-fanciers, but the tomato sauce, cheeses, peppers and mushrooms are as irresistible as in the more familiar Neapolitan version.

Salsa di Carne *(Italian)*
TOMATO AND MEAT SAUCE

In a heavy 10- to 12-inch skillet, heat the oil until it is very hot but not smoking. Add the pork and chuck, and brown them over moderate heat, turning them with tongs and regulating the heat so that the meats color richly without burning. Add the onions and garlic and, stirring frequently, cook until the onions are soft and translucent. Stir in the tomatoes and their liquid, the tomato paste, water, oregano, basil, salt and pepper, and bring to a boil over high heat. Partially cover the pan, lower the heat and simmer for 2 to 2½ hours, or until the meat offers no resistance when pierced with the tip of a sharp knife.

Remove the meat from the sauce and set it aside. The sauce may be used at once, either on pasta or as the sauce for meatballs and spaghetti, veal *parmigiana* or stuffed pasta shells *(all in Recipe Index)*. Or the sauce may be cooled to room temperature, tightly covered, and refrigerated or frozen. The meat may be served as a main course with pasta.

NOTE: To make a meatless tomato sauce, prepare the sauce as described but omit the pork and chuck and simmer the sauce for only 1 hour.

To make about 5 cups

4 tablespoons olive oil
½ pound boneless pork, in 1 piece
½ pound chuck, in 1 piece
1 cup finely chopped onions
1½ teaspoons finely chopped garlic
3 one-pound cans solid-pack tomatoes and their liquid
1 six-ounce can tomato paste
2 cups water
1 teaspoon oregano
1 tablespoon basil
1½ teaspoons salt
½ teaspoon freshly ground black pepper

POLENTA
1 quart water
1 teaspoon salt
1 cup finely ground *polenta* (yellow cornmeal)

STUFFING
3 tablespoons butter
½ cup thinly sliced onions
1 teaspoon finely chopped garlic
¾ pound ground pork
¼ cup finely chopped parsley
½ teaspoon salt

QUAIL
4 oven-ready quail (4 to 5 ounces each)
½ teaspoon salt
¼ teaspoon freshly ground black pepper
½ cup vegetable oil
1 large onion, thinly sliced
2 tablespoons flour
½ cup Marsala
1½ cups chicken stock, fresh or canned

2 tablespoons butter
1 tablespoon vegetable oil

Braised Stuffed Quail on Polenta Rounds *(Italian)*

Many Americans, although familiar with the southern Italians' love for rice and pasta, are unaware of the great popularity of polenta—or cornmeal—in the north. Polenta can be cooked as described below and served hot with a variety of sauces, but an Italian-American favorite is polenta in the Venetian style, served with small birds.

POLENTA: Combine the water and 1 teaspoon of salt in a heavy 3- to 4-quart saucepan and bring to a boil over high heat. Pour in the *polenta* in a slow, steady stream, making sure that the boiling never stops and stirring constantly to keep the mixture smooth. Reduce the heat and simmer the *polenta*, stirring frequently, for 20 to 30 minutes, or until it is thick enough so that the spoon will stand unsupported in the middle of the pan. Spoon the *polenta* evenly into an ungreased jelly-roll pan and refrigerate for about 2 hours, or until it is very firm.

STUFFING: In a 10- to 12-inch skillet, melt 3 tablespoons of butter over moderate heat. Drop in the chopped onions and garlic and, stirring frequently, cook until the onions are golden brown. Stir in the pork and continue to cook until the meat no longer shows any trace of pink. Add the parsley and ½ teaspoon of salt, and transfer to a large mixing bowl to cool to room temperature.

QUAIL: Wash the birds under cold running water and pat them completely dry inside and out with paper towels. Sprinkle the birds inside and out with ½ teaspoon of salt and the black pepper, and stuff them with the pork mixture. Close the cavities by sewing them with a large needle and heavy white thread, and truss the birds securely.

In a heavy 10- to 12-inch skillet, heat the ½ cup of oil over moderate heat until a light haze forms above it. Add the birds and, turning them frequently with tongs or a spoon, brown them delicately on all sides. Regulate the heat if necessary so that the birds color evenly without burning. As they brown, transfer the birds to a 3- to 4-quart casserole. Drop the onion slices into the skillet and, stirring frequently, cook over moderate heat until they are soft and golden brown. Thoroughly mix in the flour and, stirring constantly, pour in the Marsala and chicken stock. Bring to a boil over high heat, scraping in the brown particles that cling to the bottom and sides of the pan. Pour the contents of the skillet over the quail in the casserole. Bring to a boil over high heat, then cover the casserole tightly, reduce the heat to low, and simmer for 45 minutes.

Meanwhile, remove the *polenta* from the refrigerator and, with a 3½- to 4-inch cookie cutter or glass, cut out four rounds. In a 10- to 12-inch skillet, melt 2 tablespoons of butter with 1 tablespoon of oil over moderate heat. When the butter foam begins to subside, add the *polenta* rounds and brown them delicately on both sides, turning them with a spatula. When they are golden brown, transfer to a heated serving platter and keep warm in a low oven.

Test the quail for doneness by piercing the thigh with the point of a small sharp knife. The juice that trickles out should be pale yellow with no trace of pink; if necessary, braise the birds for 5 to 10 minutes more.

Place each quail on a *polenta* round, pour the sauce in the casserole over the birds and serve at once.

Tiny pork-stuffed quail are turned in a skillet *(above)* until they are golden brown on all sides. Tongs are used so as not to bruise the birds' delicate skins.

Rounds of *polenta* are browned lightly *(above)*. The finished birds *(below)* are perched on the *polenta* rounds and moistened with their own sauce.

Two light, creamy desserts for an Italian meal are frozen rum-flavored biscuit *tortoni (left),* adorned with nuts and cherries; and crisp, deep-fried *cannoli (right),* with a filling of ricotta and a topping of grated chocolate and pistachio sprinkles.

Biscuit Tortoni (Italian)
RUM-FLAVORED FROZEN CREAM

A popular Italian-American restaurant dessert, biscuit tortoni was introduced in Paris in 1798 by a Neapolitan restaurateur named Tortoni.

To serve 12

2½ cups heavy cream, chilled
½ cup confectioners' sugar
A pinch of salt
5 to 8 stale macaroons, crushed in a
    blender or wrapped in a towel
    and crushed with a rolling pin
    (1 cup crumbs)
¼ cup dark rum
1½ teaspoons vanilla extract
¼ cup sliced toasted almonds
6 candied cherries, cut in half
    (optional)

Place a pleated paper liner in each of twelve 2- to 2½-inch muffin-tin cups and set aside. In a large bowl, combine 1¼ cups of the heavy cream, the sugar, salt and crushed macaroons. Refrigerate for about 30 minutes, or until the macaroons are chilled and soft.

In a large chilled mixing bowl, beat the remaining heavy cream with a whisk or a rotary or electric beater until it thickens and forms soft peaks. With a rubber spatula, fold in the macaroon mixture and the rum and vanilla extract. Fill the muffin-tin liners with the cream mixture. Sprinkle the tops evenly with the sliced almonds and, if you like, top with a candied cherry half. Freeze for at least 2 hours before serving.

Cannoli (Italian)
PASTRY TUBES FILLED WITH RICOTTA

To serve 16

CANNOLI
2 cups all-purpose flour
½ teaspoon salt
2 tablespoons sugar
2 eggs
4 to 6 tablespoons white wine

Place the flour, salt and sugar in a large mixing bowl and make a well in the center. Drop in the eggs and 4 tablespoons of the white wine and, with a large wooden spoon, gradually incorporate the dry ingredients into the liquid. Continue to beat the mixture, adding up to 2 more tablespoons of wine if necessary, until you have a medium-firm dough

46

that can be gathered into a ball. Set the dough aside to rest for 30 minutes.

Meanwhile, prepare the filling: With a large spoon, rub the ricotta through a fine sieve set over a large bowl. Beat in the vanilla extract, the 1½ cups of confectioners' sugar, the citron and the orange peel, and continue to beat until the mixture is smooth. Set aside.

Transfer the dough to a lightly floured surface and, with a rolling pin, roll it into an 18-inch circle about ⅟₁₆ inch thick. With a 3½-inch cookie cutter, cut out 16 circles; if necessary, gather the scraps into a ball, roll them out again and cut out the additional circles. With the rolling pin, gently roll each circle into an oval shape about 4 inches long. Wrap the pastry ovals around metal *cannoli* forms, overlapping the edges in the center. With a pastry brush, seal the edges with the beaten egg white.

Fill a deep fryer or deep heavy saucepan with vegetable oil to a depth of 2 or 3 inches and set over moderately high heat until the oil reaches a temperature of 350° on a deep-frying thermometer. Fry two or three *cannoli* at a time for 2 to 3 minutes, turning them several times with tongs, until they are golden. With the tongs, transfer them to paper towels to drain. When the *cannoli* have cooled enough to handle, slip the pastry off the forms. Repeat, shaping and frying the remaining pastry ovals.

Put the ricotta filling into a pastry bag fitted with a plain tube equipped with a ½-inch opening and squeeze the filling into the cooled *cannoli* shells, letting it mound on the open sides. Set the filled *cannoli* on a serving tray and sprinkle the exposed filling with the grated chocolate and nuts. Just before serving, dust with confectioners' sugar.

FILLING
4 cups (2 pounds) ricotta cheese
1 tablespoon vanilla extract
1½ cups confectioners' sugar
½ cup finely chopped citron
½ cup finely chopped candied
    orange peel

1 egg white, beaten
Vegetable oil for deep frying

1 ounce semisweet chocolate, grated
2 tablespoons finely chopped
    pistachio nuts
Confectioners' sugar

by DALE BROWN

A veteran FOODS OF THE WORLD author, Mr. Brown wrote *The Cooking of Scandinavia, American Cooking* and *American Cooking: The Northwest.* To research Chapters 3 and 4 he visited many ethnic settlements, from Manitoba to New Jersey.

The Lusty Foods of Central Europe

Three Czech-American food classics—caraway-seasoned roast duck *(Recipe Index),* sliced potato dumplings and sweet-and-sour cabbage—are displayed by Mrs. Helen Zelenka of Milwaukee. While the duck is in the oven Mrs. Zelenka pierces the skin to drain off surplus fat; for a final touch, she sets the bird over a quick fire to bring the skin to crackling crispness.

Only a Hungarian would write a love poem to a pig. "Your Grace, Your Most Gracious Majesty," intoned our sturdy, well-fed host, reciting the first line of "In Praise of a Sow" by the Hungarian poet József Berda. The host's eyes moved hungrily over an array of dishes, every one of them based on pork. Then, with a lover's intensity, he continued: "Thus I courted the four-hundred-pound sow, when grunting she approached me. . . ." The dozen guests burst out laughing, and the meal began.

We had gathered to celebrate the *disznó-tor,* or "feast of the pig's wake." It is a rural Hungarian ritual dating from medieval times, and traditionally held in winter on the day a fattened pig is butchered. The neighbors come to help—the men to grind the meat and make the sausages, the women to render the lard and do the cooking. At a midmorning break, sour soup, potted pork and roast pork are served. Later in the day, after the work is over, a feast is held. A soup prepared from the pig's snout and backbone, a plate of braised pig's ears with horseradish, pork sowbelly and riblets cooked with cabbage, several roasts and at least a half dozen kinds of fresh sausage are laid out on a long, plain table and everyone sits down to food and song.

Much the same gusto marked this *disznó-tor,* but there were some important differences. The setting was not Hungary but New Jersey. We met in the dining room of a modern split-level house owned by a Hungarian-born printer and his wife—a house as American as could be, right down to the permanent-press cloth on the table. Moreover, our host and hostess had not slaughtered a pig, nor had the neighbors come to help them; instead, like most of the other Hungarian-Americans who keep the tradition of this winter feast, they had bought their pork products from the local butcher. The preparations, however, were entirely their own; all the preceding day they had been making the sausages and lining up the ingredients for the more elaborate dishes.

The meal we were about to eat was one I had long anticipated, for I was aware that food held extra meaning for the Hungarian-Americans around me. In Hungary, as in other parts of Central Europe, food had been respected as a gift of nature. Later, in the New World, it served as consolation in the uncertainty and loneliness that beset newcomers to a strange land. For immigrants from Hungary, and for the peoples from what is now Czechoslovakia and Yugoslavia (with whom this chapter will also deal), the preservation of their distinctive cuisines became a point of special pride—a way of proclaiming that, even in the Melting Pot, they were still uniquely themselves. In time they began to give up the outward signs of their old life—the big capes, the embroidered blouses, the peasant woman's babushka—and even the mother tongue seemed in danger of being forgotten. But not so the cooking; this was a tradition that could be clung to and passed on to daughters and granddaughters.

To be sure, the abundance and variety of American food —and the newcomers' increasing ability to pay for it—had their effect. Meat consumption, for instance, rose markedly; in some immigrant households the men would eat as much as three pounds a day. Dishes that had been only holiday fare in the old country now were eaten throughout the year. New foods were tried, and some found their way into cherished recipes. Old foods were eaten in new ways: many Central Europeans ate their first raw tomatoes in the New World, and had their first taste of lettuce that was crisp and fresh rather than wilted and smothered by a dressing of hot bacon fat, sugar and vinegar.

I knew of this culinary history, but from books, which is not the same as knowing it from good meals at friendly tables. Now, at this *diszno-tor* in suburban New Jersey, I could begin my direct exploration of these American inheritors of some of the world's great culinary traditions.

Our meal began with stuffed cabbage—thick, moist rolls of it, filled with chopped pork and rice, and cooked on a bed of sauerkraut. The tart, meaty juices had been thickened with a brown *roux* and poured over the rolls before serving. Spoonfuls of glowing sour cream went on top to complete a dish that was both robust and rich. It was followed by three kinds of pork sausage: *kolbász,* seasoned with garlic, black pepper, paprika and salt; *fehér hurka,* made with liver and meat from the pig's head, mixed with boiled rice; and *véres hurka,* consisting of the pig's blood combined with bits of pork and crumbled white bread. With the sausages came oven-browned potatoes and sweet-and-sour red cabbage, and there was a strong Hungarian red wine to drink.

Soon spirits were soaring, and it was the guests' turn to take a fling at poetry. "Fly into my lap," went the first verse, "let me kiss and caress you! Fly into my open mouth, heavenly vision, to roast alive upon the tip of my burning tongue." The object of this affection? A goose! The next verse praised mutton stew, "true miracle . . . to eat you demands the

50

smacking of lips!" Another celebrated "mounds of peppers with smiling bellies," and commanded, "let the essence of taste pour from you!"

"This often happens at our house," the hostess told me. "A dinner party will turn into a poetry recital. Hungarians love poetry almost as much as they love food. There have been times when we've sat at the table until five or six in the morning reciting poems and singing folk songs. A man visiting us from Hungary couldn't get over it. 'But you are even more Hungarian than we are!' he said. I had to laugh—I was born and raised in Pittsburgh."

How, then, had she come to cook like this? "I learned from my mother, who was born in Hungary—and I learned from my husband, too. He left Hungary when the Communists took over, and he hungered for the dishes of his youth. He wanted me to cook them for him, but I didn't know how. I'm glad I learned. You see, my husband was raised in the city, my mother in the country. I started cooking her way, nice and simple, as they did back in her village—then he taught me his way. I'd stand by him at the stove and try to measure out whatever he was getting ready to throw in the pot, and write it down."

She got up to clear the table, pausing to pat her husband on the shoulder. "We're a lot more relaxed about our cooking today, and he's a lot more American in his attitudes. For instance, stuffed cabbage was a main dish in Hungary, and that's how he used to want it. But he soon found so many good things to eat in America that we began to have the stuffed cabbage as a first course, or as a side dish with fried or roast chicken. In Hungary, you know, people wouldn't have dreamed of killing a young chicken for the table. My mother used to tell a joke about that: a Hungarian ate chicken on only two occasions—when he was sick, or the chicken was."

She excused herself and returned with the dessert—strudel, filled with sour cherries. As she sliced through the layers of paper-thin pastry, she continued, "Hungarians love this dessert, but it wasn't until they got to America that most of them could afford to have dessert every day." She might have added that strudel is the one Hungarian dessert that almost all Americans, of whatever origin, are certain to have heard about, and that Hungarian cooking is more widely known in America than that of the Czechs or Yugoslavs. But Hungarian food, easy to prepare and always satisfying, is its own recommendation, and Americans have borrowed much from the Hungarian kitchen. Goulash, stuffed peppers and chicken paprika have long since passed into America's culinary mainstream, while paprika, the great Hungarian seasoning, adorns every American spice shelf.

Despite this, both paprika and goulash have been misunderstood by non-Hungarians in this country. Paprika, which is produced by grinding the dried pods of a particular variety of pepper, should have spark as well as flavor, but need not be especially hot. Too many Americans use it timidly, as though it could bite, or they merely dash some on pale food for a touch of color. What is worse, some paprika sold in the United States is indeed little more than a coloring agent. The kind probably best suited to American tastes is a comparatively mild type imported from Hungary and poetically called "sweet and noble rose."

Enikö Vasvári, wearing a costume elaborately embroidered with a traditional Hungarian folk motif, samples a bowl of *gulyásleves (Recipe Index)*, a goulash-soup containing beef, potatoes, carrots and tender dumplings. A sturdy pillar of the Hungarian cuisine, goulash dates back at least to the Ninth Century. It can be served as either a soup or a stew, depending on the amount of liquid used in its preparation.

An assortment of fresh Hungarian pastries—a fraction of those turned out for the food fair— offers proof of the survival of Old World baking skills. Many of the baked goods, like the walnut coffeecake and the squares of *linzer tészta* at the center of the top tier, contain prune butter, a Hungarian favorite. To the left of the coffeecake, holeless doughnuts, plain or with prune-butter centers, spill onto the middle tier; other delicacies on this tier are crescents of spongecake topped with ground nuts and powdered sugar, and *kifli,* crisp cornucopias stuffed with cheese or a fruit preserve. Prominent on the bottom tier is a dark honey cake, a triple-layered rum torte and butter cookies—small sandwiches filled with strawberry jam.

The Dishes Are Hearty Hungarian and the Setting Is New Jersey

From the plains and mountains of Hungary to the very American city of Passaic, New Jersey, is a long leap in culture as well as geography, but the immigrants who made the journey brought a style of cooking that lost none of its vigor or flavor in transit. Hungarian-American food at its best can be seen in the dishes served at the food festival held annually by Passaic's Hungarian Reformed Church—dishes that include robust goulashes, homemade sausages, chicken spiced with paprika, sauerkraut with ground pork and sour cream, and an almost endless repertoire of pastries. All the food is prepared by women of the local Hungarian-American community, who have preserved the traditional recipes of their European forebears.

A trio of foods on a single platter *(right)* underscores the Hungarian fondness for pork and pork products. Cabbage rolls stuffed with chopped pork nestle between *kolbász* (pork sausages hotly seasoned with garlic, black pepper and paprika) and grilled boneless pork.

Paprika—and plenty of it—is a key ingredient in the beef stew called goulash; the Hungarian-born restaurateur and author George Lang places it first in what he calls the holy trinity of the Hungarian kitchen—paprika, lard and onions. A truly traditional goulash would be unimaginable without all three to give it flavor and body. It may also contain caraway seeds, and it will be better for the inclusion of some diced beef heart in addition to the chunks of beef. It should never be thickened with flour or cooked with wine. Either fresh tomatoes or tomato purée may be used, along with garlic, sliced green peppers or perhaps, for an extra tingle of excitement, hot cherry peppers. Some cooks serve goulash with potatoes, others with small homemade egg dumplings called *csipetke*—Hungarian tradition permits either or even both of them.

Csipetke are, of course, but one item in the impressive Hungarian panoply of homemade dumplings and noodles, enough to keep a cook experimenting weeks on end, and all excellent. The noodles come in a variety of shapes. One kind is rolled thin and sliced; one is stamped out with a thimble; another is produced with the aid of a grater. The basic recipe for this grated noodle is marvelously simple for something so good—a cup of flour, a large egg and a quarter teaspoon of salt. After the dough is mixed, it is shaped into a firm ball and grated, exactly like cheese. The bits are then spread on wax paper to dry. They may be tossed directly into a soup and cooked, or fried in lard with minced onion until the onion turns soft, then simmered in a little water or broth and served as a substitute for potatoes. Other types of noodles are served as a main course, mixed with boiled cabbage or potatoes. Others are eaten for dessert—though to a lesser extent in America than in Hungary—with butter, sugar, poppy seeds or ground nuts.

Next to noodles and goulash, Hungarian-Americans are perhaps fondest of soups. They have a soup for every mood and season. For hot summer days there is iced sour-cherry soup, or chilled squash soup, a smooth blend of yellow crookneck squash, fresh dill, carrots, onions, celery, potatoes, butter and heavy cream *(Recipe Index)*. Winter has its own soupy comforts: steaming bowls of cabbage soup with smoked sausage, sauerkraut-bean soup, sour-cream-and-potato soup, caraway soup—the list is almost endless. The caraway soup is cooked with water, a dark *roux,* and a tablespoonful of caraway seeds; some housewives build it up with a couple of eggs and serve it with garlic croutons. It is an old dish and—some say—an excellent hangover remedy. A more bracing soup, and one that is probably even more time-honored, is *gulyásleves,* or goulash soup, rich with beef, onions, green peppers and other fresh vegetables, and dotted with tiny *galuska,* or egg dumplings *(Recipe Index).*

Soups as sustaining as *gulyásleves* can be meals in themselves, and in the Old Country often were. In America they may be only a prelude to such hearty dishes as *gőngyőlt borjú,* a rolled steak stuffed with ground pork, ham and a whole hard-cooked egg, served with a sour-cream-and-wine gravy; or tender veal in a sour-cream-and-paprika sauce *(Recipe Index);* or stuffed veal shoulder; or one of the most rib-sticking of all, *székelygulyás,* a goulash of pork slowly cooked with sauerkraut and sour cream, spiced with paprika and topped with a dollop of more sour cream.

Sauerkraut is an important ingredient in Hungarian-American cooking. Often rinsed or soaked beforehand to rid it of some of its sourness, it is cooked either as a dish in its own right, seasoned with a little onion, pepper and paprika, or as part of another dish. Some cooks add it to the ground pork, beef and rice filling for stuffed cabbage rolls; others smother the rolls with it. In one attractive variation, a head of cabbage is hollowed out and crammed with ground meat and rice, then placed in a juicy nest of sauerkraut and slowly cooked *(Recipe Index)*. In "layered cabbage," sauerkraut cushions ground pork and sliced *kolbász;* the sauerkraut flavors the other ingredients, and in turn takes on their flavors.

Reflecting the character of the Hungarians themselves, their meals in America are spirited, full of fun and surprises. In Chicago I attended what purported to be a Hungarian winetasting at the penthouse clubrooms of the Cliff Dwellers, a local organization devoted primarily to the arts. The occasion turned out to be a harvest festival, complete with gypsy music and song. The host and chef for the evening was a local restaurateur, Louis Szathmáry, a great bull of a man with a handlebar mustache. Because Louis saw no reason to waste good wine on mere cheese and crackers, the traditional fare at a tasting, he served a lavish dinner. To prime his guests' taste buds, he served two clear brandies, distilled respectively from plums and apricots; they were accompanied by highly peppered crackling biscuits and by pastry pockets filled with minced ham. Next came a soup called *lebbencsleves,* an ancient shepherds' specialty. Louis' version contained, among other things, beef, bacon, potatoes, green pepper, paprika and noodles. To make the noodles, Louis had rolled the dough out thin and let it dry in sheets. Then he broke the sheets into fragments and browned them in bacon fat and onions before adding them to the soup. The wine with the *lebbencsleves* was a Green Hungarian, a tart American vintage made from grapes introduced to America by Agoston Haraszthy, the Hungarian count who played a major role in the creation of the California wine industry in the 1850s.

For the main course, there was a choice of either Hungarian lamb stew or chicken paprika, served with a bowl of nutty *kása* (a boiled side dish made from coarsely ground wheat) and a crisp cucumber salad. A full-bodied white wine, an imported Hungarian Debrői Hárslevelű, held its own against the strong flavors of the food. The dessert, a cake resurrected from the pages of a centuries-old Hungarian cookbook, provided a splendid climax. It resembled a jelly roll but was made from raised dough, half of which had been prepared with milk, the other half with red wine. Brushed with butter and baked with a sugar-and-almond topping, it was served in thick, colorful pink and white slices with a custardy wine sauce; to go with it, there were cracked walnuts and bunches of white grapes.

Sitting at the crossroads of Europe, Hungary was a focal point of the old Austro-Hungarian Empire; inevitably, its culinary influence spread in many directions long before reaching America. The Czechs and Slovaks to the north and the Yugoslavs to the south were much affected by it, and both developed their own versions of the great Central European dishes —the varied soups and stews, the zesty sausages, the rich baked goods. The Czechs were actually the first to bring this cooking to America. Arriving as early as the 1850s, they settled on cheap land in the Midwest and put their skills as farmers to good use. Many of their descendants still live in such states as Iowa and Nebraska. Though they speak in the accents of Middle America, they have kept their cultural heritage. They have been encouraged to do so, in part, by their numerous secular organizations, most notably the Sokol, or gymnastic society. Some groups have published cookbooks that help to perpetuate Old World foods.

In Cedar Rapids, I visited one Czech-American couple, Theodore and Bette Trefny, who seemed in all respects American—indeed, Yankee. Mrs. Trefny's kitchen was as American-looking as can be imagined: a spotless, shiny place of glittering enameled appliances and Formica surfaces. But after I sat down, she reached deep into a kitchen closet and brought out a wholly un-American object: a large, heavy mold, made of cast iron and shaped rather like a crown. "This," she told me, "is my mother's *bábovka* form. It was the heart of her kitchen."

Mrs. Trefny explained how this mold, which is used to make *bábovka,* an egg-rich cake, had come to America. Her parents emigrated from Prague in 1913, soon after they were married. In deciding what to take along, Mrs. Trefny's mother packed only a Bible, a dream book, a handful of wooden kitchen implements and the clothes she and her husband would need. But the clothes, she thought, would soon wear out, and then she would have almost nothing to remind her of the old country. Suddenly, she made up her mind: no matter how bulky it might be, she would pack her *bábovka* form, too. It would be good to have it in her kitchen; perhaps when she baked a *bábovka* she would feel at home.

Mrs. Trefny's mother did feel at home in America. She was a young woman when she was uprooted and transplanted, but the transplant worked, nourished in part by an invisible taproot that ran deep—her native cooking. She drew moral support from it, and her family grew strong on it; now that she is dead, she is survived by it. Today her daughter prepares many of her specialties—including, of course, the *bábovka.*

Still beloved by Czech-Americans are dumplings, noodles and breads. Christmas would not be Christmas for them without *houska,* an intricately braided loaf flavored with lemon rind and chock-full of raisins and nuts *(Recipe Index)*. Special occasions would seem less special if there were no caraway rye bread *(Recipe Index)* to prove for the millionth time that the only bread worth eating is the home-baked kind. Czech rye bread has body; some of the recipes for it incorporate potato water, some even call for mashed potatoes, and a few housewives add buttermilk or a little vinegar to impart a slightly sour flavor.

Of all Czech baked goods, it is probably the *koláč* that is most popular —the round bun called a kolach in America. Many Czech-American women devote their Saturday mornings to preparing kolaches—first letting the dough rise, then shaping it into balls, then waiting for the balls to double in bulk, then poking pockets in them for fillings. Almost always some of the pockets are filled with ground poppy seeds cooked in milk and honey; other popular fillings are dried prunes, dried apricots and sweetened cottage cheese. Kolaches are perfect with coffee, much lighter in texture than what generally passes for Danish pastry in this country.

No Czech-American dinner is complete without a dumpling of some kind to round it out. There must be more than a dozen different kinds. Some are prepared with yeast, others with baking powder; some are steamed, some simmered and some boiled; some contain fruit. A few use flour only as a binder, and are based on mashed potatoes, or cottage cheese. But the lord of the dumplings is *kynuté knedlíky,* invariably served with roast pork or duck. Along with milk, flour and yeast, eggs, salt and a little sugar, it contains dried bread crumbs or toasted bread cubes; these provide lightness and porosity that are essential if the gravy is to sink in. The dough is shaped into loaves about three inches thick and six inches long and allowed to rise for three quarters of an hour. Then the loaves are dropped into boiling water, cooked for seven minutes on one side and five on the other, and sliced immediately to let the steam escape and prevent sogginess. A length of heavy thread is used to slice them, rather than a knife. The thread is slipped under the dumpling loaf, both ends are brought up and over it, and crossed, and gently pulled in opposite directions. A knife might crush the dumplings; the thread does no damage, and assures light texture in every slice.

There are many places to taste Czech-American food in the Midwest, but none is more interesting than the town of Wilber, which calls itself the "Czech capital of Nebraska." With a population of 1,500—nine tenths of it Czechoslovak in origin—the town sits on a rolling plain that is reminiscent of the great plain of Central Europe. Every summer Wilber is the bustling scene of a two-day folk festival featuring dancing, singing and parades; in years past the festival has drawn upwards of 30,000

As rich and festive as its Old Country counterpart, a golden-brown *bábovka* from a Czech-American kitchen stands before the crown-shaped cake form in which it was baked. Sharing the platter is another Czech specialty—kolaches, round pastries filled with cheese or prune preserves and sprinkled with powdered sugar *(Recipe Index).*

Hungarian-American pork sausages make use of some unexpected parts of the pig. In the center bowl and grinder *(above)* are ingredients of *kolbász*—pork butt, fat and seasonings. To the left is a liver sausage that calls for rice and meat from the head and liver. The pan at right contains blood, ground skins and jowls, and white bread for a blood pudding. Below, *kolbász* is stuffed into casings of pig intestine.

visitors. Wilber's main street would ordinarily pass for any American main street, but at festival time the baker sells great quantities of caraway rye bread and kolaches, and the butcher offers *jelita,* a blood and barley sausage, *jaternice,* a type of headcheese, and cracklings, which customers buy to put in biscuits and dumplings.

Wilber's mayor, Glenn Zajicek, invited me to have dinner with him and his wife and some of their friends at Annie's Jidlike—Annie's Café. Like the town itself, the café turned out to be a perfect example of heartland America, except that on the wall a vivid mural depicted a Czech harvest scene. Annie, a stout, jolly woman who was born on a farm just outside of Wilber, knows all about hearty appetites. The meal she served us was formidable: roast duck with a crisp skin; potato dumplings; a dressing of sauerkraut flavored with onions, caraway seeds and pan drippings; tender rolls called butter horns, and kolaches for dessert.

As we ate, Annie leaned over the serving counter and watched; soon she joined our conversation, and began talking about Czech food in America. We all took up the theme, with everyone singing the praises of his or her favorites—dill sauce, made with vinegar, eggs, flour, cream and snippets of the fresh herb, and poured over new potatoes; wild mushrooms and scrambled eggs; liver dumpling soup; *kuba,* a mushroom and barley casserole *(Recipe Index);* rabbit with prune-and-raisin gravy; *bublanina,* a cake studded with sour cherries. Most of the diners were American-born. They had known hardship in the years when their immigrant parents were struggling for a living, and many remembered such spartan fare as "beggar's soup"—leftover bread, the water in which potatoes had boiled, an egg and garlic. "You know why these things tasted so good?" one woman said. "Our folks were so poor, and we were so young. . . ." But another conclusion was easy to draw: those foods tasted good because, like Annie's dinner, they were cooked with concern.

I was nearing the end of my exploration of the foods of transplanted Central Europeans; only the peoples from what is now called Yugoslavia remained to be visited. Even before then, I had come to certain conclusions.

Cooking is a form of communication, a way people have of expressing their feelings for each other and for the past. The old Central European dishes have not died out or changed drastically in America because they remain associated in many minds with family memories and traditions. They can also be a proud way of saying, "We're different"; and even of emphasizing differences within an immigrant group.

Yugoslav-Americans still cling to their old ethnic designations—Slovenes, Croats, Serbs—and each of these people has its own way of doing things. Yet each way is itself a wonderful mixture. One finds in all their cooking the influences of Austria, Hungary, Czechoslovakia, Greece and even Turkey, suggesting that the Melting Pot was a European phenomenon long before the term was coined in America.

The Slovenes, whose ancestral home is in what is now northwestern Yugoslavia, are strong in Cleveland, where nine fraternal organizations proudly help keep their culture alive. Though their cooking has much in common with that of the Austrians, they single out certain dishes they feel are Slovenian. Notable among them is the *potica,* a nut or raisin roll.

Its cooks do not stint: the raised dough for a *potica* takes as many as half a dozen egg yolks, and the walnut or raisin filling three more.

The Croats, from north-central Yugoslavia, cook with as generous a hand as the Slovenes. In Milwaukee there is a Croatian-owned super-market and catering establishment where, during a long afternoon, I watched the preparations for an enormous church supper. Pickled whole cabbages for *sarma,* the Croatian version of stuffed cabbage, were fished from barrels of brine; down in the basement, suckling pigs were roasted in a battery of ovens. The desserts at the supper itself, all prepared by the women of the congregation, were extraordinary. One was a *pita,* a rich sour-cream pastry in two layers, filled with a crunchy mixture of apples and walnuts *(Recipe Index).* There were also cookies shaped and tinted to look like apricots and peaches, with centers containing a thick paste of butter, sugar, rum, chocolate, cookie crumbs and apricot jam.

The Serbians likewise display a robust attitude toward food—and are par-ticular masters at grilling beef, pork and veal. In America, with its plenti-ful meat, they have been able to uphold the noblest traditions of their homeland in eastern Yugoslavia. Many have settled in Chicago, and sev-eral restaurants have sprung up to spread the fame of their *ćevapčići* (sau-sages of freshly ground beef), *ražnjići* (veal and pork kabobs) and *pljeskavice* (grilled patties of pork and veal). The best of the Serbian eat-ing places, though, may well be a little restaurant called the Three Brothers in Milwaukee. It is a type of restaurant that used to exist wherever im-migrants settled, the so-called mamma and papa restaurant. Three young brothers were once involved in its operation; their number has dwindled to one, but this does not matter much, for the real force has al-ways been the parents, Milun and Milunka Radicevich.

The night I met her, Milunka Radicevich, who still does much of the cooking, was wearing a big white apron down to her ankles; Milun had a green vest buttoned over his ample belly. She was wonderfully expres-sive, using her smile, her gestures and an occasional "Eh!" punctuated with a shrug of her shoulders to supplement her limited English. Eating at the Three Brothers is like being a guest in a Serbian home, and the menu reflects the varied influences that have affected the Serbian kitchen: goulash ("Less greasy than the Hungarian," Milunka's son Alex boasted), *musaka* ("Made the Serbian way with beef," noted Alex, "not the Greek way, with lamb") and *baklava,* a Middle Eastern sweet, filled with wal-nuts and honey, that may have been the prototype of the strudel.

I passed all these up for a Serbian *burek,* a flaky double-crust pie with a choice of fillings—beef, spinach or cheese; I ordered the cheese. The *burek* was as big as the plate on which it rested and it was wrapped, like a package, in layers of crisp, paper-thin pastry. It rustled at the plunge of a fork and a cloud of steam came out. The soft ewe's-milk cheese filling was not only hot, but tart and salty—and very good. According to Alex, no Serbian girl could get ahead in life without knowing how to make a perfect *burek.* As I sat eating mine, Mamma Radicevich, hands folded in satisfaction on her lap, smiled benevolently upon us, and the thought oc-curred that it was the likes of her who have made modern America so ex-citingly diverse a country in which to cook—and to eat.

Gulyásleves *(Hungarian)*
GOULASH SOUP WITH LITTLE DUMPLINGS

In a heavy 3- to 4-quart casserole, melt the lard over moderate heat. Drop in the chuck cubes and brown them on all sides. Set the beef aside on a plate, stir in the onions and garlic and cook until the onions are a light gold. Return the meat to the casserole and remove from the heat.

Place the caraway seeds and the tablespoon of salt in a mortar and, with a pestle, pound them to a fine powder. Or wrap the seeds and salt in a kitchen towel and crush them with a rolling pin. Stir this mixture into the casserole, then add the paprika. Pour in the hot water; the meat should be covered by 3 to 4 inches of liquid. Bring to a boil, then cover the casserole, reduce the heat, and simmer for 1 hour. Add the potatoes and cook for an additional 30 minutes, then add the green peppers, tomatoes and carrots, and cook for 30 minutes longer. Taste for seasoning.

Just before serving the soup, prepare the dumplings. In a mixing bowl, combine the eggs, flour and ⅛ teaspoon of salt. Beat together with a wooden spoon or whisk until the batter is smooth. Using a teaspoon, slide the batter into the simmering soup, a spoonful at a time. Simmer the dumplings for 2 or 3 minutes, or until they rise to the surface. Serve the soup directly from the casserole or a large heated tureen.

Pečená Kachna *(Czech)*
ROAST DUCK WITH SAUERKRAUT DRESSING

Preheat the oven to 450°. Pat the ducks dry inside and out with paper towels. Rub the cavities of both ducks liberally with salt and pepper, and rub the outsides with the garlic cloves. Prick the skin around the thighs, the back and the lower part of the breasts with the tip of a sharp knife. Truss the ducks and place them breast side up on a rack set in a large shallow pan. Roast in the middle of the oven for 20 minutes, until the skins brown lightly. Draw off the fat from the roasting pan with a bulb baster, and set it aside in a bowl. Then reduce the heat to 350°, turn the ducks on one side and roast for about 20 minutes. Turn the ducks on the other side and roast for about 20 minutes longer, removing the fat that accumulates with a bulb baster. Place the ducks breast side up again and roast for 20 minutes longer.

Meanwhile, prepare the dressing: Pour ½ cup of the duck fat into a 10- to 12-inch skillet and set over moderate heat. Drop in the onions and cook until they are golden brown. Mix in the flour and, stirring constantly, cook for 1 or 2 minutes. Gradually pour in the water and, still stirring, bring to a boil over high heat. Add the caraway seeds and paprika, and let the sauce boil uncovered for 15 minutes, or until it has reduced to 2 cups. Stir in the sauerkraut and cook for 5 more minutes.

To test the ducks for doneness, pierce their thighs with the tip of a small sharp knife. The juice that spurts out should be a clear yellow; if it is slightly pink, roast the birds for another 5 to 10 minutes. Transfer the ducks to a heated platter and let them rest for 10 minutes before carving. Present the dressing separately in a heated bowl.

To serve 6 to 8

2 tablespoons lard
2½ pounds chuck, cut into 1-inch cubes
2 cups coarsely chopped onions
1½ teaspoons finely chopped garlic
⅛ teaspoon caraway seeds
1 tablespoon salt
2 tablespoons sweet Hungarian paprika
2 quarts hot water
1 pound potatoes, peeled and cut into ½-inch dice (3 cups)
2 green bell peppers, halved, deribbed and cut crosswise into ¼-inch strips
2 medium-sized firm ripe tomatoes, cut into 1-inch pieces
6 to 7 medium-sized carrots, scraped and sliced crosswise into rounds (2 cups)

GALUSKA (LITTLE DUMPLINGS)
2 eggs
½ cup all-purpose flour
⅛ teaspoon salt

To serve 6 to 8

Two 4½- to 5-pound ducks
Salt
Freshly ground black pepper
2 cloves garlic, peeled and crushed with the back of a knife

SAUERKRAUT DRESSING
½ cup finely chopped onions
3 tablespoons flour
3 cups water
1 teaspoon caraway seeds
1 teaspoon sweet Hungarian paprika
2 pounds fresh sauerkraut, washed, soaked in cold water for 15 minutes and squeezed thoroughly dry

FILLING

2 cups water
¼ cup long-grain unconverted rice
2 tablespoons lard
1 pound ground pork
1 cup finely chopped onions
2 teaspoons finely chopped garlic
¼ cup sour cream
1 egg
1½ teaspoons salt
½ teaspoon freshly ground black
   pepper
1 tablespoon sweet Hungarian
   paprika

SAUERKRAUT

2 pounds sauerkraut
2 tablespoons lard
½ cup finely chopped onions
½ teaspoon finely chopped garlic
1½ teaspoons salt
2 cups chicken stock, fresh or
   canned
½ pound smoked pork butt, thinly
   sliced, or substitute 8 slices
   Canadian bacon

A 3- to 3½-pound cabbage
1 tablespoon sweet Hungarian
   paprika
½ cup sour cream

Töltött Káposzta (Hungarian)
STUFFED WHOLE CABBAGE WITH SAUERKRAUT

FILLING: Bring the water to a boil in a 1-quart saucepan, add the rice and boil briskly, uncovered, for 10 minutes. Drain through a fine sieve and set the rice aside to cool.

Place 2 tablespoons of lard in a heavy 10- to 12-inch skillet and set over moderate heat. Stir in the ground pork and, stirring frequently, cook until the meat no longer shows any trace of pink. Add the cup of chopped onions and 2 teaspoons of chopped garlic, and continue to cook until the onions are golden brown. Transfer the contents of the skillet to a large mixing bowl and stir in ¼ cup of sour cream, the egg, salt, pepper, paprika and the rice. Set the filling aside.

SAUERKRAUT: Drain the sauerkraut, wash it thoroughly under cold running water, and let it soak in a bowl of cold water for 10 to 15 minutes, depending on its acidity. A handful at a time, squeeze the sauerkraut until it is thoroughly dry.

Melt 2 tablespoons of lard in a 3- to 4-quart casserole and add ½ cup of chopped onions and ½ teaspoon of chopped garlic. Stirring frequently, cook over moderate heat until the onions are soft and translucent. Stir in the sauerkraut, 1½ teaspoons of salt, 1 cup of the chicken stock and all but 3 slices of the pork butt or Canadian bacon. Bring to a boil, then cover the casserole, lower the heat and simmer for 1 hour.

CABBAGE: Lower the head of cabbage into a large pot of boiling water and cook briskly for about 15 minutes. Drain the cabbage in a large colander, then return it to the pot and set under cold running water until the cabbage is cold.

Place a double thickness of cheesecloth, measuring about 24 inches square, on a flat surface and set the cabbage in the center. Gently peel back the outer leaves of the cabbage, but leave them attached to the center core. When you can no longer peel back the leaves easily, cut a hole in the center of the cabbage, leaving a ½-inch-thick shell, or "basket," of cabbage. Discard the cabbage you have cut out or chop it and add it to the simmering sauerkraut mixture.

Fill the cabbage basket with the pork stuffing, mounding it high. Draw up the outer leaves of the cabbage over the stuffing, reversing the order you used to pull them back, and top with the 3 remaining slices of pork butt or Canadian bacon. Draw up the ends of the cheesecloth and tie the cabbage package firmly with the loose ends of the cheesecloth.

Preheat the oven to 350°. When the sauerkraut has cooked its allotted time, remove the casserole from the heat. Set the wrapped cabbage on top of the sauerkraut, cover the casserole tightly (with a double layer of aluminum foil under the lid if necessary), and cook in the center of the oven for 1 hour. Transfer the cabbage to a plate, discard the cheesecloth, and cover the cabbage lightly with aluminum foil to keep it warm while you complete the dressing.

Place the casserole on top of the stove and pour in the remaining cup of chicken stock and the tablespoon of paprika. Bring to a boil over high heat, then remove from the heat and stir in the sour cream. Spread the sauerkraut dressing on a heated serving platter, set the stuffed cabbage on top, and serve at once.

Cold frothy beer backstops a spicy Hungarian-American specialty: whole cabbage stuffed with meat and served with sauerkraut.

Dasina Buranija *(Serbian)*
STRING BEANS IN SOUR-CREAM SAUCE

Bring the water and 3 teaspoons of the salt to a boil in a 4- to 5-quart sauce-pan and drop in the string beans, a handful at a time. Bring back to a boil over high heat and boil uncovered for 5 to 8 minutes, or until the beans are tender but still slightly resistant to the bite. Drain the beans, wash them under cold running water and set them aside.

Melt the butter in a heavy 10- to 12-inch skillet. Add the onions and garlic and cook over moderate heat, stirring occasionally, for 5 to 8 minutes, or until the onions are soft. Stir in the flour and paprika and, still stirring, cook for 2 or 3 minutes longer. Pour in the chicken stock and bring to a boil over high heat. Let the sauce boil briskly for 1 or 2 minutes, until it thickens lightly. Stir in the green beans and simmer for 1 or 2 minutes, until they are heated through. Off the heat, stir the sour cream, the remaining 2 teaspoons of salt and the pepper into the skillet. Taste for seasoning and serve at once.

To serve 6 to 8

2 quarts water
5 teaspoons salt
2 pounds fresh string beans, washed and trimmed
6 tablespoons butter
½ cup finely chopped onions
4 teaspoons finely chopped garlic
¼ cup all-purpose flour
2 tablespoons sweet Hungarian paprika
2 cups chicken stock, fresh or canned
½ cup sour cream
¼ teaspoon freshly ground black pepper

Houska *(Czech)*
CHRISTMAS SWEET BREAD

Pour the water into a small bowl and sprinkle with the yeast and 1 teaspoon of the sugar. Let it rest for 2 or 3 minutes, then stir. Set the bowl aside in a warm, draft-free place (such as an unlighted oven) for 5 to 8 minutes, or until the mixture almost doubles in volume.

Combine 4½ cups of flour, the remaining sugar, and the salt, lemon rind and mace in a large mixing bowl and make a well in the center. Pour in the yeast mixture, milk, eggs and egg yolk, and 4 tablespoons of the butter. With a large spoon, stir the dry ingredients into the liquid. Beat until the dough can be gathered into a medium-soft ball. Place on a lightly floured surface and knead, pushing the dough down with the heels of your hands, pressing it forward and folding it back on itself. Sprinkle flour over the ball by the tablespoonful, adding up to ¼ cup more flour if necessary to prevent the dough from sticking to your hands. Knead for about 10 minutes longer, or until the dough is smooth and elastic.

With a pastry brush, spread 1 tablespoon of the softened butter over the inside of a large bowl. Drop in the dough and turn it about to butter the entire surface. Drape the bowl with a kitchen towel and set it aside in the draft-free place for 1 hour, or until the dough doubles in volume. Punch the dough down with a blow of your fist and knead in the nuts and raisins. Cut the dough into five equal parts.

Roll each section of dough on a lightly floured surface into a rope 16 inches long and 2 inches wide. Brush a large cookie sheet with the remaining tablespoon of softened butter and set three of the ropes of dough side by side on the sheet. Starting at the center of the ropes and working toward each end, braid the dough loosely. Twist the remaining two ropes of dough together and set them lengthwise along the top of the braided dough. Tuck the ends under, drape with a towel and set aside in the draft-free place for 45 minutes, or until the dough almost doubles in volume.

Preheat the oven to 350°. Brush the loaf with the egg-and-milk mixture and bake in the center of the oven for 30 to 35 minutes, or until golden brown. Transfer to a wire rack to cool to room temperature.

To make one 16-inch loaf

¼ cup lukewarm water (110° to 115°)
1 package active dry yeast
1 teaspoon plus ½ cup sugar
4½ to 4¾ cups all-purpose flour
2 teaspoons salt
1 teaspoon grated lemon rind
¼ teaspoon mace
1 cup lukewarm milk (110° to 115°)
2 eggs plus 1 egg yolk
6 tablespoons unsalted butter, softened
½ cup finely chopped walnuts or pecans
1 cup seedless raisins
1 egg beaten with 1 tablespoon milk

Nokedli *(Hungarian)*
TINY DUMPLINGS

In a large bowl, combine the flour and ½ teaspoon of the salt. Pour in the eggs, milk and the cooled melted lard in thin streams, stirring constantly with a large spoon, and continue to stir until the dough is smooth.

Bring the water and the remaining 3 teaspoons of salt to a boil in a heavy 3- to 4-quart saucepan. Set a large colander over the pan and, with a spoon, press the dough through the holes of the colander into the boiling water. Stir the dumplings gently, then boil briskly for 6 to 8 minutes, or until they are tender to the bite. Drain the dumplings thoroughly.

Melt the tablespoon of lard in a heavy 10- to 12-inch skillet and drop in the dumplings. Stirring constantly, cook the dumplings for 1 or 2 minutes, or until they are dry. Serve at once, as a side dish.

To serve 4

1½ cups all-purpose flour
3½ teaspoons salt
2 eggs, lightly beaten
½ cup milk
2 tablespoons lard, melted and cooled, plus 1 tablespoon lard
2 quarts water

Houska, an intricately braided sweet bread laden with raisins and chopped nuts, is traditionally a Christmastime feature in Czech households, but Czech-Americans have turned it into a year-round favorite.

IV

by DALE BROWN

Four Fine Cuisines from Eastern Europe

Is there more than one kind of headcheese? Chester Mikolajczyk, a Polish-American sausagemaker in Chicago, finds this a foolish question. He makes about 80 different sorts of headcheese, with basic ingredients ranging from pork liver to tongue-and-ear, and they are consumed with equal gusto by first-generation Polish immigrants and their descendants. A recommended way of eating headcheese: cut a thick slab, dip it in vinegar, place it on dark bread and have a hearty meal—preferably with beer.

W hen the national anthem could not be sung, the pot on the stove sang it instead"—so said one commentator on the peoples of Eastern European lands who had survived centuries of foreign domination. The Poles, Lithuanians, Romanians and Ukrainians who emigrated (escaped might be the better word) to the United States between 1880 and 1914 carried this culinary patriotism right along with them. As Americans, their children still cherish the old ways with food as "something of our own."

Take the Poles: their homeland had not existed as a national entity since 1795, when conquering Austrians, Russians and Prussians finished dividing it among themselves. In the privacy of their kitchens, however, the Poles steadfastly maintained their time-honored cuisine—and Polish-American cooks have preserved their heirloom cuisine with loving care. In America these people of Polish birth or descent—four million in all —outnumber any other Slavic group. They are found from Maine to Alaska, with their greatest concentrations in New York, New Jersey, Pennsylvania, the Great Lakes region and southern New England. In all these places, some who left Poland in the early decades of this century are still around to pass the heritage along to their descendants.

I saw some of this faithfulness on a mushroom hunt in the Wisconsin woods that involved four generations of Polish-Americans: an 84-year-old patriarch, his son and daughter-in-law, their daughter and her two children. The great-grandfather had gathered mushrooms all of his life. After coming to the United States in 1907, he escaped the tedium of city life by trolleying to the outskirts of Milwaukee and then walking seven miles into the country to hunt mushrooms. He was still spry when I met him, and he darted through the underbrush with his glasses riding down his nose, poking among fallen autumn leaves and around decaying stumps to ferret out favorite varieties of mushrooms.

The scene might have been set in Poland itself—but I learned that not all the mushrooms gathered that day would find their way into strictly Polish dishes. Like many American-bred housewives, the daughter-in-law of the family has a gift for innovation; some of the mushrooms would go into creations of her own, such as a relish that also contains celery, scallions, and red and green peppers.

Such New World inventions, however, were exceptions. The Poles who came to America were a closely knit people, strongly Catholic in outlook. They took pains to keep their religious traditions alive, and many of these were associated with food. Although they had to find substitutes for some Old World ingredients, such as spinach and lemon juice for the sorrel used to make a sour soup, they tried to stick to the letter of recipes brought from the homeland. At Christmas each transplanted family shared the *opłatek,* or holy wafer, a feather-light rectangle of unleavened bread about three by five inches, embossed with Bible scenes. Some were lucky enough to receive these wafers directly from loved ones still in Poland, and those relatives seemed wonderfully close as the tiny flakes dissolved on the tongue. At Easter the immigrants held the *święcone,* or consecrated feast, a midday meal marking the end of Lent and consisting of foodstuffs blessed by a priest, among them festive dishes of veal, ham and *kiełbasa* (pork sausage); horseradish; hard-boiled eggs with beautifully painted shells; and cakes. The cakes always included a raised *babka,* baked with care bordering on devotion. It had to be yellow with eggs, and might contain nuts or raisins and gleam with a glaze of rum and apricot juice *(Recipe Index).* Before the feasting began, one of the painted eggs, symbol of rebirth, would be shelled and carefully divided. Each person took his portion and reverently ate it. Then there was much embracing and kissing, and a few tears for relatives still in Poland.

Reinforcing these ties were institutions that drew all Polish-Americans together. As Poles banded together in the industrial centers of the East and Midwest, there gradually emerged the Polonia Amerykańska, or Polish-American community, almost a nation within a nation, with its own churches, schools, societies and newspapers. Today, one of the most active and constructive societies is the Polanie Club of Minneapolis–St. Paul, a women's group whose cookbook, *Treasured Polish Recipes for Americans,* has gone through 13 printings and sold 110,000 copies.

On a journey to the United States in the 1870s, Henryk Sienkiewicz, the Polish author of *Quo Vadis* and winner of the 1905 Nobel Prize for Literature, was deeply moved to find a thriving Polish community along Chicago's Milwaukee Avenue. (To this day Chicago contains the largest Polish population of any American city.) Visiting there Sienkiewicz felt almost as if he were in Poland. He noted the Polish inscriptions and names on the buildings, and remarked that "only the innumerable telegraph wires and posts—a sight unfamiliar in Europe—and the limitless lake [nearby Lake Michigan] spoiled the illusion. . . . Doors and windows began to open and the illusion was restored for the first words I heard were uttered in Polish. A few minutes later I caught sight of the church of St. Stanislaus Kostka at the corner of Noble and Bradley Streets. About eight o'clock in the morning the flocks of children began to swarm here on the way to the school maintained by the priests and situated behind the church. Their childish chirping made a strange impression upon me for despite the fact that these children were studying in a Polish school an English influence was clearly perceptible in their speech."

The district he described has changed. It now seems more a neighborhood of old people than young, and its character continues to alter as Puerto Ricans, Appalachian whites and Southern blacks move in. But the inscriptions in Polish are still there, the shops have their Polish-speaking clerks, and St. Stanislaus' towers rise benevolently over the rooftops.

On a recent visit to the neighborhood I had a helpful Polish-American guide: Camille Jilke, food editor of the *Chicago Sun-Times*. Camille grew up here; in a nearby parochial school she was taught to cook by a nun of Polish descent, Sister Mary Redempta. "That great woman really got me started in the food business," Camille said. "At the age of thirteen I went home one day and made my parents the most wonderful bunch of *pierogi* [little filled dumplings] they had ever tasted. I still follow Sister's recipe. It calls for mashed potatoes, egg yolks and flour, and the filling consists of chopped mushrooms, cabbage and sour cream."

One of our first stops was a bakery. On the shelves and counters plump *babki* lolled against each other, some white with sugar icing, others glittering with honey and rum; next to them were *pączki*, sugar-dusted, raised doughnuts filled with candied fruit and nuts. In a case near the cash register were *strucle*, or rolled coffeecakes, with poppy-seed, nut and fruit fillings. On another counter lay *chrust*, crisp, flaky bows of a deep-fried cookie dough powdered with confectioners' sugar *(Recipe Index)*.

From the bakery, we crossed the street to a little sausage shop and delicatessen, wedged between a dry cleaner and a German *Wurst* factory. Chester Mikolajczyk, the owner, a short man with a dab of a mustache, gave up his job in an industrial plant to manage this family business. He offers a full range of the foodstuffs favored by the community, but his special delight is his sausages, all made by hand. Beaming with pride, he led us over to the counter where he keeps his *kiełbasy*, plump, shiny coils of garlic-flavored pork. Of all the many different Polish sausages, this is the type most familiar in America, one of the Poles' outstanding contributions to the Melting Pot. But as Chester pointed out, many people do not know how to cook it properly. He recommends that it be simmered in a little water to release the fat, then placed in a 350° oven and baked for about half an hour. It is even better, he adds, when it is baked on sauerkraut; then the juices flow into the kraut and flavor it richly. Turning reluctantly from the *kiełbasy*, Chester picked up a skinny loop of brittle sausage called *kabanosy*, and snapped off pieces for us to try. It was smoky and spicy—and the longer we chewed it, the better it tasted. Then he picked up a bulging *kiszka*, containing steamed whole buckwheat, pork, a little pig's blood, black pepper, salt, marjoram and allspice. "Try *kiszka* sometime with mustard, pumpernickel and a couple of slices of

Continued on page 76

Two Romanian winter staples: thick, tart chicken *ciorba* and a pork-and-sauerkraut casserole called *varză dela cluj*.

Keeping the Faith and the Feast Days of a Transplanted Heritage

Deprived of their village way of life, baffled by a strange new language, the Eastern European peoples who immigrated to America decades ago had to struggle to retain some sense of national identity and social organization. Some of them did not even have an "Old Country" left; the Poles and Lithuanians, for example, had seen their homelands swallowed by one conqueror after another. One thing the immigrants could and did cling to, however, was their faith. The seasonal cycle of religious festivals had always formed a major part of their cultural tradition; now, in the smoky row houses of Cleveland or Chicago, or on the lonely wheatlands of Manitoba, the familiar rituals and foods served the people both as comfort and celebration. Children grew up and became North Americans in spirit as well as fact, but the Church still drew them back to a remembrance of their heritage. And so it does today, preserving the precious legacies of an unforgotten past.

Fish, meat and dairy products are all forbidden by the Romanian Orthodox Church during Lent—but most Romanian-Americans relax the rules a bit. The Lenten delicacies above, prepared by the ladies of St. Mary's Church in Cleveland, include, for example, *icre,* a red-caviar dish topped with sliced black olives *(bottom).* Other seasonal dishes are *(clockwise from right):* a vegetable stew, or *ghivetch (Recipe Index);* marinated mushrooms; a winter *ghivetch,* traditionally made from whatever vegetables were available during the cold months; and a Lenten bread.

71

The climax of the Lenten season is, of course, Easter. For Romanian-Americans in Cleveland it is a day for religious rejoicing and partaking of special foods. Many, like those at left, are sweets. At the top are the towering Moldavian *cozonaci,* made of sweetened yeast dough and baked in cylindrical forms (as a purely American touch, the forms used here were one-, two- and three-pound coffee cans). To the right is a caramel custard, and in the center are chunks of cheesecake. At the lower right a platter contains sliced nut cake *(colac)* and small sweet rolls; a frosted nut torte with Cointreau filling is at lower left. Some or (heaven help us) all of these sweets may be served after a big Romanian Easter dinner.

EGGS FOR A LITHUANIAN EASTER

Like the Ukrainians and the Russians, Lithuanians love to decorate Easter eggs. They call them *margučiai,* and employ a special technique that involves a combination of dyeing and etching. The etching is done with a sharp knife *(above)* or a needle. The bright basket of eggs below was photographed in the Balzekas Museum of Lithuanian Culture in Chicago.

A POLISH-UKRAINIAN EASTER

From the break of dawn on Easter Day, life in a household like that of Paul and Mary Kowalsky of Westport, Connecticut, is a wonderful mixture of scents and symbolism, of family games and religious observance—and of hearty eating. Paul is half Polish and half Ukrainian; both of Mary's parents came from the Ukraine. The two traditions are closely related. On the Saturday morning before Easter, for example, both Poles and Ukrainians pack up baskets of food—eggs, sausage, bread, cheese, ham, butter, horseradish—to be blessed at church and kept for Easter breakfast.

At right, Mary prepares her basket.

Easter dinner *(left)* began with a toast offered by Paul Kowalsky, a building contractor by trade and a farmer by avocation—he runs a full-scale farm in this area of Connecticut, partly to assure himself first-rate meat and vegetables. The liquor was Żubrówka, vodka made in Poland and flavored with buffalo grass. The guests included both family and friends; the dinner ranged from stuffed cabbage and Easter soup *(żurek wielkanocny)* to ham and a whole sliced turkey. Mrs. Kowalsky's cooking is authentic but not cranky: to the white rice and *kiełbasa* in the cabbage, she also adds wild rice, an American delicacy. The innovation has obviously found favor with her parents, pictured at right.

At St. Anthony's Church in Fairfield, a priest blesses Mary's basket. On Easter morning she staged an egg hunt for children.

crisp bacon," he said. "Wow! Or *kiszka* American style, with a couple of eggs, sunny-side up. A wonderful breakfast!"

Chester also makes *pierogi* (the filled dumplings)—sometimes as many as a hundred dozen in a week. Some *pierogi* he fills with meat, using just a touch of garlic and pepper to season them; others he fills in true Polish style with cheese, sauerkraut, fruit or mushrooms. That the love of mushrooms runs as deep in Polish-Americans as it does in native Poles was obvious from a glance at the shelves behind him. There stood dozens of jars of them, pickled, salted, marinated—all of them brown, glossy and appetizing, and nearly all imported from Poland. Hanging next to them were garlands of dried wild mushrooms, also imported from Poland, where they grow in abundance. Strung on threads, they formed crinkly necklaces, delicious with forest aromas. Most Polish-Americans agree that these imported mushrooms are the most flavorful; a couple, they say, can make all the difference in a barley soup, a meatless borscht or a gravy.

After Camille made her purchases, we strolled through her old neighborhood to build an appetite for the evening ahead. She had arranged for a food-tasting at a local restaurant, the Turewicz. We arrived at sunset and entered a dim, candlelit dining room, where the proprietress, Mrs. Rosemarie Turewicz, emerged from the shadows to greet us. She showed us to our table, brought drinks—martinis made with Polish vodka—then began to serve our specially prepared meal. To start there were three soups: one made of tripe (and thick enough to be a stew), the second a clear, lemon-flavored borscht, and the third a Polish classic called *czernina,* or black soup. They were excellent, especially the *czernina,* though its ingredients might seem odd to the uninitiated—duck blood, giblets, vinegar, prunes and raisins. Despite the difficulty of finding duck blood, *czernina* remains a favorite dish in Polish-American households.

The soups were followed by a selection of other specialties: *gołąbki* (literally, little pigeons), stuffed cabbage Polish style, with a rich mushroom sauce; *zraziki,* beef pounded thin and rolled around a bread stuffing containing bits of pickle; *kasza,* or buckwheat groats; and *bigos,* or hunter's stew. The latter is traditionally prepared from game, but in this American version consisted of pork, bacon and slices of the garlicky *kiełbasa,* all cooked in sauerkraut and seasoned with onions, garlic and bay leaf.

Even limiting ourselves to the smallest portions left little room for dessert, but Mrs. Turewicz insisted we try her *naleśniki,* or pancakes *(Recipe Index).* They were limp, tender and very thin, just a bit crisp around the edges, and filled with a cheese filling. *Naleśniki*—which may also be served as an appetizer or as an entrée when filled with meat, calves' brains, cabbage or mushrooms—require skill to prepare. Mrs. Turewicz pours only enough batter into the pan to create a paper-thin film and, when it is done, she spreads it with sweetened farmer cheese, as she did for us, or with strawberry or cherry jam, and quickly rolls it up. When the last luscious *naleśniki* disappeared, we toasted the delights of Polish-American cooking with a spiced honey liqueur called *krupnik.*

More than most American cities, Chicago personifies the Melting Pot. Besides its Polish-Americans, it has many other citizens of Eastern European birth or descent to color its life and add to its vitality. Among them are the Lithuanians, 100,000 strong (there are not quite a million in all of the United States, but considering that their ancestral home on the Baltic has a population of only three million, this is indeed a lot). They are a proud non-Slavic people, whose history is entwined with that of the Poles, their neighbors in Europe. Like the Poles, Lithuanian-Americans tend to cluster in their own neighborhoods. There is a touch of serenity to these areas, stemming perhaps from the fact that not long ago many Lithuanian immigrants were desperate displaced persons who had lost everything to the Nazis and Communists. Along Chicago's 69th Avenue, the houses are neat, flowers poke their heads over picket fences, and toward one end of the community rises a yellow-brick church with needle-sharp copper-clad spires. There are several bookshops, a small theater, a large hospital, a cultural center, a museum and a dozen or so taverns that serve the local population as social clubs.

The shopper finds in this area an assortment of unusually appetizing foods. The bakeries turn out some of the best rye bread in America. It is made with flour that has been scorched at a temperature of 170° to bring out its sweetness; the scorching also colors the flour, giving it a grayish cast. A sourdough starter gives the bread a special tang. The loaves are fed into a deep brick oven and baked at 450° to 500° for an hour. They weigh several pounds each and have shiny crusts that crackle when cut.

Like other ethnic neighborhoods, this one has its own restaurants. The food usually consists of such everyday Lithuanian dishes as a bowl of chilled sour milk with a boiled potato on the side. It is good, but I wondered: what of the more lavish Lithuanian fare? The answer came at a dinner with Mr. and Mrs. Stanley Balzekas Jr. and a few of their friends. A first-generation Lithuanian-American, Stanley is a highly successful automobile dealer; as a hobby, he raises wine grapes on a 400-acre farm outside Chicago. His activities in the Lithuanian community are many and varied. One of his pet projects is a museum of Lithuanian culture, which houses a large display of arts and crafts; it also sponsors courses, including one in the art of dyeing and decorating Easter eggs.

The Balzekases live in a large, handsome house, and the night of their party they led their guests into the living room, where logs blazed in the fireplace. With the predinner drinks, Mrs. Balzekas served a tart, crumbly Lithuanian cheese—made by pressing the moisture from a block of farmer cheese—containing flecks of caraway. "But don't eat too much of it, please," she warned. "We have a big menu tonight."

Her dinner began with a chilled borscht, followed by several appetizers —herring in sour cream, a sour-cream-and-cucumber salad, hard-boiled eggs capped with halved tomatoes to look like mushrooms, fresh rye bread and home-baked bacon buns. The last had a good, strong, smoky taste. The appetizers were followed by a gefilte fish, a Jewish specialty that Christian Lithuanians long ago adopted as their own. Mrs. Balzekas had taken an American fish, a walleyed pike, skinned and boned it, and reduced the flesh to a paste, which she mixed with eggs, salt, pepper and cracker crumbs. Then she squeezed the paste back into the skin, wrapped the re-created fish in cheesecloth and simmered it in stock. Served sliced, the fish was smooth and pleasantly bland. Next came dumplings, some

As if it were indeed a tree, growing layer by layer, a Lithuanian "tree cake" takes shape with accretions of egg-rich batter on a spit in Chicago's Brighton Bakery. A single cake calls for 320 egg yolks, and takes between three and three and a half hours to complete—after which it remains on the spit up to two days "to cool and settle."

filled with chopped liver, others with cottage cheese, both kinds swimming in butter.

The same spirit of plenty marked the main dishes. First there was a course of roast pork, sauerkraut, gravy, homemade applesauce, creamed wild mushrooms and potato sausages flavored with onions and bacon. Then a second wave arrived—roast breast of veal, a salad of beets, peas and carrots in sour cream, and the famed *kugelis*, a crusty pudding of grated potatoes baked with milk. When it seemed no one could eat another thing, Mrs. Balzekas carried in a torte, a Baltic version of the classic French Napoleon. It was a good two feet across, and consisted of 13 crisp layers, slathered with custard cream with a touch of lemon juice to cut the richness. As guest of honor I had the privilege of slicing it, and I did, but after all that food it seemed wise to cut very small wedges.

The tenacity with which the Lithuanians cling to their traditions has its match among the Romanian-Americans, who are also non-Slavic and claim the ancient Romans among their ancestors. Most Romanians in this country—as small a minority as the Lithuanians—come from the region of Transylvania bordering present-day Hungary. Not surprisingly, they share several dishes with the Hungarians, but they also have many that could only be Romanian—and one that never could have evolved in its present form without assistance from America. *Mamaliga,* a favorite Romanian dish for centuries, is made from corn, originally taken to Europe from the New World. A thick cornmeal mush, *mamaliga* is often baked with layers of goat cheese and topped with sour cream, but Romanians in this country have added another New World touch by substituting Wisconsin brick cheese for the stronger goat cheese.

Other venerable dishes still cherished by Romanian-Americans include a varied repertoire of sour soups. An enduring favorite is *ciorba,* whose traditional recipes call for such ingredients as sauerkraut juice or pickled-cucumber juice; in America, where citrus fruit is plentiful, lemon juice is commonly used instead. One delicious version calls for lettuce, a vegetable that is not usually cooked. Torn leaves of romaine lettuce, braised briefly in bacon fat with minced onion and garlic, are simmered briefly in water with lemon juice. The soup is thickened with a mixture of egg yolks and sour cream and served sprinkled with minced parsley.

Many Romanians in America are of the Eastern Orthodox faith, and observe two main meatless and dairyless fasts, one before Easter, another before Christmas. As a result, perhaps, they have a special resourcefulness with vegetables. Their predilection for fresh vegetables finds its greatest expression in *ghivetch (Recipe Index),* a poem of a baked vegetable casserole generally made "from all the vegetables you can get your hands on." *Sarmale,* the Romanians' version of stuffed cabbage, has its Lenten counterpart, too: mushrooms are substituted for meat, and dill and savory accent the mushrooms' flavor.

The six-week pre-Christmas fast is broken joyfully by many Orthodox Romanians on Christmas Eve. In Cleveland, where some 7,000 Romanians live, it is the custom for groups of carolers to visit the homes of the faithful and collect money for St. Mary's, their church. They start out after the vesper service, carrying a large illuminated star on a long pole; at its center there is a vivid transparency of the Virgin and Child through which candlelight shines. After singing at a front door, they step inside to partake of a holiday table, spread with appetizers and baked goods. There are such old Romanian treats as the *sarmale,* homemade liver and garlic sausages, jellied pigs' feet, eggplant caviar and an appetizer made of chopped eggplant, green pepper, pimiento, onions and other piquant ingredients, and baked under a layer of tomato sauce. Among the cakes will be a yeast-raised *cozonac,* which in one of its richest versions is filled with a mixture of nuts, raisins, sugar and lemon peel *(Recipe Index).*

North Americans of Ukrainian descent—a million and a half of them live in the United States, and half a million more in Canada—are another proud group whose food traditions contribute to the diversity of the Melting Pot. Wherever they have settled, these Slavic people still seem to belong spiritually to the Ukraine, now part of the Soviet Union.

In Winnipeg, a Ukrainian stronghold, a priest invited me to have a drink with him in his quarters. He had been away from the Ukraine long enough to switch from vodka to Scotch—but he poured the whisky out Ukrainian fashion, by the glassful, and insisted that we drink it neat. Then he offered food: Ukrainian-style rye bread, sliced dill pickles and a big slab of raw home-cured bacon, showing a quarter inch of dark lean meat and an inch and a half of white fat. He cut off some slices, then hand-

A finished "tree cake," stubbly with dark bumps where batter has dripped and singed, is four feet tall and weighs 18 pounds. Slices of it will sell for $2.50 a pound—or you may take the whole tree for $40.

79

The Ukrainians in Manitoba have maintained their own customs and also influenced other Canadians— particularly in matters of food. A Christmas Eve-feast, however, is still a purely Ukrainian affair. Above, in their Winnipeg home, Ahafia Kostyshyn and her daughter Luba ladle out *vushka,* little mushroom dumplings, to be served in borscht. They are one of 12 canonical foods (symbolic of the Apostles) for the dinner. The table *(opposite)* is ready for guests with *(clockwise from top):* fried pickerel, *prosfora* (bread bits blessed by a priest and eaten at the start of the meal), *kalach,* a braided Christmas bread (an extra item), *holubtsi* (stuffed cabbage rolls), *pyriszhky* (small breads stuffed with mushrooms or cabbage), *varenyky* (sauerkraut-filled dumplings), mushroom sauce, jellied pike, *kutia* (a wheat pudding), marinated herring, clear borscht with *vushka,* stewed fruit (an extra item), *nalysnyky* (pancakes stuffed with cabbage and onions) and peas.

ed me my glass—the stiff drink was intimidating enough without the bacon. The priest made a toast and gulped the Scotch, and I did likewise. The whisky ignited my stomach, and a blaze was roaring there before I even tasted the bacon. Then he poured me a second glass and passed the bacon, "to line the stomach." The fat was not so offensive after all; in fact, it was smooth, even buttery. I had a second slice, and a third, before the time came for another drink. I could even stand without wobbling for a final toast; the bacon fat had not only insulated the stomach, but had canceled out the alcohol. "Now," he said as he bade me farewell, "you will know you have been with Ukrainians!"

This initiation served me well. Whenever I have met Ukrainians since, I have found them warm, generous to a fault, ever ready to share their food and drink. And they have much that is delicious to share. They greet their guests with a great array of appetizers: pickled or jellied fish, cold meats, cheese, relishes, salads, canapés, breads, rolls and *pyriszhky* —pastries made of yeast dough or puff paste, and containing such savory fillings as ground liver, sauerkraut and mushrooms. Their soups are marvelous. They claim to have invented borscht, and well they may have. One favorite version is like the soup from which all other soups sprang, a paean to the Earth Mother, red with beets and tomatoes, heaped with meat and vegetables—cabbage, parsley root, parsnips, celery, potatoes. It is a soup not to sip, but to slurp.

Ukrainian meat dishes are wonderfully varied as well—veal cutlet with brain sauce; steak stuffed with ground veal and bacon, bread crumbs and eggs, and cooked in stock and sour cream on a bed of diced carrots, celery, parsley root, green pepper and onions; *pashtet,* finely ground meat (usually veal, pork and lamb), spiced and steamed in a mold. Ukrainian meatballs, called *zrazy (Recipe Index),* may be stuffed with freshly grated horseradish, sieved egg yolks and buttered bread crumbs, and baked in a sauce of seasoned stock and sour cream. At the press of a fork they break open to reveal their fillings: smooth in texture, sharp in flavor. They are a delightful complement to a baked potato *babka,* a golden, glorious puff consisting of mashed potatoes, cottage cheese, egg yolks and stiffly beaten egg whites folded in for lightness *(Recipe Index).*

When Ukrainian immigrants first settled in the Canadian province of Manitoba in the 1890s, they were astonished to see its prairies planted with the same variety of hard red spring wheat that they themselves had cultivated back in the Ukraine. Known in Canada as Red Fife wheat, after David Fife, the farmer who had introduced it there, it had been brought over by a route that led from the Ukraine to Danzig on the Baltic Sea to Scotland, and ultimately to the New World. This hardy strain established itself as a standard Canadian wheat for bread flour, and from it more than 80 North American varieties have been developed.

Given such familiar material to work with, it is no wonder that the Ukrainian settlers produced breads as appetizing as any they had baked in their homeland, and their descendants still bake breads that restore one's faith in the staff of life. Some are works of art—gorgeous braided rings and twists glazed with egg white, or loaves decorated with birds and floral ornaments made of yeast dough.

The vitality of Ukrainian-Americans' food traditions derives in part from their religion. For most of them, the Ukrainian Orthodox Church or the Ukrainian Catholic Church serves as custodian of their culture, and they observe a round of religious holidays with all the love and pageantry of centuries-old ritual. For Easter they produce the world's most exquisite Easter eggs, covering them with intricate designs. Days are given over to preparing nut bars, tortes, cheesecakes and strudels to be eaten at the end of Lent. And every housewife, even one who does not regularly attend church, is sure to go to church for the priest's blessing on her basket of *paska* (the rich Easter bread) and decorated eggs, cottage cheese, horseradish and other foods for the Easter breakfast. Each basket contains a lighted candle, and when many baskets are massed in the aisle, they create a sea of flames that seems to wash against the gilded frame of the sacred iconostasis, or altar screen.

Christmas involves another feast and other specialties. The centerpiece for the table is usually a three-tiered stack of *kalach,* a braided bread, with a burning candle inserted into the top of the loaf. Wisps of hay are spread under the tablecloth as a reminder of the manger in which Christ was born, and 12 dishes are served, representing the 12 Apostles. These may vary from household to household, but all are Lenten dishes. The meal, called the Holy Supper, begins with *kutia,* a dish of pre-Christian origin. It consists of cooked wheat, mixed with honey, ground poppy seeds and, occasionally, chopped walnuts, and it is surprisingly flavorful, a natural food that would please a natural-food enthusiast. A few New World Ukrainians still observe a custom dating back to pagan times. Toss a spoonful of *kutia* at the ceiling: if it sticks, the bees will swarm, the harvest will be good and good fortune will be yours in the year to come. The person who told me about the custom invited me to visit his father's house for a look at the dining-room ceiling; the stain from last year's *kutia* was still visible.

For all Orthodox and some Catholic Ukrainians, Christmas falls on January 7, in keeping with the old Julian calendar, but it is on the night before—soon after the first star appears—that the big dinner is served. Last January I attended evening Mass in an Orthodox Ukrainian church in New York, then joined the parishioners downstairs for their Christmas meal. All the meatless dishes were there, including borscht, cabbage rolls stuffed with rice, and *kutia;* and perhaps because these had been cooked in quantity, they were not memorable. But the priest's wife invited me to the parish house to sample her own Christmas borscht. On her table there was one extra plate, set in honor of a sister who had recently died. "Sit down, please," said the priest's wife. "Be at home. I will come."

She returned a few minutes later and placed a bowl of crimson borscht before me. Among the shredded cabbage leaves floated *vushka,* or "little ears"—tiny dumplings stuffed with chopped wild mushrooms. She then produced a large, well-worn spoon. It had belonged to her mother. "And the soup," she said, "is my mother's soup—from my mother's recipe." The borscht was tart and so full-bodied that it seemed meaty, though there was not a bit of meat in it. Never did simple food taste better, or seem to hold more meaning.

Grybai *(Lithuanian)*
MUSHROOM-SHAPED SPICE COOKIES

To make about 30 cookies

In a large mixing bowl, cream 4 tablespoons of the butter with the sugar by beating them together vigorously against the sides of the bowl with a wooden spoon. When the mixture is smooth, beat in the eggs, one at a time, then gradually beat in the lukewarm honey and the sour cream.

Sift together the flour, baking soda, cinnamon, cloves, ginger, nutmeg and cardamom, and beat into the creamed mixture ½ cup at a time. When the ingredients are well combined, stir in the grated lemon rind and orange rind. Gather the dough into a ball, cut the ball in half, and wrap each half in wax paper. Chill for at least 1 hour.

Preheat the oven to 350°. With a pastry brush, lightly coat two cookie sheets with the remaining tablespoon of softened butter.

Remove the dough from the refrigerator and pull off walnut-sized pieces from one of the halves. Shape the pieces of dough into balls varying from 1 to 1½ inches in diameter. With your thumb, indent one side of each ball to make a mushroomlike cap. Set the balls rounded side up, 1 inch apart on a cookie sheet. Bake in the center of the oven for 10 minutes, then transfer to wire racks to cool to room temperature.

Meanwhile, shape the remaining half of dough into mushroomlike stems. Pull off walnut-sized pieces of dough and roll them in your hands to make stems of varying thickness and ranging from 1 to 1½ inches long. Set the stems 1 inch apart on the second cookie sheet and bake in the center of the oven for 10 minutes. Transfer to wire cake racks to cool.

ICING: Place the confectioners' sugar in a bowl and, with a wire whisk or a rotary or electric beater, beat in the water, a teaspoon at a time. Continue to beat until smooth, then beat in 4 teaspoons of lemon juice. Taste the icing; if you prefer a tarter flavor, beat in up to 2 more teaspoons of juice. Divide the icing in half and stir the cocoa into one half.

When the mushroom caps and stems have cooled, dip one end of each stem into the white icing and fit it into the indentation on the bottom side of the caps. Set the cookies side by side on a platter until the icing has set. Then, with a small icing spatula or the flat of a knife, gently coat the stems and underside of the caps with the remaining white icing. Set aside again to dry, then ice the tops of the caps with the cocoa icing.

Ingredients:

5 tablespoons unsalted butter, softened
½ cup sugar
2 eggs
1 cup honey, heated and cooled to lukewarm
¼ cup sour cream
4 cups all-purpose flour
1½ teaspoons baking soda
1 teaspoon cinnamon
½ teaspoon ground cloves
½ teaspoon ginger
½ teaspoon nutmeg
½ teaspoon ground cardamom
1 teaspoon finely grated lemon rind
1 teaspoon finely grated orange rind

ICING
2 cups confectioners' sugar
5 teaspoons cold water
4 to 6 teaspoons strained fresh lemon juice
2 teaspoons unsweetened cocoa

Pieninis Krupnikas *(Lithuanian)*
MILK LIQUEUR

To make 20 two-ounce servings

Combine the vodka, milk, sugar, orange and lemon pieces, and vanilla extract in a large glass or ceramic mixing bowl and stir with a wooden spoon to dissolve the sugar. Cover tightly with plastic wrap and set the bowl aside at room temperature for 3 weeks, stirring the mixture daily.

Strain and discard the fruit. Insert a funnel of filter paper—the kind used to filter coffee—in one or more bottles and ladle in the liquid. Let it filter through undisturbed. The liqueur can be served at once, or it can be corked and kept at room temperature indefinitely.

Ingredients:

1 quart vodka
1 quart milk
4 cups sugar
2 oranges, unpeeled, washed and cut into small pieces
2 lemons, unpeeled, washed and cut into small pieces
1 tablespoon vanilla extract

Piled high in elegant baskets, these well-formed "mushrooms" are perfectly edible, but they were plucked from neither a field nor a forest floor. Instead, they originated in a hot oven—soft and redolent of honey and spices. Baked separately in the shape of stems and caps, the mushroom cookies *(Recipe Index)* are coated with lemony white and chocolate icing.

To serve 4 to 6

8 fillets of white firm-fleshed fish, such as pike, perch or sole
6 tablespoons unsalted butter, plus 1 tablespoon butter, softened, and 1 tablespoon butter, cut into ¼-inch bits
4 to 6 slices white bread, trimmed and cut into ¼-inch dice (2½ cups)
3 tablespoons finely cut chives
¼ teaspoon thyme
½ teaspoon tarragon
½ teaspoon salt
¼ teaspoon white pepper

SAUCE
½ cup sour cream
1 tablespoon flour
1 teaspoon strained fresh lemon juice
½ teaspoon salt
1 tablespoon tomato purée

Rolled Stuffed Fish Fillets *(Ukrainian)*

Wash the fish fillets under cold running water and pat them thoroughly dry with paper towels. Place the fillets side by side on a flat surface and trim them evenly to 8- or 9-inch lengths. Gather all the fish you have trimmed from the fillets and chop it fine.

In a 10- to 12-inch skillet, melt 2 tablespoons of the butter over moderate heat. Stir in the chopped fish and, stirring it constantly, cook over moderate heat for 4 or 5 minutes, until the flesh becomes opaque. Transfer to a bowl and set aside.

Add 4 tablespoons of butter to the skillet and drop in the bread cubes. Toss them constantly with a wooden spoon until they are a light gold, then add them to the bowl of fish. Sprinkle the fish and bread cubes with the chives, thyme, tarragon, ½ teaspoon of salt and the pepper, and toss together lightly but thoroughly.

Preheat the oven to 400°. With a pastry brush, lightly coat the bottom and sides of a 9-by-12-inch flameproof baking dish with the tablespoon of softened butter. Place 2 tablespoons of the herbed stuffing on the narrow end of each fillet and gently roll up the fillets. Arrange them seam side down in the baking dish, and dot with the tablespoon of butter bits. Bake in the center of the oven for 12 to 15 minutes, or until the fish feels firm when prodded gently with a finger. With a spatula, transfer the fish rolls to a heated platter and keep them warm in the turned-off oven while you make the sauce.

In a small bowl, combine the ½ cup of sour cream with the 1 tablespoon of flour. Place the flameproof baking dish over moderate heat and, with a wire whisk, gradually beat in the sour-cream-and-flour mixture, the lemon juice and ½ teaspoon of salt. Stir in the tomato purée and taste for seasoning.

Spoon the sauce over the fish rolls. Or, if you prefer, present the sauce separately in a heated sauceboat.

To serve 6 to 8

6 medium-sized leeks
4 tablespoons butter
3 medium-sized onions, finely chopped
6 cups chicken stock, fresh or canned
1 pound potatoes, peeled and cut into ½-inch cubes
1 cup dry white wine
½ teaspoon white pepper
1 cup heavy cream
2 tablespoons finely chopped parsley
2 tablespoons finely cut chives

Ciorba de Praz *(Romanian)*
CREAM OF LEEK SOUP

Wash the leeks thoroughly under cold running water and pat them dry with paper towels. Cut off the green leaves and discard the very tough or damaged leaves. Chop the leaves fine and set them aside. Slice the white part of the leeks crosswise into ¼-inch-thick rounds.

In a 2½- to 3-quart enameled or stainless-steel casserole, melt the butter over moderate heat. When the foam begins to subside, add the leek rounds and the chopped onions and, stirring frequently, cook for 5 to 8 minutes, or until they are soft and translucent. Stir in the chopped leek leaves and cook for 2 or 3 minutes more. Add the 6 cups of chicken stock, the potato cubes and the wine, and bring to a boil over high heat, then partially cover the casserole, lower the heat and simmer for 1 hour.

Purée the soup through a food mill or fine sieve set over a mixing bowl, and again through a fine sieve back into the pan. Stir in the white pepper and bring to a simmer over moderate heat. Stir in the heavy cream, sprinkle with the parsley and chives, and taste for seasoning. Ladle the soup into a heated tureen or individual soup plates.

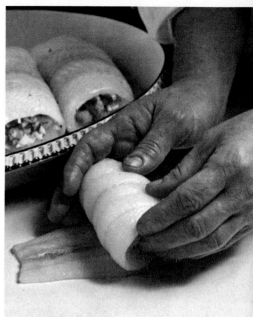

A neatly trimmed rectangle of fillet of sole *(above)* is filled with an aromatic mixture of golden-brown bread cubes, herbs and lightly cooked bits of the trimmed fish itself. Starting from one of the narrow ends, the fillet is loosely rolled up *(above, right)*, laid seam side down and baked.

At the table the delicate fish rolls *(below)*, with their slightly crunchy stuffing, are bathed in a lemony, tomato-accented sour-cream sauce.

For a dish of savory Ukrainian-inspired stuffed pork chops, herb-flavored bread crumbs are placed in pockets that have been cut in loin pork chops *(above)*. The pockets are then secured with toothpicks or bamboo skewers, and the chops are cooked to a golden turn. Bathed in a mustardy sour-cream sauce, a finished chop is served with a complement of boiled green beans.

Stuffed Pork Kotlety *(Ukrainian)*
HERB-STUFFED PORK CHOPS

With a small knife, slit each chop through its side to create a pocket about 3 inches deep. Sprinkle the pocket and outside of the chops with the lemon juice and set aside.

In a small skillet, melt 2 tablespoons of the butter over moderate heat. Stir in the bread crumbs and, stirring constantly, brown the crumbs lightly. Transfer to a mixing bowl and toss with the chives, ¼ cup of parsley, the celery, ½ teaspoon of salt and the pepper. Taste for seasoning. With a small spoon, pack the stuffing evenly into the pork-chop pockets and secure the openings with toothpicks or small skewers.

Combine the remaining 3 tablespoons of butter with 2 tablespoons of oil in a heavy 10- to 12-inch skillet. Place over high heat until a light haze forms above it, then add the chops and cook them for about 3 minutes on each side until golden brown. Lower the heat, cover the skillet and simmer for 10 minutes. Then turn the chops over and cook, covered, for 10 more minutes. Transfer the chops to a heated platter, cover with foil, and keep warm in a low oven. Pour off the fat remaining in the skillet, replace it with 2 tablespoons of butter and set over low heat. In a small bowl, beat together the sour cream, flour and mustard and, with a wire whisk, beat the mixture into the melted butter. Stir in the heavy cream and ½ teaspoon of salt and, whisking constantly, bring to a boil. Pour the sauce over the pork chops, garnish the chops with the lemon slices and chopped parsley, and serve at once.

To serve 4

4 center-cut loin pork chops, cut 1 inch thick
¼ cup strained fresh lemon juice
5 tablespoons unsalted butter
1 cup fine dry bread crumbs
¼ cup finely cut chives
¼ cup finely chopped parsley
¼ cup finely chopped celery
½ teaspoon salt
¼ teaspoon freshly ground black pepper
2 tablespoons vegetable oil

SAUCE
2 tablespoons butter
½ cup sour cream
1 tablespoon all-purpose flour
1 tablespoon prepared mustard, preferably Dijon-style
¼ cup heavy cream
½ teaspoon salt
4 thin lemon slices
2 tablespoons finely chopped parsley

Naleśniki *(Polish)*
ROLLED PANCAKES WITH FRUIT PRESERVES

To make the pancake batter in an electric blender, combine the flour, eggs, milk, water, sugar and salt in the blender jar and blend them at high speed for a few seconds. Turn off the machine, scrape down the sides of the jar with a rubber spatula, and blend again for 40 seconds.

To make the batter by hand, stir the eggs and milk together, then beat in the flour, water, sugar and salt with a whisk or a rotary or electric beater. Strain the mixture through a fine sieve set over a bowl.

In a small mixing bowl, stir together the fruit preserves and grated lemon rind. Set aside.

Heat a 6-inch crêpe pan or skillet over high heat until a drop of water flicked onto it evaporates instantly. With a pastry brush, lightly grease the bottom of the pan with about ½ teaspoon of the melted butter. Pour 3 tablespoons of batter into the pan and tip the pan so that the batter quickly covers the bottom; the batter should cling to the pan and begin to firm up almost immediately. Cook the pancake for a minute or so, until a rim of brown shows around the edge. Turn it over with a spatula and cook for another 1 or 2 minutes, or until the pancake is lightly browned. When the pancake is done, spread it with 2 heaping tablespoons of the fruit-preserve filling, roll it loosely into a cylinder, and place it in a baking dish in a 200° oven to keep warm. Repeat the process with the rest of the pancake batter, adding butter to the skillet as needed. Serve the pancakes warm, sprinkled with confectioners' sugar.

To make 28 pancakes

1½ cups all-purpose flour
3 eggs
1 cup milk
1 cup water
1 tablespoon sugar
1 teaspoon salt
12 ounces fruit preserves (cherry, raspberry or strawberry)
1 tablespoon grated lemon rind
5 tablespoons unsalted butter, melted and cooled
Confectioners' sugar

by ISRAEL SHENKER

Born in Philadelphia of Russian-Jewish parents, Mr. Shenker has had a distinguished career as a journalist in many countries. He served as TIME magazine bureau chief in Moscow and Rome and is currently a feature writer for *The New York Times.*

Only in America:
Joys of Jewish Cooking

A persistent legend has it that Columbus was a Jew—and a persistent joke is that he never settled in the New World simply because he could not find a Jewish delicatessen here. Historians, who try to stick with the facts and ignore the legends and jokes, point out that the first group of Jews—23 of them—came to America from Portugal, via the Netherlands and Brazil, in 1654. For more than a century and a half, most of those who followed them (only about 1,000) came from Western Europe. In the 19th Century larger numbers came from the German states. The years between 1881 and the outbreak of World War I were a period in which more than two million of the eventual total of three million Jewish immigrants came here, a great wave of them arriving from Central and Eastern Europe. It is with the cuisine of these Jews of the "New Immigration" that this chapter will deal.

The newcomers came largely from the *shtetlach* (villages) of Poland and Russia, Romania and Austria-Hungary. Poverty had been their way of life at home, and religious oppression so common that it sometimes seemed to be ordained by heaven. Barred from many professions and agriculture, rarely permitted to attend a university or even to live in some principal cities, Eastern Europe's Jews practiced trades that depended on the skill of their hands and their skills at trading. In the *shtetlach* the common meal was based on bread, potatoes and onions, relieved at times with salty herring; only on Friday evening, when each family had its Sabbath dinner, was this spartan fare varied. Sholom Aleichem, whose stories of Tevye the dairyman became the theme of *Fiddler on the Roof,* dealt

As he reads aloud from the Haggadah, a sacred narrative that recounts the Old Testament story of the exodus of the Jews from Egypt, Benjamin Finkelstein of New York City blesses a goblet of wine at the beginning of the Seder, or Passover feast. Each of the foods before him, including the matzo (unleavened bread) in the foreground, is symbolic of an element of the Biblical story *(page 93).*

again and again with this aspect of Jewish life in Eastern Europe. One of his finest tales is a dialogue between a husband and wife in which they describe what he would like to eat and she would love to cook—if only they could afford the ingredients. The husband's fancy ranges from fried fish swimming in butter to golden blintzes (pancakes) with cheese—a litany that goes on and on in a dream of hopelessly remote delights. They have no money—and therefore no fish, no butter, no cheese, no flour, no fat —only unsated appetites and incontinent nostalgia.

In America, the Golden Land, matters were to be different. To be sure, the immigrants lived in ghettos—most notably on the Lower East Side of Manhattan, where the vernacular was Yiddish (a blend of old German and Hebrew) and the immigrants set up their own synagogues, schools and shops. In these slums the air throbbed with a chorus of cries from men and women selling their wares from pushcarts, and the streets were redolent of herring and pickled vegetables. From America's riches, the immigrant was beginning to enjoy a plenty unknown in Europe. If the reality was less glittering than the promise (some immigrant Jews had heard stories of streets paved with gold), it was sumptuous enough. Jewish mothers from lands where no one needed encouragement to eat were entreating their children to dig in—and there was much more to dig into. "Fix yourself!" they cried—meaning "Eat more and put on weight!"

The food they ate made up a surprisingly cosmopolitan cuisine, differing from family to family according to the influence of non-Jewish European cuisines. In Austria-Hungary and the Balkans, Jews had come to appreciate stuffed cabbage, strudel and paprika; in Russia and Poland they had learned to make cabbage and beet borschts, blintzes and *pirogen*. In a sense, the world of Eastern and Central Europe was their hinterland, and its best products entered their cuisine.

But Jewish cooking is not simply Polish or Russian or Hungarian or Romanian cooking—if it were, it would have been described in the two chapters preceding this one. The crucial difference lies in the Jewish dietary laws, part of the invisible baggage of belief and tradition that every Jew brought with him in steerage to America. Based on passages in the Old Testament and subsequently elaborated by rabbinical commentary, these regulations dictate which foods and cooking methods are kosher (fit and proper to eat) and which are *trayf* (not kosher, and forbidden).

Leviticus 11:3 declares: "Whatsoever parteth the hoof, and is cloven-footed, and cheweth the cud, among the beasts, that shall ye eat." Thus pork and all its products are forbidden, for the pig does not chew its cud. The Bible also prohibits the eating of fish without both fins and scales —which, for observant Jews, means no lobster or shellfish. Certain methods of butchering also are enjoined. The hindquarters of any animal may not be eaten unless certain veins and arteries are removed by a difficult and expensive process, and kosher butchers sell only the front cuts. Blood is forbidden, and animals must be killed and processed in a way that maximizes the loss of blood. Liver, an organ especially rich in blood, must be salted and seared over an open flame before further cooking.

In three different passages the Old Testament prohibits "seething" a kid in its mother's milk, and this thrice-voiced warning developed into a

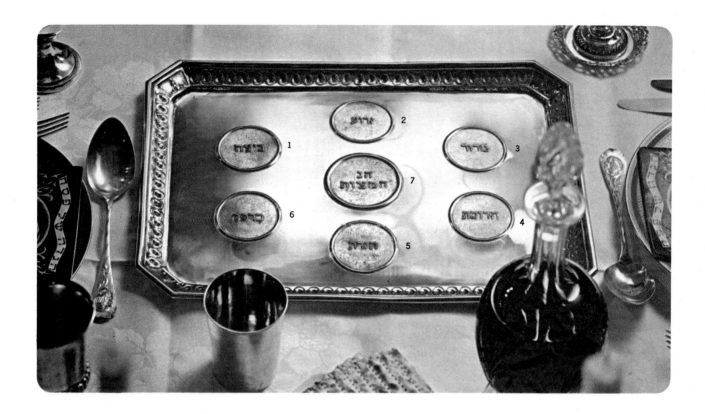

prohibition against serving meat and dairy dishes at the same meal. Even the dishes that are used to serve dairy food cannot be used for meat. Fortunately, there is a third category of food, lying between meat and dairy; the foods in this *pareve* (neutral) category, which comprises eggs, fish, vegetables, fruits and grains, can be included in either meat or dairy meals. In this case, the dietary restrictions proved a blessing in disguise. Using dairy and *pareve* ingredients, ingenious Jewish cooks have developed a rich and varied "dairy" cuisine based on fresh or smoked fish, eggs, cheeses, sour cream, salads, pancakes, dumplings, butter-rich "Danish" pastries and creamy cheesecakes.

Today, the dietary laws are often honored in the breach as well as by observance. Many Jews dismiss the laws as obsolete and academic; others practice selective observance, eating no pork but loving lobster, or shunning shellfish at home but eating it in restaurants. But even these Jews, along with their co-religionists who do honor the dietary laws, are the beneficiaries of a very special culinary heritage. Interacting with individual European cuisines, the laws have produced a great cuisine that is identified with the cooking of Jews in America.

In Jewish cooking, Romanian pork and lamb *pastramă* became beef pastrami—the form in which it is best known in the United States. Russian and Polish meat borschts are served without their usual dollop of sour cream (but luckily there is the beloved beet borscht, with lots of sour cream). Jellied pigs' feet becomes *p'chia*, or calves' feet. Jewish meats are generally potted (stewed or braised), a slow cooking method that is ideal for the tougher forequarter cuts favored by the dietary laws. American supermarkets now sell Jewish-style *flanken*, which is short ribs of beef cut

The focal point of Benjamin Finkelstein's Seder table *(page 90)* is a silver tray inscribed to show the position of seven symbolic foods used in recounting the story of Passover. Their order is as follows: (1) a roasted egg, and (2) a lamb shank, representing ritual sacrifices of the ancient Passover; (3) bitter herbs (such as grated horseradish) to recall the bitterness of bondage in Egypt; (4) *charoset,* a mixture of chopped apples, nuts and wine, representing the mortar the Jews made as slaves of the Pharaohs; (5) leafy greens, a symbol of earth's regeneration in springtime; (6) parsley dipped in salt water, representing the waters of the Red Sea, which parted to allow the Jews' escape from bondage; and (7) matzo, for the bread left unleavened by the Jews in their haste to flee.

across the bones, but few Americans have learned to savor the boiled-beef dish based upon it, cooked with fragrant soup greens and served with horseradish or a tart compote of stewed fruit. Even better to some tastes, as befits a basically humble cuisine, is leftover *flanken,* rubbed with salt, pepper and garlic and baked with vegetables and dumplings until it is dark brown and crusty.

Best of all is the fact that individual Jewish dishes compose marvelously into varied full-course meals. Perhaps the finest—and certainly the most regular—of these grand meals is the Friday Sabbath dinner. Even in Europe this had been the hallowed occasion when the women of the house scrubbed the kitchen clean and the mother lit the Sabbath candles and intoned a prayer over them, then served the most substantial meal of the week. If there was no money, others had to provide, for the celebration of the Sabbath is a holy command: in the rabbinical writings the Sabbath is likened to a queen, and during her weekly visit the head of every Jewish household is a king. This, then, was one day of the week when food was rich and everyone had enough . . . or ultimately in America, more than enough. From the days of the tenement kitchens, the Sabbath meal has featured many of the highlights of the Jewish cuisine. In America, a menu might include all this: gefilte fish; chopped liver; chicken soup with *lukshen* (thin noodles), *kreplach* (boiled dumplings filled with chopped beef or liver) or *knaidlach* (balls of matzo meal, egg and fat); chicken or meat; *kishke* (beef intestine stuffed solidly with flour, onions and fat) or stuffed *heldzel* (the skin of the chicken neck); *tsimmes* (a combination of dried fruits, white or sweet potatoes or carrots, and onions); *kugel* (potato or noodle pudding); *challah* (a special egg bread); and sponge or honey cake.

Every one of these courses and foods has its own traditions and associations. Take the *challah,* for instance—a yeast bread made rich and golden by the presence of eggs. At least two cloth-covered loaves should be on the table under the stately Sabbath candles when the head of the house takes his place, fills small goblets with sweet kosher wine and blesses the day and the bread. Only then is the cloth removed and the tops of the loaves revealed, glistening with a glaze of egg and sometimes garnished with poppy seeds. But why the cloth? It is said to symbolize the dew that gathered on the manna from heaven in the desert.

With the *challah* uncovered, the Sabbath diners are ready for their first course—in an especially sumptuous meal, a double-barreled course of chopped liver *(Recipe Index)* and gefilte fish, served separately. The liver is chicken liver, chopped by hand with a curved-bladed *hockmesser,* or chopping knife—never (heaven forbid!) mashed or ground to a heavy purée. Enriched by chicken fat, brightened by bits of egg and sharpened by crisp nuggets of fried or raw onion, Jewish chopped liver bears no relation to the imitation "terrines," adulterated by mayonnaise and puréed to peanut-butter consistency, that are served by many restaurants.

An even nobler dish is gefilte fish *(Recipe Index),* round or oval *quenelles* of fish forcemeat swimming happily in a sea of jellied fish broth and sliced carrots. In its original form the fish was literally *gefilte,* or stuffed, with a forcemeat of fish fillets ground with onions, then chopped with eggs, salt, pepper and matzo meal, and finally worked back into the reserved fish skin. Whatever its form, the forcemeat was ideally made with a combination of three different fish—pike, whitefish and (absolutely essential) flavorful, fatty carp—all fresh-water fish, reflecting the inland-European origins of the dish. An awesome amount of work went into the original way of preparing the dish. After killing, filleting and grinding her own fresh fish, the housewife would chop it for at least half an hour to get the proper texture—not too airy, not too dense. She would simmer the fish up to three hours in a stock of water, fish trimmings, carrots, seasonings and aromatic vegetables, then drain the fish and strain the stock and leave the two to chill until the broth turned to a shimmering, loose gelatin. The finished dish would look like the masterpiece it was: ovals of sand-colored fish, speckled with black dots of pepper and rimmed with dark bands of skin, perched in a pool of amber jelly and bright orange carrot slices and accompanied by white or red (beet) horseradish sauce that was strong enough to draw tears.

With chicken soup, the next course of the Sabbath meal, a central foodstuff of a traditional Jewish kitchen comes into its own. Jewish gourmets argue that if the state of Israel ever adopts a national bird it should be the chicken; others claim that the chicken, not the lion, is the king of beasts. It is no lean fryer or broiler, but a plump fowl, a soup chicken, and once it was by far the most important purchase of the week. The skin of the neck is carefully removed in one piece to be stuffed with a thick paste of flour, onions, chicken fat and seasonings. The yellow fat is cut away and rendered with onions to produce *schmaltz,* a Jewish balm that is used as cooking fat, as seasoning or as an incredibly rich spread on bread or matzos. (In nostalgic tribute to its richness, the words schmaltz and schmaltzy have oozed into English to designate anything excessively sentimental.) As a bonus there are *grebenes,* or the *schmaltz* cracklings, to be mixed into the chopped liver with the *schmaltz,* onions and hard-cooked eggs.

But it is the soup that makes the greatest demands upon the chicken. The heart, neck, gizzard and feet go into the pot as well as the chicken itself; for a special treat there are the small unlaid eggs that are found in any proper fat hen; and the flavor of the final product is enhanced by onions and such "soup greens" as celery tops, parsley, parsnips and carrots. Filled as much with thin noodles as with soup, a bowl of it may be crowned with the tiny egg yolks, cooked to a pale yellow, and its surface glitters with light reflected from globules of chicken fat. It is a "golden soup," the proud cook will tell you—and it is also, in the opinion of many Jewish mothers, the panacea for all the physical ailments of mankind. Author Charles Angoff recalls that his great-grandmother used to say: "If chicken soup and sleep can't cure you, nothing will."

When this miracle of medicine is not served with noodles, its accompaniments, especially on holidays, may be *knaidlach* or *kreplach.* Some like their *knaidlach* light, while others feel shortchanged by *knaidlach* that are "light as feathers." The resident expert in a Jersey City matzo factory once told me in an almost threatening tone, "I wouldn't eat a matzo ball that didn't weigh a ton." But some people prefer *kreplach* to any weight of matzo ball. Usually reserved for especially festive occasions,

At a Holiday Held in a Straw Hut, Jews Give Thanks for Fruits of the Earth

The power of food to call up vivid memories was known to the Jews long before Marcel Proust based his multivolume *Remembrance of Things Past* on a single tea pastry. In Jewish family rituals, which are in part designed to instruct children in traditional lore and inherited legend, foods play a key role, and it may be no coincidence that the Jewish religion has survived under greater pressure and for a longer time than any other. Sukkoth, the Holiday of the Huts, is an autumn harvest festival that also commemorates the time when the Jews lived in the Sinai desert in temporary huts of straw after fleeing from Egypt. Today, for this holiday, many orthodox Jewish families build small straw huts outdoors—in a backyard, like the *sukkah* (hut) shown at the right, or on a terrace or rooftop—and for seven days eat all their meals there. The roof is thinly covered with reeds to allow the light of the stars and moon to filter through at evening mealtime. And extra chairs are placed around the table so that neighbors can be invited in for cakes, fruit and wine.

The harvest holiday of Sukkoth is a time of hospitality and joy—but it is also a time of deep symbolic meaning. At left, 11-year-old James Dworskin holds a traditional bouquet of willow and myrtle branches tied with palm fronds in one hand, and a citron fruit in the other. Together, they symbolize the fruitfulness of the earth. In their *sukkah,* decorated with autumn gourds, dried corn and chrysanthemums *(opposite),* Mr. and Mrs. Harry Bialick of Brooklyn, New York, entertain young James and three other neighborhood children around a table piled with fruit, candies and a variety of cakes. The richly decorated Bibles in the foreground, bound in silver and turquoise, were made in Israel.

the luscious little relatives of ravioli and *wonton* form a curious link between the Jewish cuisine and those of Italy and China.

After the triumphs of the fish and soup, the main course may at first seem an anticlimax. Often it is simply the boiled chicken from the soup pot, served as is or rubbed with fat, paprika and garlic, and roasted in the oven; alternatively, there are such perennial favorites as braised beef and stuffed breast of veal. But it is the side dishes that give this course its quality. One may be a *tsimmes* braised along with the meat. During the long cooking over a low flame, the fat of the meat permeates these fruits and vegetables to create a sort of glazed essence, sweet yet savory. For those with heartier tastes and stronger physiques there is the denseness of a length of *kishke*. Cooked with the *tsimmes, kishke* comes to the table infused with all the juices and flavors of both the meat and the fruits and vegetables—but it goes down with a thump, producing the impression that a diner will never be hungry again.

The meal is almost over, though. Those with ever-replenishing appetites may linger over a moist potato *kugel* with a thick, crisp, brown crust. Or they may turn to a sweet *kugel* made with noodles, eggs, fruit and cinnamon, remembering the saying that *kugel* is the perfect food because if it holds together you have a marvelous pudding and if it doesn't you have marvelous ingredients. (More solemnly, the poet Heinrich Heine called it "this holy national dish.") Finally, there are the classic cakes for a meat meal, *lekach* (honey cake) and spongecake. The latter is perhaps the only dish in the Jewish cuisine on which all cooks are in absolute agreement: it should be light, and the more eggs the better.

The splendid Sabbath meal comes once a week; the far more splendid Passover feasts come once a year, during the week-long holiday at which Jews all over the world celebrate their deliverance from bondage in Egypt and recall their flight across the Sinai desert to Israel. The entire holiday is a time of joy and part of the joy is in eating, for the first two evenings of Passover are given over to magnificent family meals accompanied by singing and ritual. These two meals, called Seders, are the high point of the Jewish culinary year.

Because the ancient Jews fled Egypt with bread dough that had had no time to rise, modern Jews eat only the flat unleavened bread called matzo during the Passover. Matzos are eaten throughout Passover week, not only with meals but also in light snacks of matzo-meal pancakes called *chremzlach* and in such special dishes as a fried-egg-and-matzo mixture called *matzo brei (Recipe Index)*. In an orthodox home, all leaven (such as baking powder) and all food that has come into contact with leaven must be removed before the holiday begins. Earlier, special orders of food for the holiday begin to arrive, and in the old days the fire escapes of the Lower East Side would be crowded with jugs of wine and jars of pickles and preserves. From his own childhood on the East Side, author Sam Levenson recalls this phase of the holiday with special vividness:

> *About three days before the Passover there was a knock on the door: "Your order is here." The Israelites took less out of Egypt with them than Mama brought in for the holidays. We were prepared for forty years of desert living. For weeks we*

felt our way amongst crates of eggs, sacks of [matzo] flour, farfel [matzo bits] and matzos—matzos in closets, on mantelpieces, under beds, under tables, under sinks, on the fire escape, on the piano: egg matzos, plain matzos, long matzos, short matzos, round matzos, square matzos.

Now comes an orgy of cleaning and cooking. As sundown approaches on Passover eve, each household throbs to the sounds of preparations: the rapping of *hockmessers* against thick wooden bowls, chopping livers and *charoset,* a ritual combination of apples, nuts and wine that symbolizes the mortar used by the Hebrew slaves in Egypt; the rasping of potatoes rubbed on graters for *kugel;* the swish of knives cutting homemade thin egg pancakes into noodles. Fluffy masses of egg white are folded into batter to provide the only "leavening" in cakes that must be made with potato flour or matzo cake flour. And then, at the last moment, batches of *chremzlach* begin to sputter in skillets of chicken fat.

Because a long religious service precedes the meal at a Seder, the *chremzlach* are served early as a snack to ward off starvation. Children love them, and the first guests to arrive will have a few pancakes and perhaps a thimbleful of holiday fruit brandy. The table shines with virgin dishes reserved for Passover use alone, set out with silver and the best cut glass on a white tablecloth. At the head of the table stands a tray of the ritual foods used in the Seder service, and a napkin-covered dish of matzos, the unleavened "bread of affliction." And there are wine glasses, for as part of the Seder service each diner must drink four glasses of wine. An extra wine glass, preferably the largest and most ornate, is set out for Elijah the Prophet, who, according to tradition, may visit any Jew this night.

On this most glorious evening of the year, Jewish families celebrate the central experience of Jewish history—the passage from bondage to freedom and the revelation of God's laws. For Jews, the words "This year we are slaves—next year, free men" have never lost their meaning. It is natural and right that the celebration should take the form of a feast, and that the ethnic patriotism that is celebrated is not only religious and cultural, but also culinary.

While the Passover feast reigns as the high point of the Jewish culinary year, day-to-day meals are much more humble affairs. Perhaps the humblest is a quick snack at a dairy restaurant—though even there the menu can easily expand to a leisurely six-course dinner or an enormous smorgasbord-style brunch. Your dinner may include some odd items—imitation "chopped liver" based on the high-protein mixture called Protose, and "cutlets" of finely chopped vegetables—for dairy restaurants have specialties that look like meat, try to taste like meat, and have everything in them except meat. But watch those around you at a place like Ratner's Restaurant on Second Avenue or the Garden Cafeteria on East Broadway, both well within the boundaries of Manhattan's Lower East Side. There the old men of the New Immigration—and a healthy sampling of their offspring to the fourth generation—sit over coffee or glasses of hot tea. They choose their side dishes with a connoisseur's eye: perhaps a piece of noodle *kugel,* or a dish of broad noodles mixed with fresh chalk-white farmer cheese and swimming in butter, or a bowl of mushroom-and-

Brunch Means
Bagels and Lox

*For many Jews—and for growing
numbers of non-Jews—Sunday
brunch means a visit to an
"appetizing store," whose salty,
smoky foods seem to taste best on a
leisurely weekend morning. The
featured breadstuff is the bagel—a
chewy ring of baked dough, now
available fresh or frozen throughout
the country; but man cannot live by
bagels alone, and so rolls are also
served. All are eaten with sweet
butter, cream cheese and smoked
fish: salmon, winter carp, sable,
whitefish or sturgeon. A happy
alternative is herring—pickled,
or in wine or sour-cream sauce.*

barley soup made with dried mushrooms—all accompanied by baskets of bread (black or rye) and rolls (soft or hard).

You yourself may settle for one perfect main dish, perhaps blintzes *(Recipe Index)*—those golden pancakes, less delicate than crêpes, rolled around sweet creamy fillings of white cheese, or tarter ones of blueberries or cherries, sautéed in butter and served with sour cream. Or you may try a single cold dish and a dessert. At the Garden Cafeteria the glassed-in counters displaying these dishes seem endless. There are plates of smoked whitefish, carp or sable, and a whole galaxy of chopped salads—salmon or tuna; egg with mushrooms or onions or spinach; herring with apples, eggs and onions. There are the white cheeses—farmer, pot and cottage —served with sour cream and/or chopped raw vegetables for a spring salad *(Recipe Index)*. The next section is piled high with cakes—cheese and prune "Danishes" (in New York's pastry heaven, "Danish" will mean "Jewish"); coffeecakes bursting with cinnamon, poppy seeds and raisins; sinfully rich cheesecakes topped with strawberries *(Recipe Index)*. And just beyond there are rice puddings, bread puddings, noodle puddings, egg-barley puddings with bright red fruit sauce.

Of all the dairy delicacies, the one best known to the non-Jewish world is the familiar trio of bagel, lox and cream cheese. The bagel is a doughnut-shaped roll that is first boiled and then baked. Lox is simply smoked salmon; the cream cheese, curiously enough, is an American invention.

100

No one knows for sure how the combination became a Jewish specialty, or when and how the bagel originated. The name presumably comes from *bougel,* an old German word for ring. But even an amateur authority on the "appetizing store" (one buys appetizing things in an appetizing store, just as one "eats dairy" in a dairy restaurant) can point out some very Jewish—and far less well known—contributions to an elaborate brunch. Instead of bagels he may suggest puffy round "bialys" (the name comes from the Polish city of Bialystok), which have the crisp yeasty texture of a pizza crust; or soft onion rolls, flecked with dark-brown bits of crisp baked onion and concealing other bits of nearly raw onion at the heart. Instead of lox and its less salty version, Nova Scotia salmon, he may have you try smoked whitefish (which is actually shiny gold on the outside) or sable or winter carp. All have enticing, silky textures, and all are far more delicate in taste than lox, which calls out for the blandness of cream cheese to neutralize the ardor of its flavor.

You don't have to be Jewish to enjoy any of these delights—or to enjoy a Jewish delicatessen. What is more, you probably won't have to go far to find one, wherever you live. There are now almost six million American Jews, and sometimes there seem to be almost that many delicatessens, too. Detroit alone has threescore and ten of them, including one that calls itself a "corned-beef happening"; in Hollywood, delicatessens honor the stars of the season by naming sandwiches for them.

Flanking a halved bagel slathered with cream cheese and rich with sliced lox and onions is an array of brunch specialties. In the dish at far left are thick slices of smoked whitefish with black olives, pickled herring and herring in a sour-cream sauce. At right are slabs of smoked salmon, with the delicate Nova Scotia type below the fattier belly lox. At the top is a parade of bagels: from left to right, the simple classic bagel; variations seasoned with salt, sesame seed, poppy seed, garlic and onion; and—a relatively new variety—the pumpernickel bagel.

Nostalgia on Rye— the Jewish Deli

Devotees of the kosher or "kosher-style" delicatessen claim (only half-humorously) that it is the most important contribution Jews have made to the American scene. Purists seek out traditional shops where grills are redolent of juicy, all-beef frankfurters and rotund knishes; steam boxes puff out the fragrances of pastrami and corned beef; huge beef tongues and batteries of salamis and rolled beef await the knife, and all the meats are surrounded by a dazzle of pickles, salads and breads. The Jewish deli has become as much an integral part of the Melting Pot culture as the pizzeria.

This popularity is not only deserved but completely understandable, for the Jewish delicatessen as we know it was created in America. It was here that Jews altered the frankfurter, replacing its pork with beef and adding new spices (a small, fat *Wurst* is generally called a "special"). Salamis, too, were made here from beef rather than pork. Kosher-style beef pastrami, corned beef and pickled tongue were developed here. Delicatessens catered to American tastes by adding turkey, roast beef, Russian dressing and coleslaw to their bills of fare.

The result is a sort of subcuisine of the Jewish meat diet, according to one friendly critic, "bad for the digestion, vitaminless and delicious." Even to the mild charges in that assessment, however, one delicatessen owner had a ready answer; asked when the vegetables would be served, he indignantly countered, "What's the matter, a pickle isn't a vegetable?" And indeed, the appetizing store and the delicatessen have made an art of such pickled vegetables as cucumbers, green tomatoes, sauerkraut and cherry peppers. In the pickle factories of the East Side's Hester Street, a shopper can select a cucumber pickle from several degrees of "sour," ranging from the bland, bright-green "quarter sour" to the potent, garlicky, olive-green pickle that most Americans call "kosher dill."

But it is the meats, not the vegetables, that make a delicatessen. Served in a sandwich these meats provide ecstasy as they are eaten, and pangs of nostalgia later on; it is no wonder that movie stars fly the stuff to remote

shooting locations, or that there are two delicatessen restaurants known as Lindy's East in Hong Kong. For a perfect sandwich the bread or roll should be very fresh, and the bread thinly sliced. The pastrami and corned beef must be "hot"—that is, warm enough to keep their substantial content of fat from congealing—while salami, rolled beef and tongue can be served at room temperature, or better, the temperature of a nice warm room. Piled an inch high and topped with a "shmear" of distinctively sharp mustard (the secret is a little pickle brine mixed into the mustard as a stretcher), the meat in a delicatessen sandwich is a meal in itself, with the thin bread almost disappearing into the mammoth mound. Nevertheless, true devotees insist on supplementing it with potato salad (rich in mayonnaise, with a dash of sugar), coleslaw (the sugar more pronounced here), baked beans and pickles, and on drowning it in great draughts of cream soda, "celery tonic" or plain soda.

The Sabbath dinner and the Passover feast, the dairy brunch and the delicatessen mini-orgy—these meals represent the four corners of the Jewish gastronomic experience. On the one hand there is food that accompanies and completes the religious rites of one of the world's most ancient peoples. On the other, there is a secular ritual of delight—Enjoy! Enjoy! —that embraces a host of exotic though increasingly Americanized foods. But there are certain occasions, most notably a Bar Mitzvah, that can embrace all of these elements: a solemn sacred service, a galaxy of

Spicy warm pastrami, lean corned beef and center-cut tongue *(opposite)* are the classic fillers of a deli sandwich, shown at center with an initial dollop of hot mustard, a hearty portion of corned beef and the traditional accompaniments. These, shown above, include *(clockwise):* sweet red peppers, pickled green tomatoes, sour and half-sour pickles, potato salad and coleslaw.

103

noshes (snacks) and a glorious banquet. As fully developed in modern America, it is unmatched by anything in any other cuisine.

The Bar Mitzvah celebrates the coming-to-manhood of a Jewish boy. More specifically, it marks the moment when, at the age of 13, he is fully received into the religious community and becomes a "son of the Commandment." Neither a ceremony nor a feast is called for in Jewish religious law, but the Jews of Germany and Eastern Europe began very early on to mark the day with a ceremony at the synagogue and a simple party. In America, the ceremony was retained and the party has been expanded by some families to awesome proportions.

The ceremony itself remains relatively simple; it is, in fact, no more than a part of the weekly Sabbath service in the synagogue. On a Sabbath morning after the boy's 13th birthday, his father, as well as the rabbi (spiritual head) of the congregation, reads designated parts of the regular service; the boy himself is called upon to read part of the Torah (the first five books of the Bible) and, usually, to give a speech. At the close of the service it became customary for the boy's parents to invite the congregation to a *kiddush,* the traditional Sabbath sanctification over bread or wine. Gradually, this phase of the Bar Mitzvah grew into a modest party. The parents and the congregation would enjoy *schnapps* (liquor), wine and sweets, perhaps a lunch; the boy would receive gifts such as a prayer shawl, which he was now allowed to wear for the first time.

The modern kosher caterer has transformed this simple party out of all recognition. His slogan seems to be: more is better, less is a lousy advertisement. His clients (who may spend thousands of dollars on Bar Mitzvah day) seem to agree with him. Hours after the synagogue service, when the Sabbath has ended, the guests assemble for a cocktail reception, often in the caterer's own establishment. There will be music and a reception line at which the Bar Mitzvah boy receives gifts—usually substantial checks rather than the prayer shawls and prayer books of earlier days. A lofty-hatted chef may be on hand to carve the lox or the turkey. The caterer may produce an impressive centerpiece for the burdened table—perhaps a fountain spurting punch or wine, or (though this is maybe only a legend) a statuette of the Bar Mitzvah boy himself sculpted in chopped liver. But the heart and soul of this cocktail party is food —and now, in a movement that has been called "the charge of the bagel lancers," the guests go on the attack.

Take the cold cocktail foods first. They could include chopped liver, chopped or marinated herring, smoked fish and caviar, the roe of sturgeon, whitefish or carp. The cold cuts include roast beef, turkey, tongue, pastrami, corned beef and salami, some of which may be rolled around pickles or even water chestnuts, to be dipped in mustard, Russian dressing or mayonnaise. To round out this part of the table there are coleslaw, potato salad and deviled eggs, and raw vegetables with a cocktail dip.

With the hot cocktail food, new and wonderful influences join in this apotheosis of the delicatessen and the appetizing store. Traditionalists will find their old favorites in miniature: little potato and meat *knishes,* tiny sweet-and-sour meatballs and stuffed cabbage rolls, baby potato pancakes with applesauce. There is more: sautéed sweetbreads in a wine sauce, mushrooms stuffed with meat and bread crumbs, and such pastry-wrapped savories as little frankfurters in blankets of dough. Finally, there are dishes brought in as though by a net cast over the varied ingredients of the American Melting Pot: Southern fried chicken, for instance, or egg rolls and fried rice, or barbecued beef ribs.

The real meal, remember, has not yet begun. With the guests half sated, the party moves into a dining room, where the Bar Mitzvah boy and his immediate family take their places on a dais or at a head table. The musicians come with them, for dancing will follow every course—a custom that is not only good for the digestion but gives the waiters a chance to change the plates. Now, seated at festive tables, the guests address themselves to a dinner that makes a conscious attempt to combine Jewish and certain non-Jewish elements. Indeed, the most interesting thing about their meal is the extent to which it assimilates the good foods that Jews have come to know in America.

Typically, it will begin with a fresh fruit cup followed by an imitation creamed-seafood dish, with the filling either rolled in a crêpe and called *crêpes de fruits de mer* or stuffed in a shell and called *coquilles St.-Jacques*. (Since shellfish is forbidden, the basic ingredient will be a bland white fish, and the "cream" a vegetable-based product.) The main course is likely to be based on an all-American favorite, perhaps filet mignon or roast beef or Rock Cornish hen stuffed with wild rice; string beans amandine is a popular accompaniment. There may also be honeyed carrots, a reminder of the *tsimmes* of yore—there may, in fact, be a serving of *tsimmes* itself, and a slice of good hot *kishke* to go with it. The diners may turn from their meat to a sweet noodle *kugel,* or a dish of spiced stewed fruit offsetting the richness of what has come before.

As the evening moves on to the pastry table and the after-dinner dancing, it is likely to be the *tsimmes* and the *kishke* and the *kugel* and the compote that the older guests remember with the greatest affection. Like the great Jewish "spreads" at the cocktail party, these dishes bring the old days back to a people that has been largely caught up in the mainstream of American life. For many, the new folkways and foods cannot compare with the pioneer delights of the Lower East Side in the days of the immigrants; the pushcarts have almost disappeared, but not the heartburn of nostalgia. Memory's delights are now sold bottled, canned and frozen; supermarkets offer commercial borscht, gefilte fish, pastrami and frozen bagels (there is not yet a prayer to intone over a thawing bagel but someone, somewhere, is surely working on it).

What is far more important, a new generation of Jews, often with the help of grandmothers and great-grandmothers, is learning to prepare the good old foods in the good old ways. That, after all, is how the Melting Pot works. Not long ago, a vivacious third-generation girl told me that she had just made her first batch of *knaidlach.* She described her fears as the little matzo balls refused at first to rise from the bottom of the pot of simmering chicken stock, and told of her delight in the finished product —fluffy, but not too light, and rich with the flavors of this, her own golden chicken soup. "And you know," she ended triumphantly, "just as my grandmother used to say of *her* cooking, 'es est sich' ['it digests itself']!"

To make 10 blintzes

COTTAGE-CHEESE FILLING

1 pound dry cottage cheese, or
    substitute 1 pound creamed
    cottage cheese, wrapped in
    cheesecloth and squeezed dry
2 tablespoons sour cream
1 egg yolk
2 tablespoons sugar
½ teaspoon vanilla extract
¼ teaspoon salt

BLINTZES

3 eggs
½ cup water
¾ cup sifted all-purpose flour
¼ teaspoon salt
2 tablespoons butter, melted and
    cooled
4 tablespoons melted butter,
    combined with 1 tablespoon
    flavorless vegetable oil

1 cup sour cream

Blintzes (Jewish)

ROLLED PANCAKES FILLED WITH COTTAGE CHEESE

To prepare the filling: With the back of a large wooden spoon, force the cottage cheese through a fine sieve into a deep bowl, or put the cheese through a food mill set over a bowl. Add 2 tablespoons of sour cream, the egg yolk, sugar, vanilla extract and ¼ teaspoon of salt. Stirring and mashing vigorously, beat with a large spoon until the ingredients are well blended and the mixture smooth. Set aside.

To make the batter for the blintzes: Combine the eggs, water, flour, ¼ teaspoon of salt and 2 tablespoons of cooled melted butter in the jar of an electric blender and blend them at high speed for a few seconds. Turn the machine off, scrape down the sides of the jar with a rubber spatula and blend again for 40 seconds.

To make the batter by hand, stir the flour and eggs together in a mixing bowl and gradually stir in the water and ¼ teaspoon of salt. Beat with a whisk or a rotary or electric beater until the flour lumps disappear, then force the batter through a fine sieve into another bowl and stir in the 2 tablespoons of cooled melted butter.

However you make it, the batter should have the consistency of heavy cream; dilute it if necessary by beating in cold water a teaspoon at a time.

To cook the blintzes, heat a 6-inch crêpe pan or skillet over high heat until a drop of water flicked onto it evaporates instantly. With a pastry brush or crumpled paper towels, lightly grease the bottom and sides of the pan with a little of the combined melted butter and oil.

Pour about 3 tablespoons of batter into the pan and tip the pan so that the batter quickly covers the bottom; the batter should cling to the pan and begin to firm up almost immediately. Cook the blintz for a minute or so, until a rim of brown shows around the edge. Then, without turning it over, slide the blintz onto a plate. Brush the combined butter and oil on the skillet again and proceed with the rest of the blintzes. As they are cooked, stack the blintzes one on top of the other.

When all the blintzes have been browned on one side, fill and roll each of them in the following fashion: Place about 3 tablespoons of filling on the cooked side of the blintz an inch or so from the top edge. With a knife or metal spatula, smooth the filling into a strip about 3 inches long and 1 inch deep. Fold the sides of the blintz toward the center, covering the ends of the filling. Then turn the top edge over the filling and roll the blintz into a cylinder about 3 inches long and 1 inch wide.

Pour the remaining butter-and-oil mixture into a heavy 10- to 12-inch skillet and set over moderate heat. Place four or five blintzes, seam side down, in the pan, and fry them for 3 to 5 minutes on each side, turning them with a metal spatula and regulating the heat so they color quickly and evenly without burning. As they are browned, transfer them to a heated serving platter.

Serve the blintzes hot, accompanied by the cup of sour cream, presented separately in a bowl.

The cheese-filled pancakes called blintzes, shown with their classic accompaniment of sour cream, are a popular Jewish-American specialty.

CHICKEN SOUP
A 5- to 5½-pound stewing fowl,
    cut into 6 or 8 pieces, plus the
    neck, giblets and feet
3½ quarts cold water
2 medium-sized onions, peeled
2 medium-sized carrots, scraped and
    each cut crosswise into 3 pieces
1 celery stalk, including the green
    leaves, cut crosswise into 2 pieces
½ medium-sized parsnip
8 parsley sprigs
3 dill sprigs, or substitute
    1 teaspoon dried dill weed
1 tablespoon coarse (kosher) salt,
    or substitute 1 teaspoon regular
    salt

MATZO BALLS
6 egg yolks
8 tablespoons chicken stock, fresh
    or canned
2 teaspoons regular salt
Freshly ground black pepper
8 tablespoons chicken fat, melted
    and cooled (see gehakte leber,
    page 24)
1½ cups matzo meal
6 egg whites
2 tablespoons coarse (kosher) salt,
    or substitute 2 teaspoons regular
    salt

4 matzos, broken into 1½- to
    2-inch pieces
4 tablespoons unsalted butter
¼ cup finely chopped onions
4 eggs
1 teaspoon salt

Chicken Soup with Matzo Balls (Jewish)

Place the pieces of fowl and the neck, giblets and feet in a heavy 8- to 10-quart pot and pour the cold water over it. The water should cover the pieces completely; if necessary, add more water. Bring to a boil over high heat, meanwhile skimming off the foam and scum as they rise to the surface. When the soup is clear, add the onions, carrots, celery, parsnip, parsley, dill and 1 tablespoon of coarse salt. Return the soup to a boil, reduce the heat to low and simmer, partially covered, for 2½ to 3 hours, or until the fowl shows no resistance when a piece is pierced with the point of a small sharp knife.

Meanwhile, make the matzo balls in the following fashion: With a whisk or a rotary or electric beater, beat the egg yolks until they are well blended. Whisk in the chicken stock, 2 teaspoons of regular salt, a few grindings of black pepper and the chicken fat. Whisking constantly, add the matzo meal, ¼ cup at a time. In a large bowl, beat the egg whites with a clean whisk or a rotary or electric beater until they are stiff enough to form firm, unwavering peaks on the beater when it is lifted from the bowl. With a wooden spoon or rubber spatula, lightly stir the whites into the matzo-meal mixture until they are well incorporated; do not overstir. Refrigerate the mixture for at least 30 minutes, or until it is stiff enough so that a spoon will stand unsupported in the bowl.

In a 6- to 8-quart pot, bring about 4 quarts of water and 2 tablespoons of coarse salt (or 2 teaspoons of regular salt) to a boil over high heat. For each matzo ball, pinch off about a tablespoon of the dough and roll it between your hands. Drop the balls into the boiling water and stir gently once or twice so that they do not stick to one another or the bottom of the pot. Cook covered and undisturbed for 40 minutes. With a slotted spoon, transfer the matzo balls to a bowl of cold water to prevent them from drying out. Set them aside.

When the soup has cooked its allotted time, remove the fowl and vegetables with tongs or a slotted spoon. Discard the vegetables, gizzard, neck and feet, and either reserve the pieces of fowl for later use or serve them, skinned, boned and sliced, with the soup.

Strain the soup through a fine sieve and return it to the pot. With a large spoon, skim as much fat as possible from the surface. Taste the soup for seasoning. Drain the matzo balls, add them to the soup and bring it to a simmer over moderate heat. Reduce the heat to low and cook gently, uncovered, for 15 minutes to heat the matzo balls through.

To serve the soup, place three matzo balls in each of six large soup plates and ladle the soup over them.

Matzo Brei (Jewish)
SCRAMBLED MATZO AND EGGS

Place the matzo pieces in a large mixing bowl and pour in just enough cold water to cover them. Let them sit for 1 minute, then pour off the water. Squeeze the matzos in your hands to remove any excess water.

In a 10- to 12-inch skillet, melt the butter over moderate heat. When the foam subsides, stir in the onions and, stirring frequently, cook over moderate heat until they are soft and translucent. Drop in the matzos and, tossing the pieces constantly, cook until they are heated through. Reduce the heat to low.

Beat together the eggs and salt, and pour them into the skillet. Stirring constantly with the flat of a table fork or a rubber spatula, cook the mixture until the eggs begin to form soft, creamy curds. Transfer the *matzo brei* to a heated serving platter and serve at once.

NOTE: If you prefer sweet *matzo brei,* prepare as above but omit the onions. Serve with cinnamon and sugar or fruit preserves.

Lindy's Strawberry Cheesecake *(Jewish)*

Since dietary laws forbid the use of milk-based dishes in a meal that also features meat, cream- or butter-enriched desserts have never been emphasized in the Jewish cuisine. But rich creamy cheesecake—served after a "dairy" meal—has become a cherished Jewish-American specialty. The fruit-topped version below was featured for many years at Lindy's, until recently a restaurant landmark in New York's theater district.

To make one 9-inch cake

COOKIE CRUST: Place 1 cup of flour, ¼ cup of sugar, 1 teaspoon grated lemon rind, ¼ teaspoon of vanilla extract, 1 egg yolk and 8 tablespoons of butter in a large mixing bowl. With your fingertips, rub the ingredients together until they are well combined and can be gathered into a ball. Dust with a little flour, wrap in wax paper, and refrigerate for at least 1 hour. Preheat the oven to 400°.

Place the chilled dough in an ungreased 9-inch springform pan. With your hands, pat and spread the dough evenly over the bottom and about 2 inches up the sides of the pan. Bake in the center of the oven for 10 minutes, then remove and set aside to cool to room temperature.

FILLING: Lower the oven temperature to 250°. Place the cream cheese in a large mixing bowl and beat vigorously with a wooden spoon until it is creamy and smooth. Beat in ¾ cup of sugar a few tablespoons at a time and, when it is well incorporated, beat in 1½ tablespoons of flour, 1 teaspoon of lemon rind, the orange rind, ½ teaspoon of vanilla extract, the eggs and egg yolk, and the heavy cream. Pour the filling into the cooled cookie crust and bake in the center of the oven for 1 hour, then remove from the oven and set aside to cool in the pan.

STRAWBERRY TOPPING: Wash and hull the strawberries and place them, 1 cup at a time, in a fine sieve set over a large bowl. With the back of a wooden spoon, press just enough berries through the sieve to get ¾ cup of purée. Set the purée aside. With the cake still in the springform pan, arrange the remaining whole strawberries, stem side down, over the surface of the cake.

Beat ½ cup of sugar, the cornstarch-and-water mixture and the salt into the puréed berries, and pour the mixture into a 1- to 1½-quart enameled or stainless-steel saucepan. Bring to a boil over high heat, stirring frequently, then boil the syrup undisturbed for 2 minutes. Remove from the heat and, if you prefer a deeper red color, stir in a drop or two of red food coloring.

Spoon the hot glaze over the whole berries and refrigerate the cheesecake for at least 3 hours before serving.

COOKIE CRUST
1 cup all-purpose flour
¼ cup sugar
1 teaspoon finely grated
  lemon rind
¼ teaspoon vanilla extract
1 egg yolk
8 tablespoons (1 quarter-pound
  stick) unsalted butter, chilled and
  cut into ¼-inch bits

CHEESE FILLING
1¼ pounds cream cheese, softened
¾ cup sugar
1½ tablespoons all-purpose flour
1 teaspoon finely grated
  lemon rind
1 teaspoon finely grated
  orange rind
½ teaspoon vanilla extract
3 eggs plus 1 egg yolk
2 tablespoons heavy cream

STRAWBERRY TOPPING
1 quart fresh strawberries
½ cup sugar
4 teaspoons cornstarch dissolved in
  ¼ cup cold water
Dash of salt
Dash of red food coloring
  (optional)

To make about 12 oval cakes

3 pounds fish trimmings: the heads,
　　bones and tails of the pike,
　　whitefish and carp *(below)*
5 large onions (2½ pounds), 2
　　cut into ⅛-inch-thick slices and
　　3 quartered
4 tablespoons coarse (kosher) salt,
　　or substitute 4 teaspoons regular
　　salt
1 tablespoon white pepper
1 pound each of skinned filleted
　　pike, whitefish and carp
2 tablespoons matzo meal
1 egg, lightly beaten
¼ cup cold water
8 medium-sized carrots, scraped: 1
　　cut on the diagonal into about
　　12 ¼-inch-thick ovals, 6 cut
　　crosswise into ½-inch-thick
　　rounds and 1 finely grated

To make about 1⅓ cups

3 medium-sized beets (1½
　　pounds)
¼ pound fresh horseradish root
4 tablespoons red wine vinegar
2 teaspoons coarse (kosher) salt, or
　　substitute 1½ teaspoons regular
　　salt
1 teaspoon sugar

Gefilte Fish *(Jewish)*
POACHED FISH CAKES

*Centuries ago in Eastern Europe, gefilte fish was, as the name implies, a
stuffed fish. The meat was meticulously removed from a whole fish, then
chopped and seasoned, and stuffed back inside the skin to be cooked. In
some Jewish-American households traces of this practice still remain: a
strip of fish skin is wrapped around the oval of ground or chopped fish before it is poached.*

Place the fish heads, bones and tails in a sieve or colander and wash them
under cold running water. Then transfer them to a heavy 8- to 10-quart
pot and scatter the onion slices, 2 tablespoons of the coarse salt (or 2 teaspoons of regular salt) and 2 teaspoons of the white pepper over them.
Pour in just enough cold water to cover the fish trimmings and onions
and bring to a boil over high heat. Reduce the heat to low and simmer, partially covered, for 40 minutes.

Meanwhile, put the filleted pike, whitefish and carp and the quartered
onions through the fine blade of a meat grinder twice. Combine the
ground fish and onions in a deep mixing bowl.

To make the gefilte fish mixture by hand, chop the fish and onions fine
and, with a pestle or the back of a large wooden spoon, mash them into a
fairly smooth paste.

Beat the fish and onions with a spoon until the mixture is well combined, then beat in the matzo meal, egg, the remaining 2 tablespoons of
coarse salt (or 2 teaspoons of regular salt) and the remaining teaspoon of
white pepper. Beat in the ¼ cup of cold water a tablespoon at a time.

Divide the fish mixture into 12 equal parts and shape each into an oval
cake about 4 inches long, 2 inches wide and 1 inch thick. Press an oval carrot slice flat on the top of each fish cake.

When the trimmings and onions have cooked their allotted time, scatter the carrot rounds into the pot. Arrange the fish cakes in one layer on
top of the carrots; if they do not all fit comfortably, reserve some and
cook the fish in two batches. Bring the liquid in the pot to a boil over
high heat, reduce the heat to low, cover tightly and steam the fish cakes
for 30 minutes, or until they are firm when prodded gently with a finger.

With a slotted spoon, arrange the fish cakes attractively on a large platter. Strain the remaining contents of the pot through a fine sieve set over
a large shallow bowl. Stir the grated carrot into the strained stock.

Refrigerate the poached gefilte fish and strained cooking stock separately for at least 3 hours, until they are both thoroughly chilled and the
stock is a firm jelly.

Just before serving, chop the jelly fine and mound it on the platter
around the fish cakes. Serve with bottled white horseradish or beet horseradish sauce *(below)* as a first course or a light luncheon dish.

Fresh Horseradish Sauce with Beets *(Jewish)*

With a small sharp knife cut the tops off the beets, leaving about 1 inch
of stem on each. Scrub the beets under cold running water, then place
them in a 2- to 3-quart saucepan and add enough cold water to cover

Gefilte fish are poached fish ovals garnished with carrots and chopped fish jelly, and complemented by beet horseradish sauce.

them by 2 inches. Bring the water to a boil over high heat, reduce the heat to low, cover the pan tightly and simmer until the beets show no resistance when pierced with the point of a small sharp knife. This may take anywhere from 30 minutes for young beets to as long as 2 hours for older ones. The beets should be kept constantly covered with water; add additional boiling water if necessary.

Drain the beets in a colander and, when they are cool enough to handle, slip off the outer skins and, with a small sharp knife, trim the tops and tails. With the fine side of a four-sided stand-up hand grater, grate the beets into a deep bowl.

With a small sharp knife, trim off the stem and tail end of the horseradish root, then scrape it with the knife or a vegetable peeler with a rotating blade. Grate the horseradish as fine as possible.

Stir the grated horseradish into the beets, then add the red wine vinegar, coarse or regular salt and sugar. Taste for seasoning. Cover tightly and let the sauce stand at room temperature to develop flavor for at least 2 hours before serving.

Tightly covered, it can be kept in the refrigerator for several weeks. Beet horseradish sauce is traditionally served with gefilte fish *(opposite)*, and can also accompany boiled beef.

~ Prices ~

Osushi	$1.00
Udon	.75
Pizza	.30
Taco	.30
Burritto	.30
Tostada	.30
Coke	.15
Coffee	.15
Donut	.10

VI

A Cook's Tour of Six Communities

Dorothy Sasaki, a young American of Japanese descent, munches a taco— a snack food of Mexican origin— at the Japanese-American Nisei Week Festival held annually in Los Angeles. The sign behind her provides further evidence of the ethnic and culinary diversity of America's Melting Pot: along with *osushi* and *udon,* two Japanese specialties, it lists several Mexican-inspired foods, Italian pizza and the ubiquitous American Coke.

The chapter that follows is different from the others in this book. Each of the previous chapters deals with one great wave of people (Italians, Slavs or Jews, for example) who came to America in the New Immigration starting in the 1880s and spread over their new nation. But that is only part of the story of the Melting Pot. (The final chapter, on the Puerto Ricans, tells another part.) The New Immigration contributed a sizable number to the scores of ethnic strains in the New World. Many of these peoples were absorbed into the American mainstream, while some of the small ethnic communities worked out their own unique versions of the U.S. experience.

This chapter is divided into six parts; generally, the people it discusses represent only small samples of larger ethnic groups, but each has a special meaning in the Melting Pot. The Basque shepherds and the Greek sponge fishermen have followed familiar occupations in a new land. In California the Armenian and Portuguese settlers enjoy a climate similar to that of their homelands—and a bounty that exceeds it. The forebears of one group of German-Americans made an arduous journey from Europe to the valley of the Pedernales River in Texas, where their descendants now reap the rewards of persistence. From the opposite direction came the early Oriental immigrants, whose food has become one of the most popular of all "naturalized" American cuisines.

In short, this "sampler" chapter is intended to present, in smaller helpings than the other chapters, a variety of communities whose delightful cooking should be better known to everyone.

The Basque Shepherds
of the Mountain States

The Basques who came to America's mountainous West from the mountainous borderlands between Spain and France added a fascinating bit of spice to the Melting Pot. They did not come to the New World in a single great wave, nor did they settle in big-city slums as unskilled laborers. Instead they came in a trickle, most of them bearing contracts to work as sheepherders—a basic Basque occupation, but one that attracts few native-born Americans. The influx was so small that even today, almost a century after it began, the Basque immigrants and their descendants total scarcely 60,000. Yet this handful of Basques dominates sheepherding in the Western United States.

The herders went to live where they had to, in remote regions of the Far West where mountain meadows and sagebrush flats provided ample cheap pasturage. Families were often quartered in Basque boardinghouses in nearby towns, such as Mountain Home, Idaho, and Bakersfield, California. It was at best a lonely life for all of them. In their little enclaves, the women and children were alone most of the year while the men roamed afield with their flocks. The herders themselves were ready to accept loneliness as an occupational hazard, knowing that in many ways it was worse than storms or savage beasts. But even the weatherbeaten veterans among them were unnerved by their first encounter with America's endless open spaces. Dominique Laxalt, a retired sheepman and the father of former Governor Paul Laxalt of Nevada, received his baptism of solitude as a 16-year-old immigrant back in 1910, and has never forgotten it. "Those first few months," he said, "you thought you would go insane. Then, suddenly, your mind turned the corner and you were used to it, and you didn't care whether you ever saw people again."

As with all peoples, the life style of the Basques influenced the way they cooked and ate. Shaped by centuries of rigorous existence in the rugged Pyrenees, their cuisine had always been strong and simple, featuring dishes that were filling and easy to prepare. In America, Basque cooking was further simplified by becoming for a time an almost exclusively male province, particularly in the field, where the herders cooked for themselves. Still, a cuisine flourished. It is now perhaps the world's best outdoor fare, and a repertory of only a few of its dishes would work wonders for the mealtime morale of American campers and hikers. Yet in town, a good Basque meal is not an impromptu, sketchy affair, nor is its enjoyment restricted to Basques and Bascophiles. Boardinghouse restaurants have become meccas for non-Basque gourmets from miles around, and they are often the best mealtime bet for highway travelers heading through the big, thinly settled country west of Cheyenne.

These boardinghouse restaurants are overwhelmingly generous (all you can eat for about four dollars) but sternly unpretentious. All the guests —boarders, locals and food-wise wayfarers—may sit together, family style, at long tables. There may be no menu; each diner helps himself from big communal serving plates and even bigger jugs of red wine, usually California Burgundy. Before the meal, many Basques indulge in a glass of picon punch, a bittersweet potation with brandy floated on top, over a mixture of club soda, the French apéritif Amer Picon (flavored with quinine, orange essence and gentian) and sweet red grenadine syrup. The drink—which looks as harmless as soda pop—has the kick of a herder's pack mule.

The dinner itself invariably starts with soup. It will probably be a thick leek-and-potato soup, or a clear beef or chicken broth with barley or vermicelli—but if the cook is in a creative mood he may present an aromatic purée of potatoes, beans and garlic, poured over slices of dried bread that have been spread with potatoes and grated cheese. The next course, served in an order peculiar to the Basque boardinghouse, may be a salad, usually crisp greens and onion rings with a light olive oil and vinegar dressing, but even this simple course may be enhanced: instead of a green salad, some cooks bring to the table a potato salad enriched by cold cooked vegetables, or fresh asparagus in season, very cold and accompanied by dollops of mayonnaise.

At a lofty summer grazing range in the Challis National Forest in southern Idaho, José Martín Celeya, a Basque sheepherder, drives his flock with the help of his border collie Brucie. The altitude here is 8,500 feet, too high and cold for a stay later than mid-September.

The main course comes in two or more parts. One of the dishes may be a rich stew of oxtail or tripe with beans and tomatoes. The stew, mopped up with plenty of fresh bread, may be accompanied by an inch-thick sirloin steak, roast lamb, sautéed chicken or fried liver. Frequently, a feature of this course is fish. An especially elegant dish of Pacific halibut, baked slowly with onions, peas and parsley, is prepared at the Valencia restaurant in Boise, Idaho, by chef Jesús Lejarcegui, a young Basque who recently arrived from the Spanish port of Bilbao. More typical of the Basque cuisine are the many dried-cod dishes. One of the most famous of them presents the fish simmered in a garlicky white sauce produced by its own gelatinous parts; another calls for cutting soaked and desalted cod into small squares, which are lightly fried, then baked in a lively mixture of diced cooked vegetables and tomato sauce.

Dessert, served with strong coffee, is drawn from two or three different Basque favorites, most often *flan* (caramel custard), ice cream or cheese with fresh fruit. The cheese usually gets the biggest play from the men; they would most like to have one of the Basques' own ewe's-milk cheeses, but since they are not imported or made here, they content themselves with liberal helpings of dry Jack or Cheddar cheese. Pastry is seldom served with the meal.

Simple as it is, a boardinghouse meal demands a greater variety of ingredients and more preparation time than the sheepherders can ever bother with out in their wilderness camps. In Idaho, for instance, a two-man herding team will head out for the high summer ranges in June, with more than 2,000 ewes and newborn spring lambs. These two men will generally cook for themselves until September, when they join ranks for a few days with other teams to send the weaned lambs to market; then the men are assigned a camp cook to prepare food for all of them. But out on the range, each team must make do with a minimum of portable foodstuffs and cooking equipment. Dyed-in-the-wool epicures and skilled cooks, the herders ingeniously mix their long-keeping staples with a few perishables and the one food that they have in never-ending abundance —lamb on the hoof. The result is a variety of flavorful, nourishing dishes, many of them one-pot or one-skillet meals.

Every staple and virtually every part of the lamb is used in several combinations. A busy herder may make a hasty meal a tasty one by cooking chick-peas or pinto beans with slices of *chorizo,* a garlicky Iberian sausage. The leftover chick-peas or beans may be warmed up as a side dish to lamb chops, or go into a lamb stew, or turn up—along with more *chorizo* slices—in a pancake-style Basque omelet. In a restaurant or a home kitchen, this famous dish is almost a cuisine in itself, for it adapts splendidly to any filling that comes to hand, including diced ham, dried cod, fried eggplant, sliced potatoes and onions *(Recipe Index)*, sautéed mushrooms, asparagus, pimiento and sardines. The trick common to all these variations is to cook the omelet to a firm golden brown on both sides, turning it over with the aid of an inverted plate.

Numerous Basque versions of lamb stew *(Recipe Index)*, strongly influenced by Western American cooking, are simply prepared and enthusiastically consumed whenever time permits. Chunks of the choicest lamb are coated with flour and browned with garlic and onions in a cast-iron Dutch oven. The cook then adds his vegetables—perhaps beans or a few potatoes, some tomatoes, carrots and green peppers—and douses, but does not cover, the whole with red wine. The pot is covered and set to cook on a wood-burning camp stove or in a pit lined with hot coals and heaped over with the earth. About two and a half hours later, the coals have cooled and the stew is ready for the herders to dig in. It is the typical main meal of their day, usually consumed in the evening, after the flock has been driven to its overnight "bedding ground."

The same pot used to cook the stews also serves as an oven for baking sourdough or yeast bread, an indispensable staple that plays a part in all of the herders' meals. Breakfast, eaten at first light under the pressure of moving the flock to its grazing ground, may be no more than a bowl of strong coffee with condensed milk, but it is turned into a souplike food by the addition of dried, crumbled bread. Coffee is one of the herders' two indispensable beverages. The other is red wine—the same wine that is used in cooking—and it is drunk copiously as long as the supply lasts. To keep wine handy out on the trail, many a herder carries the Basques' traditional goatskin *bota* and squirts himself a drink now and then. A fresh wine supply is the most welcome item that a camp foreman brings with him when he comes out with supplies for the trail-weary herding teams. "I could forget the beans or the bread," said one foreman, "but if I didn't bring the wine I'd have to go back and get it. Some of the old boys can put down a gallon of red Burgundy a day."

For the herders, the only real vacation from work comes in the fall or winter. After they have brought their breeding stock in from the high ranges, most of the men are free to spend some time in town. But the high point of the year comes in the summer, when Basque celebrations are held in centers throughout the sheep-raising country. Ranchers excuse as many herders as they can spare to attend the festivities, as a relief from the loneliness of sheepherding.

The celebration serves several purposes. It reunites friends long scattered by their work, permits parents to introduce marriageable daughters to eligible youths, and gives oldtimers a chance to marvel or grumble at how much things have changed. Many celebrations are simple picnics to which housewives with kitchens of their own contribute a few homemade dishes. But some communities put on grandiose folk festivals at which the Basques welcome their non-Basque neighbors. Men wearing American Levi's and Basque berets sing their mournful old songs; boys and girls in colorful costumes perform the strenuous *jota, arin-arin* and other dances; men proud of their strength compete in wood-chopping and weight-lifting contests *(pages 120-121)*.

Of course every big festival features plenty of good Basque food and Basque-style drinking. Whole lambs, spit-grilled on the spot or wrapped in foil and cooked underground, are consumed at an astonishing rate and washed down with long draughts of red wine. Traditional toasts in the difficult (some say impossible) Basque language can be heard everywhere. One of the fancier ones is translated: "May the happiest day of your past be the saddest day of your future." But a simple and more popular toast expresses a wish that many Basque-Americans seem to have realized in the present: "Osagarria!"—"The good life!"

—*Gerald Simons*

A ball of sourdough slowly rises in a Dutch oven.

When the dough has risen, the cook claps the lid on the Dutch oven and buries it in a trench filled with hot coals *(above)*. The result, after about an hour of undisturbed baking, is the loaf shown below, decoratively dented by the studlike protrusions of the oven lid.

Braised Lamb and Bachelor's Bread

It is very much a man's world in the high timberlands of southern Idaho, where Basques tend sheep and wait for the rare festive occasions when they can socialize a bit *(pages 120-121)*. Meanwhile, they must feed themselves. Their cooking could be a perfunctory as well as a lonely process, and sometimes it is, but mostly it is not. Traditionally the Basques make the best use of what they have, inspired to do so both by the ways of their homeland and by the customs of other Western outdoorsmen. This solid culinary standard means the crusty lightness of sourdough bread baked in a Dutch oven, lamb in every form from braised to fried, and plenty of hearty stews, heavy with sweet peppers, garlic, tomatoes and onion. If such urban niceties as tables and chairs are lacking—as they often are—well, no matter. The wine rarely runs out.

Aboard a convenient log in their temporary summer camp, five herders eat a midmorning snack of bread, Cheddar cheese and red wine.

Sheepherders work hard, and eat accordingly. At left is a special lunch—eggs and tomatoes *(foreground)* and braised lamb shoulder, enhanced with garlic, onions and pimiento. That evening, lunch having settled, the men disposed of a lamb stew *(below)*, including ham, tomatoes, pinto beans, onions and garlic, with macaroni or potatoes to be added.

Every summer the sheepherders come down from the
mountains to break the solitude and join their friends
at a Basque picnic. At this fete in Mountain Home,
Idaho, ex-sheepherder John Chacartegui fixed his
special combination of ham, sausage and *garbanzos*.

Most of the entertainment at the picnic consists of contests of strength—weight lifting, tugs-of-war and *(above)* wood chopping. Standing shoeless to improve his toehold, a young sheepherder blasts his way through a 10-inch-thick log in less than a minute.

Two brothers, John and Moises Oleaga, of Boise, Idaho, prepare to dispatch a bowl of a typical Spanish dessert, *flan,* a rich baked custard made of milk, eggs and sugar.

121

Tender morsels of ham and shrimp add their flavors to golden-brown chicken in *pollo vascongado,* a subtle Basque specialty.

Pollo Vascongado *(Basque)*
CHICKEN-AND-SHRIMP CASSEROLE IN WINE SAUCE

To serve 4

A 2½- to 3-pound chicken, cut
    into 8 pieces
½ teaspoon salt
¼ teaspoon freshly ground black
    pepper
½ cup olive oil
¾ cup finely chopped onions
1½ teaspoons finely chopped
    garlic
3 tablespoons all-purpose flour
½ pound boiled ham, cut into
    ¼-inch dice (1 cup)
¼ teaspoon sweet Hungarian
    paprika
1 cup dry white wine
½ pound medium-sized shrimp
2 tablespoons finely chopped parsley

Wash the pieces of chicken under cold running water and pat them thoroughly dry with paper towels. Sprinkle the pieces of chicken with the salt and pepper. In a heavy 10- to 12-inch stainless-steel or enameled skillet, heat the olive oil over moderate heat until a light haze forms above it. Add the pieces of chicken to the skillet and cook for 4 or 5 minutes on each side, or until the chicken is golden brown. Transfer the chicken to a 2½- to 3-quart casserole and set aside.

Drop the onions and garlic into the skillet and cook over moderate heat until the onions are golden brown. Mix in the flour and, stirring constantly, cook for another 1 or 2 minutes.

Stir in the ham and paprika, pour in the wine and bring to a boil over high heat. Pour the contents of the skillet over the chicken and set the casserole over high heat. Bring to a boil, then cover the casserole tightly, lower the heat and simmer for 30 minutes.

Shell the shrimp. Devein them by making a shallow incision down their backs with a small sharp knife and lifting out the black or white intestinal vein with the point of the knife. Wash the shrimp under cold running water and set them aside.

To test the chicken for doneness, pierce a thigh with the tip of a small sharp knife. The juice that spurts out should be clear yellow; if it is tinged with pink, cook the chicken for 5 minutes longer. Arrange the shrimp on top of the chicken, cover the casserole again and cook for 5 minutes longer, until the shrimp are pink.

Arrange the pieces of chicken and the shrimp attractively on a heated serving platter and ladle the sauce in the casserole over them. Sprinkle with parsley and serve at once.

Chilindrón *(Basque)*
LAMB STEW WITH HAM

Dust the pieces of lamb with the flour. In a heavy 10- to 12-inch skillet, heat the olive oil until a light haze forms above it. Add the pieces of lamb and, turning them frequently, cook over moderately high heat until they are golden brown.

Transfer the browned lamb to a 2- to 2½-quart casserole. Stir the onions, garlic, salt, pepper and ham dice into the fat in the skillet and cook over moderate heat, stirring constantly, until the onions and ham are golden brown. Watch carefully for any signs of burning, and regulate the heat accordingly.

Stir in the boiling beef stock or water, red wine and tomato paste, and bring to a boil over high heat, meanwhile scraping in any browned bits that may be clinging to the bottom or sides of the pan. Pour over the lamb, cover the casserole and simmer for 1 hour, or until the meat shows no resistance when pierced with the tip of a sharp knife. Taste the stew for seasoning, sprinkle with the chopped parsley and serve hot.

To serve 4 to 6

3 pounds boneless lamb, cut into 1½-inch pieces
½ cup all-purpose flour
2 tablespoons olive oil
1 cup finely chopped onions
1½ teaspoons finely chopped garlic
1½ teaspoons salt
½ teaspoon freshly ground black pepper
½ pound boiled ham, cut into ¼-inch dice (1 cup)
1½ cups boiling beef stock, fresh or canned, or substitute 1½ cups boiling water
1 cup dry red wine
2 tablespoons tomato paste
1 tablespoon finely chopped parsley

Tortilla de Patatas *(Basque)*
POTATO-AND-ONION OMELET

Heat 4 tablespoons of the olive oil in a heavy 10- to 12-inch skillet (preferably one with a nonstick surface) until a light haze forms above it. Stir in the sliced onions and potatoes and, tossing them about gently with a spatula, cook them over moderate heat until they have colored lightly. Cover the skillet tightly and cook over low heat for 12 to 15 minutes, or until the potatoes are tender and offer no resistance when pierced with the tip of a small sharp knife.

Sprinkle the potatoes with the salt and pepper. In a small bowl, beat the eggs vigorously with a table fork or whisk until they are frothy. Pour into the skillet and cook uncovered for 3 to 4 minutes, or until the eggs are set. Place an inverted plate over the pan and, grasping plate and skillet together firmly, turn them over. Add an additional tablespoon of oil to the pan if necessary, then slide the omelet back into the skillet, browned side up. Cook the omelet over moderate heat for another 3 or 4 minutes.

Traditionally, *tortilla de patatas* is served in wedges, directly from the skillet. It is also popular at room temperature, and is a favorite picnic staple served sandwich-style on French bread.

To serve 4

4 to 5 tablespoons olive oil
1 medium-sized onion, thinly sliced
3 medium-sized potatoes (1 pound), peeled and cut crosswise into ⅛-inch-thick slices
1 teaspoon salt
¼ teaspoon freshly ground black pepper
4 eggs

Armenians at Home in the Golden West

There is a musical ring and rhythm to Armenian family names: Gulbenkian and Khachaturian, Saroyan and Mardikian . . . and California's San Joaquin Valley, home of a big Armenian-American community, is as full of such names as it is full of grapes and raisins and figs. But—Normart? How did that blunt name get in there? Around Fresno there are, nevertheless, authentically Armenian Normarts. They evidently descend from a mystery man who in the late 1870s was one of the first Armenians ever to lay eyes on the valley. When he came to this country he was asked his name in the difficult language of the new land, and misunderstood the question. Thinking he was being asked how he felt to be on American soil, he joyfully replied, in Armenian, "Nor mart!"—"newborn" or, more literally, "like a new man."

Some who later followed him west actually carried on the name. And all the Armenians who later settled around Fresno were "newborn" to a better life. A resourceful people, they had learned to adapt and improvise through centuries of hardship in their oft-conquered homeland, once an empire that reached toward the Black, Caspian and Mediterranean Seas, and included the fertile Tigris and Euphrates Valleys in civilization's cradle. Certainly they adjusted quickly to the American environment. They soon came to love the San Joaquin flatlands, the hot dry climate and the fertile irrigated soil that made the big, low, sun-baked plain far better than Armenia's small high ones for raising figs, melons and grapes. And the newcomers made the most of what they found. As many had at home, they cultivated vineyards and orchards, and several families became powers in the fruit business, the Seropians as packers and shippers of figs, the Markarians as fig growers, the Arakelians as melon kings. Such success came naturally, since, in the words of Father Kourken Yaralian, pastor of the Holy Trinity Armenian Apostolic Church in Fresno, "The instinct to build and rebuild is very strong among Armenians. Wherever an Armenian hand touches the soil, a Garden of Eden flourishes."

Inevitably, the new life meant a rebuilding of cooking and eating habits. How extensive these changes have been, and whether they are good or bad, are subjects of much earnest discussion among the San Joaquin Valley's Armenian-Americans, now about 30,000 strong. All agree, however, that their robust ancient cuisine, whose heart and soul are *bulghur* (cracked wheat) and lamb, is changing in two ways. First, the Armenian-Americans are consuming fewer strictly Armenian meals and more strictly American ones, featuring beefsteak, chops and roasts. Second, Armenian dishes are being modified by American foodstuffs, condiments and cooking techniques. A few ardent traditionalists are pessimistic about

the future of Old Country cooking. But their fears may be exaggerated.

"I've seen plenty of changes since I was a little girl, but in some ways Armenian cooking has become more unified and stable," says Mrs. Mard Peloian of Dinuba, the American-born wife of a leading private packer of raisins. To begin with, she says, cookery in Armenia varied considerably from region to region, depending on local produce. Her husband, who came from a mountain village, was brought up on a far more restricted diet than the one her family enjoyed in the milder lowlands. Even in their home, dishes varied widely with the seasons. In summer, cooks had plenty of fresh vegetables. They made vegetable *dolma* of hollowed-out eggplant, squash, bell peppers or tomatoes, stuffed with *bulghur* or rice and chopped lamb *(Recipe Index)*. Wintertime *dolma* of dried tomatoes or small eggplants were similarly stuffed, but with preserved meat, and thus lacked the full, rich tastes of summer. But here in America, says Mrs. Peloian, the seasons have been abolished, for an unlimited selection of vegetables is always available.

Common-sense changes in old recipes are no bugaboo to George Mardikian, who left Armenia during the famine in 1920, and who worked his way up from journeyman chef to famous restaurateur (he once had an Omar Khayyam in Fresno, now owns the one in San Francisco). On the grounds that Armenian cookery is essentially international, he has no compunctions about modifying old dishes to suit American tastes. And to show that the culinary interchange is a two-way affair, he has also Ar-

Skewered separately, tomatoes, peppers, eggplant and marinated lamb chunks are roasted over glowing coals in a classic Armenian shish kabob. The scene is the patio of Mr. and Mrs. Edward Garry (the name was Americanized from Garabedian) of Del Rey, California, and the occasion is a birthday party for Mr. Garry, who is one of many Armenian-Americans prominent in California's vast fruit industry.

125

Armenian *bulghur* is processed from whole wheat in the Old Country way at the California Sun Dry Bulgur Company. The wheat is first boiled vigorously in 1,000-pound batches for a half hour *(top)* to puff the grains to three times their normal size. The cooked wheat is then spread on screens to cure in the sun. Then the dried grain *(above)*, crisp and brown, is hulled; the hulls are sifted out and the wheat is ground into four grades: coarse, medium, fine and extrafine.

menianized American dishes. He serves Thanksgiving turkey with a dressing of rice or *bulghur pilaf,* flavored with currants, cinnamon and allspice.

The pragmatic attitude of most home cooks around Fresno is typified by Mrs. Yaralian, the wife of the pastor. Mrs. Yaralian does not deny herself a big rare T-bone today merely because beef was traditionally scarce in the Old Country. She feels it is easier to serve the family a grilled steak than to make a time-consuming Armenian classic such as *hariseh,* for which *bulghur* is cooked in chicken broth, then combined with shredded chicken and beaten for hours to the consistency of oatmeal. But she is not without devotion to her culinary heritage, and for a company dinner she always cooks Armenian. When she makes shish kabob, the dish is a model of authenticity. She cuts generous chunks of lamb and marinates them overnight in a mixture of red wine, oil and tomato sauce, seasoned liberally with salt, black pepper, paprika, chopped onion, oregano or mint, and minced garlic. Skewered and grilled with onion and pepper slices speared on separate skewers, the meat is not only tender but tangy enough to surprise any guest who knows only the milder Americanized version.

Mrs. Yaralian and other church women cook shish kabob and other dishes for Fresno's grape-blessing festival, which her husband conducts at the local fairgrounds on the Sunday closest to August 15, the Feast of the Assumption of the Virgin Mary. For the ceremony, held to give thanks for the vineyards' prosperity, Father Yaralian begins by blessing the four corners of the earth in a prayer for universal peace. Then he

blesses the grapes, offered up by local growers in rotation. After the blessing comes a picnic. There is shish kabob cooked over open fires, rice *pilaf, bulghur pilaf,* loaves of *peda,* a bread *(Recipe Index),* and *choerek* (sweet buns), both sprinkled with sesame seeds, watermelon, grapes and cantaloupe. In a recent year, the festival drew some 4,000 guests, and each went home with a little bag of blessed grapes. Fresno has them to spare: Fresno County produces 80 per cent of the country's raisin crop.

The Armenians have always loved celebrations of every kind, and they outdo themselves at wedding feasts. The wedding guests may sit down at once to a bowl of *havabour,* a steaming chicken broth in which rice or vermicelli has been cooked, with beaten eggs and lemon juice added just before serving. Then comes a series of courses featuring lamb and—of course—*bulghur.* The beverages include wine and the wildly potent, mildly anise-flavored spirit, arak. It is not unusual to have many desserts on hand, including honey-filled *baklava.* The bride herself may not be ready to make a perfect *baklava,* which by one standard is supposed to have 56 layers, each one thin to the point of transparency; but according to an old Armenian saying, she is unprepared for marriage until she can make at least a 40-layer *baklava.* If the food at a wedding differs little from Old Country cooking, the celebration itself has changed a good deal. Back in Armenia, the partying might whirl along for three days and nights. But in and around Fresno the party never lasts beyond the small hours; and the newlyweds are rarely around when it ends.

Beneath appropriate paintings in his Valley Bakery in Fresno, Sam Saghatelian displays two kinds of Armenian breads, both baked in brick ovens from old family recipes. *Lavash (left)* is made from unleavened dough rolled out into thin sheets 14 to 16 inches in diameter. At right, *peda (Recipe Index),* made with vegetable shortening and yeast, appears in round and long shapes. Both *lavash* and *peda* are sprinkled with sesame seeds before they are baked.

127

Skilled cook though she is, Jessie Garry took on a formidable job when she decided to prepare—with no help whatever—an Armenian buffet feast of some two dozen major dishes for the 14 celebrants at her husband Ed's birthday party. Many of the dishes had to be made from scratch on the day of the party; an example is the platter Mrs. Garry displays at left—*keyma kufta,* a highly seasoned mixture of freshly ground raw sirloin and extrafine *bulghur,* garnished with chopped parsley and scallions. Other dishes, partially prepared in advance, required last-minute attention; for example, the pastry-wrapped cheese *boerek (overleaf),* made and frozen days before the party, had to be baked and served hot, and the *kadayif* pastry *(page 133)* got a dousing of sugar syrup late enough to make it moist but not soggy. To bring all the dishes to the table at their prime, Mrs. Garry's timing had to be—and was—faultless.

To make *dolma (Recipe Index),* Mrs. Garry stuffed a spiced mixture of rice and ground lamb into hollowed-out eggplants, tomatoes, green bell peppers, yellow Armenian peppers and zucchini *(right).* Then she baked the stuffed vegetables for about an hour. She served the *dolma* on a platter trimmed with grape leaves and tendrils from the Garrys' own vineyard.

Among the relishes were pickled cucumbers *(left)* and three types of peppers, shown with the raw vegetables on which they are based.

Twelve of the buffet dishes are shown overleaf. *Top row (from left): lavash* bread; cheese *boerek (Recipe Index),* triangles of pastry encasing soft white cheese; cold salad; *peda,* sliced *(Recipe Index). Middle row:* string-bean salad dressed with dill; *sarma,* grape leaves (from the Garrys' vines) wrapped around ground meat and spiced rice; a rice *pilaf* containing oven-browned vermicelli and almonds, and ringed with cooked dried apricots; shish kabob *(page 125). Bottom row:* Armenian *moussaka,* a baked casserole of braised ground lamb and broiled eggplant, topped with tomato and green pepper; *bulghur pilaf,* cracked wheat cooked with chopped onion and vermicelli; Armenian "string cheese" (a mixture of mozzarella and skim milk), and black olives; and *dolma (page 125).*

To make about 30 four-inch twists

2 to 2¼ cups all-purpose flour
¼ cup sugar
1 teaspoon salt
2 teaspoons double-acting baking
  powder
4 tablespoons unsalted butter,
  melted and cooled, plus
  1 tablespoon butter, softened
6 tablespoons milk
1 egg, plus 1 egg beaten with
  1 tablespoon milk
½ cup sesame seeds

To make about 3 dozen pastries

PASTRY
2 to 3 cups all-purpose flour
½ teaspoon cream of tartar
1 teaspoon salt
½ pound (2 quarter-pound sticks)
  unsalted butter, cut into ½-inch
  bits and thoroughly chilled
10 to 12 tablespoons ice water

FILLING
½ pound Cheddar cheese, grated
  (3½ cups)
1 egg
6 tablespoons finely chopped parsley

1 egg, lightly beaten

Simit (*Armenian*)
SWEET SESAME-SEED BREAD TWISTS

Combine 2 cups of flour, the sugar, salt and baking powder in a large mixing bowl and make a well in the center. Drop in the 4 tablespoons of cooled melted butter, the milk and 1 egg and, with a large wooden spoon, gradually stir the dry ingredients into the liquid. Continue to stir until the dough can be gathered into a ball. If the dough sticks, add up to ¼ cup additional flour by the tablespoon. Cut the dough into five parts.

Preheat the oven to 400°. With a pastry brush, lightly coat a large cookie sheet with the tablespoon of softened butter. Roll each section of dough into a long round rope about ½ inch thick and 2 feet long. Cut each rope into 4-inch lengths and twist each length slightly. Brush the twists lightly with the egg-and-milk mixture. Spread the sesame seeds on a sheet of wax paper and gently roll the twists in the seeds. Set the twists about 1 inch apart on the cookie sheet and bake in the center of the oven for about 20 minutes, until they are golden brown. Transfer the twists to wire racks to cool to room temperature.

Boerek (*Armenian*)
CHEESE-FILLED FLAKY PASTRIES

PASTRY: Sift 2 cups of flour, the cream of tartar and salt together into a large chilled mixing bowl. Drop in the butter bits and, working quickly, use your fingertips to rub the flour and butter together until the mixture looks like flakes of coarse meal. Pour 10 tablespoons of ice water over the mixture all at once, and working from the outer edges of the bowl toward the center, mix the ingredients together with a fork or rubber spatula. If the dough crumbles, add up to 2 tablespoons more ice water, 1 teaspoon at a time, until the particles adhere. Refrigerate the dough, wrapped in wax paper, for 30 minutes.

Sprinkle a board or table lightly with flour and roll the dough into a rectangular shape about ⅛ inch thick. With a pastry brush, brush off any excess flour. Starting with one of the narrow ends of the dough, fold it into thirds to form a three-layered rectangular packet. Brush each fold to remove excess flour. Again starting from a narrow end, fold the dough into thirds to form a square, brushing each fold. Cut the dough in half. Wrap the halves separately in wax paper; refrigerate for 1 hour.

FILLING: Meanwhile, prepare the filling. Place the grated cheese in a large mixing bowl and, with a wooden spoon, beat in the egg and parsley. Continue to beat until the mixture is smooth, and set it aside.

Preheat the oven to 425°. Place one half of the pastry at a time on a lightly floured surface and roll it out to an approximately 8-by-15-inch rectangle about ⅛ inch thick. With a pastry wheel or sharp knife, cut the dough into 2-by-3-inch rectangles.

Place 1½ teaspoons of the filling on the bottom half of each rectangle and fold over the top. Seal the edges of the pastry with the back of a fork and set the pastries side by side on an ungreased cookie sheet. Similarly roll out, cut, fill and shape the other half of the dough.

Brush the pastries with the beaten egg and bake in the center of the oven for 12 to 15 minutes, until golden brown. Serve at once.

The desserts shown here brought the Garrys' birthday party to a festive close. At top is a plate of locally grown fruit: purple Ribier grapes, lighter Red Malaga grapes, yellow Calimyrna figs, brown Turkish figs and greengage plums. Below the fruit are a round bowl of dried pears and dried apricots, and a plate of *kadayif*, a nut-filled, syrupy pastry that was served as the birthday cake (with a single candle). In the next row, an oval dish of *simit (Recipe Index)*, its twists of sweet dough sprinkled with white sesame seeds, stands beside a plate of *choerek*, small seeded rolls of various shapes. At bottom are a dish of shelled walnuts and a plate of crisp multilayered *baklava* pastry.

133

A refreshing Armenian salad combines chilled cooked *bulghur* (cracked wheat) with colorful bits of garden-fresh vegetables.

To serve 6 to 8

2 cups water
1 cup *bulghur* (cracked wheat)
1 small cucumber
1 medium-sized firm ripe tomato
1 small green bell pepper
1 bunch large scallions
¼ cup finely chopped parsley
2 teaspoons salt
½ teaspoon freshly ground black
    pepper
3 tablespoons strained fresh lemon
    juice
¼ cup olive oil

Bulghur Salad (Armenian)

Bring the water to a boil in a 1½- to 2-quart saucepan and drop in the *bulghur* in a slow, thin stream so that the water continues to boil. Cover the pan, lower the heat and simmer the *bulghur* for 10 minutes, or until all of the water has been absorbed. Uncover the pan and, stirring frequently, cook over low heat for another 1 or 2 minutes to dry the grains.

Transfer the *bulghur* to a large mixing bowl and cool to room temperature. Then cover with plastic wrap and refrigerate for at least 30 minutes, or until it is thoroughly chilled.

With a small sharp knife or rotary peeler, peel the cucumber. Cut it crosswise into ½-inch slices, then cut each slice into ½-inch cubes. Cut the stem out of the tomato, then cut the tomato into ½-inch pieces. Halve the green pepper, cut out and discard the ribs and scoop out the seeds. Cut the pepper into ½-inch pieces. Trim the root ends from the scallions and wash them under cold running water. Cut them, including 2 inches of the green stems, crosswise into ⅛-inch-wide slices.

Add the cucumber, tomato, green pepper, scallions and parsley to the *bulghur,* and season with the salt and pepper. Just before serving, sprinkle the salad with the lemon juice and pour in the olive oil. With a rubber spatula or wooden spoon, toss the salad together lightly but thoroughly. Taste for seasoning, and transfer the salad to a serving bowl or platter.

134

Combination Dolma *(Armenian)*
STUFFED GREEN PEPPERS, TOMATOES AND ZUCCHINI

"Dolma" means "stuffed" in Armenian—and the Armenians, as well as most Mediterranean peoples, are fond of using some foods as edible containers for other foods. In addition to the green peppers, tomatoes and zucchini specified in the recipe below, Armenians also stuff grape leaves, cabbage leaves and eggplant.

STUFFING: In a small saucepan, bring 1 cup of water to a boil over high heat. Pour in the rice in a slow, thin stream, stir it once or twice and cook briskly, uncovered, for 8 minutes, or until the rice is softened but still somewhat resistant to the bite. Drain the rice in a sieve and set it aside to cool to room temperature.

In a large mixing bowl, combine the ¾ pound of ground chuck, ¾ pound of lamb, 3 tablespoons of parsley, ¾ cup of tomato purée, 2 teaspoons of salt, ½ teaspoon of paprika, 2 tablespoons of lemon juice and several grindings of black pepper. Stir in the cooled cooked rice and knead the ingredients together with your hands, then beat vigorously with a wooden spoon until the mixture is smooth and thoroughly combined. Taste the stuffing for seasoning.

VEGETABLES AND SAUCE: With a small sharp knife, cut out the stem and the ribs of the green peppers; be careful not to cut through the walls of the peppers. Scrape out the seeds, wash the peppers in cold water and invert them on a double thickness of paper towels to drain.

Cut a ¼-inch slice off the stem ends of the tomatoes and set the slices aside. With a spoon, hollow out the tomatoes and discard the inner pulp and the seeds. Sprinkle the tomato cavities with ½ teaspoon of the salt and invert them on a double thickness of paper towels to drain. Pat the sliced tomato caps dry with additional towels.

Scrub the zucchini under cold running water and pat them thoroughly dry with paper towels. With a small sharp knife, cut about ½ inch off both ends of each zucchini. Cut each in half lengthwise, and scoop out and discard the inside, leaving a boatlike shell.

Stuff the hollowed-out green peppers, tomatoes and zucchini with the ground meat-and-rice mixture, dividing it evenly among them, packing it down firmly and smoothing the open ends with a spatula. Cover each tomato with its reserved slice.

Arrange the green peppers and zucchini, stuffed side up, side by side in a baking dish large enough to hold them in one layer. Set the tomatoes on top of the peppers and zucchini.

Place the tomato purée in a mixing bowl and beat in 1 cup of cold water. Stir in the 4 tablespoons of lemon juice, the chopped green pepper, the onions and the remaining ½ teaspoon of salt. Pour into the baking dish; if the sauce does not reach ½ inch up the sides of the dish, stir in additional water. Bring to a boil over high heat, then partially cover the baking dish and reduce the heat to low. Simmer for 45 minutes, basting the vegetables once or twice with the cooking liquid, until the vegetables are tender enough to be easily pierced with a fork.

To serve, arrange the stuffed peppers, zucchini and tomatoes attractively on a heated platter and pour the tomato sauce over them.

To serve 8 to 10

STUFFING
1 cup water
3 tablespoons long-grain unconverted rice
¾ pound ground chuck
¾ pound ground lamb
3 tablespoons finely chopped parsley
¾ cup tomato purée
1 to 3 cups cold water
2 teaspoons salt
½ teaspoon paprika
2 tablespoons strained fresh lemon juice
Freshly ground black pepper

VEGETABLES AND SAUCE
3 medium-sized green bell peppers
3 large firm tomatoes
1 teaspoon salt
3 large zucchini
¾ cup tomato purée
4 tablespoons strained fresh lemon juice
¼ cup finely chopped green pepper
¼ cup finely chopped onions

German Feasts in Tex-Mex Style

Since the whole Melting Pot is such an unlikely combination, the presence of German food deep in the heart of Tex-Mex country is not so incredible. It does exist there, and in the little town of Fredericksburg, Texas, it takes some fascinating forms.

Consider sauerkraut, that pillar of German cooking. In Fredericksburg, it is sometimes mixed with pimiento, chopped bell peppers and hot chilies to make a startlingly spicy salad.

Many German towns produce variations of the fruited bread called *Stollen,* especially popular at Christmastime; the best known, perhaps, is Dresden *Stollen.* Less well known is Texas *Stollen (Recipe Index),* a wonderfully light coffee ring, decorated with white icing and raisins; it was developed in the Fredericksburg area and appears on ranchers' breakfast tables along with their venison steaks and scrapple.

A favorite party snack in Fredericksburg is *Kochkäse,* a homemade cheese cooked with butter, milk and caraway seeds. The women of the town age and prepare it with painstaking care (the job can take weeks) in memory of their immigrant forebears, who brought the recipe from Germany. Sharp in taste, deliciously soft and clinging in texture, hot *Kochkäse* goes perfectly with jerky, the dried venison or beef originally developed by the Indians.

How did these "Hans-across-the-sea" culinary alliances come about? The story is a romantic one.

In the 1840s a wave of enthusiasm for emigration to the Republic of Texas swept across what is now Germany. It was stimulated in part by an emigrant society popularly called the Adelsverein, the Association of Nobles, because its founders were rich noblemen. Few of these founders intended to settle in Texas or even to visit there. Some had the somewhat absurd dream of turning a part of the Texas republic into a Germanic dependency; some may have hoped to profit from land speculation.

Whatever the original motives, in practice the Adelsverein showed little more than recklessness and ineptitude. To accommodate its emigrants it obtained a grant of nearly four million acres of land, but the title to the land was uncertain. What was worse, the region was the stronghold of the fearsome Comanche Indians, who for more than a century had fought Spaniards, Mexicans and Americans in turn to a standstill.

The first emigrants sailed from Germany in 1844 and landed at a swampy spot on the south Texas coast, where they milled about in total confusion. Everything they needed was lacking, especially organization. The venture would probably have failed miserably except for Ottfried Hans Freiherr von Meusebach, a tall, imposing man with bright red hair

and beard. Although he himself was a nobleman of ancient lineage, Von Meusebach sympathized more with the emigrants than with the Adelsverein. At sea he changed his name to plain John O. Meusebach and resolved to become a Texas citizen. Once in the New World he brought order out of chaos and began to organize the settlers at New Braunfels, a newly founded inland colony near San Antonio. This first (and still flourishing) settlement was outside of the Association's land grant, for by this time the settlers knew all about the ferocious Comanche.

Cautiously Meusebach explored the wild country beyond New Braunfels and picked a pleasant site near the Pedernales River for the town of Fredericksburg. Early in 1847 he asked the Comanche chiefs for a formal meeting on the day of the next full moon. When that day came, Meusebach and a small party rode to the Indian camp where the chiefs sat, surrounded by hundreds of armed warriors. As Meusebach and his companions entered the camp, they emptied their rifles in the air. The gesture of confidence (and, it is said, Meusebach's bright red hair) impressed the chiefs. After a long parley, the Germans promised the Comanche presents worth $3,000, and each side promised not to molest the other. Except for a little horse stealing, the treaty was never broken.

Since that time, descendants of the German pioneers have spread all over Texas, but New Braunfels and Fredericksburg remain largely German towns, where German lettering appears on signs and the German lan-

Wherever Germans have settled in numbers you may find a town called Fredericksburg, named after such Old Country rulers as Frederick the Great of Prussia. This town, as the Stetson hat and string tie on the man at the left suggest, happens to be Fredericksburg, Texas, where members of the local historical society have gathered for a Christmas *Fest* in the kitchen of the Pioneer Museum. Along with cookies baked from recipes handed down by pioneer grandmothers, the party fare includes jerky, dried sausages and bowls of homemade cooked cheese called *Kochkäse*.

137

A German Christmas dinner, Texas style, includes an American bird, roast wild turkey, stuffed with apples and raisins, and surrounded by peaches and prunes; spinach topped with egg slices and a stuffed-cabbage loaf called *Kohl-im-Sack* (literally, cabbage-in-the-sack). The Christmas tree in the background is decorated in the thrifty German tradition with strings of popcorn and cranberries, cookies, candy canes and candles—all things that can be eaten or used afterward.

guage is often heard. Fredericksburg in particular boasts a cuisine that blends German and Texan, itself a mixture of American and Mexican.

American and Mexican influences were there from the start. The inevitable German sausages are likely to be made with Texas venison and to be hot with chili peppers, a Tex-Mex touch. Dishes made with cornmeal, almost unknown in Germany, include cornbread in the Texas fashion, with chopped chilies in it. Many German-speaking housewives make Mexican tamales and Tex-Mex chili con carne. "Don't forget," says Mrs. Rodolph Smith (née Stieler), who lives on a ranch near Fredericksburg, "we are now Texans first, Americans second, Germans third."

On festive occasions German cooking takes over—in forms considerably different from those of Germany itself. A Christmas dinner in the house of Mr. and Mrs. Fritz Stieler began with a delectable hybrid—an *Eierstich* ("egg drop") soup based on venison rather than beef broth. The dinner featured a roast of venison. The second featured dish, wild turkey *(Recipe Index),* is never eaten in Germany. But both venison and turkey were cooked in the German way, the venison spread with sour cream and the turkey stuffed with apples, raisins and dark German bread. And to go with the meats there was that sauerkraut salad with pimiento, which shows the Mexican influence.

Some of the pleasantest meals in Fredericksburg are served in cottages called "Sunday houses." In the late 1800s many German families went

138

With two of her grandchildren looking on, Mrs. Rodolph Smith brings the carved Christmas turkey to the table. It will be served by her rancher husband, who bagged it two weeks earlier. Most of the recipes that Mrs. Smith uses have come down to her through three generations of Fredericksburg cooks, and in the process they have taken on an unmistakable Tex-Mex flavor. As Mrs. Smith puts it, "We are now Texans first, Americans second, Germans third."

into cattle breeding and moved to ranches many miles away, but they retained their Fredericksburg houses or built small wooden ones for marketing and weekend visits. A recent breakfast in Mrs. Smith's Sunday house offered such German dishes as apple strudel and cottage cheese with sour cream. Also served were American-style pan-fried venison steaks. sausages and scrapple. Finally, there were purely Texan contributions: jams of wild grapes, wild plums and agarita, a flavorsome Texas berry.

One of the most festive occasions of the Fredericksburg year is a Christmas party held in the Pioneer Museum, a quaint old general store and residence crammed with relics of the frontier past, from faded flour sacks to cooking utensils big enough to feed a wagon train of pioneers. Many guests come in costumes lovingly preserved or faithfully copied from those of the early days. German songs are sung and German dances danced. The food includes an array of German-style cakes and cookies baked from recipes that came over the ocean with the pioneer women. But also served at a recent celebration, perhaps to remind the guests that they were "Texans first," was the jerky that the local people love to have with their *Kochkäse*. The history of this thin-sliced dried beef goes back before the first Texans or the first Spaniards came to the region. Jerky was made of buffalo and other game by the Indians, who hung the meat on trees to cure in the sun. It is perhaps the oldest food in Texas—and in Fredericksburg it comes as naturally as sauerkraut or *Stollen*.

—Jonathan Norton Leonard

Sunday Breakfast in a Fairy-Tale Cottage

"Sunday houses" are among Fredericksburg's most charming features. In the 1880s many German-Americans who had settled in the town became ranchers and farmers, and moved out to the surrounding countryside. They would return once a week for the Saturday market. So that they could stay the night and attend church on Sunday, some families held on to old town homes like the one shown at right and below, built in 1847. On Sunday mornings, before the tiring ride back to the farm or the ranch, the family would partake of a big, filling breakfast.

In a Sunday house *(left)* Robert and Barbara Heinem and their three daughters sit down to the sort of breakfast their forebears might have eaten generations ago. Counterclockwise from bottom left, the meal *(right)* includes a bowl of cottage cheese and sour cream; poached eggs; apples; a plate of sausages, scrapple and venison steaks; an apple strudel; sweet butter; homemade bread and a Texas *Stollen* surrounded by wild plum, wild grape and agarita jams, peach preserves, honey and a bowl of molasses. Hanging on the wall is a Christmas wreath that combines a traditional German ring of bread with an equally traditional Mexican sunburst design also made of baked dough.

To serve 8 to 10

STUFFING

12 tablespoons butter

2 cups coarsely chopped onions

6 to 8 slices white bread, trimmed and cut into ¼-inch dice (3 cups)

8 to 10 slices black or pumpernickel bread, trimmed and cut into ¼-inch dice (3 cups)

3 medium-sized apples, peeled and cut into ¼-inch dice

½ cup seedless raisins

1 teaspoon salt

¼ teaspoon freshly ground black pepper

TURKEY

A 10- to 12-pound wild turkey, or substitute a 10- to 12-pound oven-ready domestic turkey, thoroughly defrosted if frozen

1 teaspoon salt

Freshly ground black pepper

12 tablespoons butter, melted

½ cup coarsely chopped onions

To serve 6 to 8

1 pound fresh sauerkraut

1½ cups sugar

½ cup distilled white vinegar

½ cup finely chopped celery

½ cup finely chopped bell pepper

½ cup finely chopped onions

A 7-ounce can pimientos, finely chopped

Roast Wild Turkey with Raisin-and-Apple Stuffing (German)

STUFFING: Melt 4 tablespoons of the butter in a heavy 10- to 12-inch skillet, add 2 cups of chopped onions, and cook over moderate heat for 6 to 8 minutes, or until the onions are soft and have colored lightly. Scrape them into a large mixing bowl. Melt 8 tablespoons of butter in the skillet and drop in both the white and black bread cubes. Cook the bread cubes over moderate heat, turning frequently, until they are lightly golden, then transfer to the bowl of onions. Add the apples, raisins, 1 teaspoon of salt and ¼ teaspoon of pepper to the onions and bread cubes, and toss together lightly but thoroughly. Taste the stuffing for seasoning.

TURKEY: Preheat the oven to 400°. Wash the turkey under cold running water and dry it thoroughly inside and out with paper towels. Rub the inside of the turkey with 1 teaspoon of salt and a few grindings of pepper, and fill the body and breast cavities with the stuffing. Close the openings with skewers or sew them with thread, and truss the bird securely.

With a pastry brush, brush the outside of the turkey with 2 or 3 tablespoons of the melted butter. Place the bird on its side on a rack in a shallow roasting pan and roast uncovered in the middle of the oven for 15 minutes. Then turn it on its other side and roast for 15 minutes more.

Reduce the oven temperature to 325°, turn the turkey breast side down, and roast for 30 minutes, basting it every 10 minutes or so with the rest of the melted butter and the drippings that accumulate in the pan. Now turn the bird breast side up and scatter ½ cup of chopped onions around it. Roast a wild turkey for about 1 hour longer, a domestic bird about 1¼ hours longer, basting every 15 minutes with the pan juices.

To test for doneness, pierce the thigh of the bird with the tip of a small sharp knife. The juice should spurt out a clear yellow; if it is slightly pink, roast the turkey for another 5 to 10 minutes. Transfer the turkey to a heated platter and let it rest for 10 minutes before carving.

Sauerkraut Salad with Pimientos (German)

Sauerkraut salad is an example of an "evolved" ethnic recipe: the sweet-and-sour dressing for the sauerkraut is classic Eastern European, while the pimientos are a Mexican influence.

Drain the sauerkraut through a large sieve set over a mixing bowl, and set the juice aside. Wash the sauerkraut thoroughly under cold running water, and let it soak in a bowl of cold water for 15 to 20 minutes, depending upon its acidity. A handful at a time, squeeze the sauerkraut until it is dry. Place it in a large mixing bowl and set it aside.

In a 1- to 1½-quart enameled or stainless-steel saucepan, combine the sauerkraut juice, sugar and vinegar and, stirring constantly, bring to a boil over high heat. When the sugar is thoroughly dissolved, remove the pan from the heat and cool to room temperature.

Add the celery, bell pepper, onions and pimiento to the sauerkraut in the bowl, then pour in the cooled dressing. Toss the salad to distribute the dressing evenly, cover it tightly with plastic wrap and refrigerate until ready to serve. Sauerkraut salad can be kept in the refrigerator for as long as 2 weeks.

Texas Stollen (German)
CINNAMON-AND-RAISIN COFFEE RING

Pour the lukewarm water into a small shallow bowl and sprinkle with the yeast and ½ teaspoon of the sugar. Let the mixture stand for 2 or 3 minutes, then stir to dissolve the yeast. Set the bowl in a warm, draft-free place (such as an unlighted oven) for 5 to 8 minutes, or until the mixture almost doubles in volume.

Combine 4 cups of the flour, ½ cup of the remaining sugar and the salt in a deep bowl, and make a well in the center. Pour in the yeast mixture, the 2 eggs, ¾ cup of lukewarm milk and the 8 tablespoons of softened butter bits and, with a large spoon, gradually incorporate the dry ingredients into the liquid.

Gather the dough into a ball and place it on a lightly floured surface. Knead the dough, pushing it down with the heels of your hands, pressing it forward, and folding it back on itself. Meanwhile, sprinkle in up to ½ cup more flour, adding it by the tablespoon until the dough no longer sticks to your hands. Continue to knead for 10 minutes, or until the dough is smooth and elastic.

With a pastry brush, spread 1 tablespoon of the softened butter inside a deep bowl. Place the dough in the bowl and turn it about to grease all sides evenly. Drape the bowl loosely with a kitchen towel and set it aside in the warm, draft-free place for about 45 minutes to 1 hour, or until the dough has doubled in volume. Punch it down with a single blow of your fist, and set it to rise again in the warm, draft-free place for another 30 to 45 minutes.

With a pastry brush, lightly coat a large baking sheet with 1 tablespoon of the softened butter and set it aside.

On a lightly floured surface, roll out the dough to a rectangle measuring 20 inches long and 15 inches wide. Spread the surface of the dough with the remaining 6 tablespoons of softened butter, then sprinkle it evenly with the remaining cup of sugar and the cinnamon. Scatter the raisins evenly over the top.

Starting at one of the 20-inch sides, roll up the dough, jelly-roll fashion, into a cylinder. Transfer the cylinder to the buttered baking sheet and bring together the ends of the dough to make a ring. With a sharp knife, cut two thirds of the way through the ring, from its outer edge inward, at 1-inch intervals, gently turning each cut pastry "leaf" to its right to reveal the filling. Drape the ring with a kitchen towel and set it aside in the warm, draft-free place for about 45 minutes to 1 hour, or until it doubles in volume.

Preheat the oven to 375°. With a pastry brush, coat the surface of the coffee ring with the egg-and-milk mixture and bake in the center of the oven for 25 to 30 minutes, or until it is golden brown.

While the coffee ring is baking, prepare the frosting. Place the confectioners' sugar in a large mixing bowl and, with a spoon, gradually beat in the water, a tablespoon at a time. Continue to beat until the frosting is smooth and has the consistency of heavy cream.

Transfer the coffee ring to a serving dish and, while it is still warm, spoon the frosting over the top, letting it run down the sides. Serve the *Stollen* at room temperature.

To make one 12-inch ring

¼ cup lukewarm water (110° to 115°)
1 package active dry yeast
½ teaspoon plus 1½ cups sugar
4 to 4½ cups all-purpose flour
1 tablespoon salt
2 eggs
¾ cup lukewarm milk (110° to 115°)
8 tablespoons butter, cut into bits and softened, plus 8 tablespoons butter, softened
4 teaspoons cinnamon
1 cup seedless raisins
1 egg, lightly beaten with 1 tablespoon milk

FROSTING
2 cups confectioners' sugar
5 to 6 tablespoons cold water

143

A Portuguese Family amidst California's Good Life

Portuguese cooking found a hospitable home in North America long before there was a United States of America. It was brought over as early as the colonial period by groups of intrepid whalers and fishermen, and the Atlantic ports where their ships put in—ports like Newport and New Bedford—in time became major Portuguese-American centers. In the 19th Century, numbers of Portuguese settled around San Francisco Bay and in California's fertile interior valleys, and many of them rose to prominence as farmers and dairymen. The cuisine these hard-working immigrants brought with them is comfortable and nourishing. It is based on olive oil rather than butter, it is rich in soups and stews, and it exploits such preserved foods as dried salt cod (*bacalhau*) and highly seasoned sausages. While the ingredients are common to other cuisines of the Iberian Peninsula, even Spanish guests at a Portuguese-American table are usually surprised, and pleasantly so, by the unusual tastes produced by unexpected additions to familiar foodstuffs.

Anyone lucky enough to be invited to dinner at the suburban home of Mr. and Mrs. Arthur Goncalves in Santa Clara, California, will taste this cuisine at its best. Good food is an old tradition on both sides of the family. Born in eastern Portugal, Mrs. Goncalves was an accomplished cook when she arrived in America in 1922. Arthur Goncalves, whom she met and married in 1927, had left his family's ancestral farm in northern Portugal to better himself; he had turned from growing food to producing Portuguese sausages in a one-room shop. Their family firm, incorporated as the Neto Sausage Company (Neto, Arthur's nickname, is actually the Portuguese word for grandson), has prospered over the years, and its annual gross business exceeds one million dollars. Attached to the plant is a retail store that smacks of old Portugal. The aromas of garlic and smokehouse wood fill the place, emanating from such Neto sausages as pork *lingüiça* and the spicier *chouriço picante*. There is a colorful and fragrant assortment of foods imported from Portugal: *queijo São Jorge,* a Cheddarlike cheese; and frozen sardines, octopus and *pescada* (hake). The Neto complex and seven households representing four generations of Goncalves relatives are all clustered within a mile or so of the campus of the University of Santa Clara.

When Mrs. Goncalves cooks for guests, she goes well beyond the simple meals that usually suffice for the family on workdays. The first course is likely to be the traditional *caldo verde,* a hearty green soup made with sausage, kale and potatoes. For the second and main course, Mrs. Goncalves may present an *arroz de galinha,* fricasseed chicken with rice. Like most of her favorite rice dishes, the dish begins with an *estrugido*—a

basic sauce of onion and garlic sautéed in olive oil, then simmered with chopped tomato. The chicken, cut into serving portions, is added to the *estrugido* along with a little water. When the mixture has simmered until the chicken is almost done, the rice and more water are added. Finally the pot is covered and left to simmer as the rice expands and softens, sopping up the rich flavors in the pot. Mrs. Goncalves often gives this dish a special touch, adding shrimp to the chicken-and-rice mixture, and topping the dish with hard-cooked eggs and black olives. Because her version is finished off in the oven (*forno*), she calls it *arroz no forno.*

The main course, consumed with a good Portuguese white wine, is usually followed by a crisp salad, perhaps with home-grown lettuce, tomato wedges, green-pepper rings and sliced onions, dressed with olive oil and wine vinegar. (Mrs. Goncalves says her fellow Portuguese-Americans eat many more salads in California than they did in the Old Country.) Then come dessert and strong black coffee. Mrs. Goncalves may offer a sweet rice pudding (*arroz doce*) cooked with cinnamon and egg yolks, or light meringue cookies that live up to their name, *suspiros (Recipe Index),* by melting away like "sighs." Or she may have a Portuguese sweet bread, made for the occasion by the mother of her son-in-law Manuel Costa. (Manuel and Beatrice Goncalves Costa are next-door neighbors, and the senior Mrs. Costa lives just across the street.) Among the 30-odd Portuguese families in the immediate neighborhood, Manuel's mother is as

Arthur and Maria Goncalves, prominent members of an enclave of Portuguese-American families in the San Francisco Bay Area of California, sit for a picture under their orange tree, surrounded by their family. In the front row are their daughter Beatrice Costa, 43, holding her two-week-old granddaughter, Janine Romano; Mr. and Mrs. Goncalves; their granddaughter Susan Costa Romano, 22, holding her daughter Nanette, 2; and the Costas' son Edward, 19. Behind them are Beatrice's husband, Manuel, 43; Susan's husband, Everist, 23; and the Costas' daughter Mary, 14.

The Five Wounds Catholic Church, built in 1919, serves as the religious and social center for some 750 Portuguese-American families in the San Jose-Santa Clara area.

Opposite: The Portuguese desserts that climaxed a Goncalves family barbecue included *(clockwise from top left)* egg-rich, sugar-coated *cavacas* (cookies), more lengthily called *cavacas das Caldas da Rainha* after a famous spa in Portugal; *pão de ló (Recipe Index),* a spongecake whose name may be translated as "bread of the sea"; meringue cookies so light the Portuguese call them *suspiros,* or "sighs" *(Recipe Index);* and *arroz doce,* a rice pudding sprinkled with cinnamon.

famous for her baked goods as Mrs. Goncalves is for *arroz de galinha* and for *cozido à portuguêsa*—a rich combination of pork cuts, *lingüiça* from the family store, several vegetables and sometimes a whole chicken, all boiled together in one pot.

All the Portuguese-American families in the community visit often and share freely, and they seldom drop in on each other empty-handed. One visitor may bring a head of home-grown red-leaf lettuce, another a jar of tomato preserves. Flourishing backyard gardens also provide indispensable cooking greens such as *coentro* (coriander) and kale. Mint, too, is grown in shareable quantity, and is an essential ingredient of the thick meat soup generally called *sopas e carne.* The meat, usually a chuck roast or brisket of beef, is braised in a little water with lots of onions, chopped mint, allspice and garlic; when the dish is ready, the meat is sliced and served with the thick, rich cooking liquid over fresh mint leaves and chunks of firm, crusty bread.

Sopas e carne is also known as *sopas de Espírito Santo,* because it is traditionally served at the Festa do Espírito Santo, or Festival of the Holy Ghost. This event is celebrated with great verve on the last Sunday in June, and all the clan—the Goncalveses, the Costas and a set of grandchildren, the Romanos—joins the proceedings at their church in nearby San Jose, the Church of the Five Wounds. (The name of the church is a devout reference to the wounds that were suffered by Christ on the Cross, but it is nonetheless startling to telephone the church and hear a cheery voice answer, "Five Wounds.")

The *festa* begins with a splendid procession around the elegant church. Presently the crowd, swollen by busloads of Portuguese from every part of the San Francisco Bay area, spills out into sunny East Santa Clara Street and marches for several blocks, past Portuguese-owned shops. Then, at one of the buildings in the church complex, the feasting begins. The celebrants are served with all they can eat, and they eat plenty. The number of cows slaughtered to make the *sopas de Espírito Santo* is a good index to the size and the success of the *festa,* and according to Father Charles Macedo, associate pastor of the Five Wounds Church, the 1970 festival was a record-breaking triumph. "We killed 14 cows," said the Azores-born priest with a rapturous smile, "and we put everything in the *sopas* but the hides and the heads."

Between the *festas* and the family's own business and personal affairs, the Goncalveses have no trouble keeping busy. They try to make an annual visit to Portugal, but though the trips to the Old Country are always happy adventures, the couple is happier still to return to Santa Clara. Mrs. Goncalves was once so moved to see her California home again that, she said, "I kneeled down and kissed my kitchen floor!" Near her kitchen, on a wall hung with brightly colored Portuguese ceramics, is one tile that sums up the Goncalveses' satisfying present and their tranquil outlook on the future. Inscribed on it in Portuguese is a simple verse:

> Our sons are our life,
> Our grandsons, new hope;
> With this beloved certainty
> Life never tires us.

146

For Gourmet Compadres, a Hearty Carne de Espêto

On an August day, patriarch Arthur Goncalves and his son-in-law Manuel Costa gave a buffet on their adjoining patios in Santa Clara for 30 relatives and friends. The main course was a *carne de espêto* ("Why don't you call it barbecue? It sounds better than the literal translation, 'meat on a spit,' " said Mrs. Goncalves). The *carne* was *carne de vinho e alhos,* or grilled pork with white wine and garlic *(Recipe Index),* made by Joaquin Sameiro, one of several guests who, in the informal Portuguese manner, contributed dishes for the feast. Joaquin prepared the pork in the Portuguese way, by marinating chunks of it in the wine, and slaved over the grill until everyone had eaten his fill. At the small tables where the *compadres* ate, lively discussions of Portuguese cooking produced a consensus of opinion summed up by Mrs. Rose Sameiro: "If you don't do the dishes the old way, they don't turn out right."

Joaquin Sameiro tests his pork for doneness as it sizzles beside garlicky *lingüiça* sausages. The sausages were grilled 20 minutes, as compared with an hour for the pork.

Portuguese nuns, teachers at the school attached to the Five Wounds Church, fill their plates across the buffet table from Manuel Costa *(left)*, Carlos Aguiar and Susan Costa Romano, whose daughter Nanette stands in the foreground. The buffet dishes shown at left include *(clockwise from far left)* Mrs. Goncalves' *salada à portuguêsa,* composed of lettuce, sliced onion and tomato wedges, and dressed with vinegar and Portuguese olive oil; Joaquin Sameiro's barbecued pork and sausage, placed next to a bottle of young white Portuguese wine; Beatrice Costa's Portuguese beans-and-sausage dish, *feijão com lingüiça (Recipe Index).* Finally, there are three more dishes by Mrs. Goncalves: her much-admired Portuguese rice, cooked with tomato and chopped onion, which had been sautéed in olive oil; her *morcela frita,* consisting of blood sausage (made by the Goncalves family company) fried slowly on both sides and served with pickled onions; and *bacalhau à Beira Alta (Recipe Index),* baked salt cod in tomato sauce with potatoes and hard-cooked eggs. The *bacalhau* is a classic dish made in the style of—and named after—the province in Portugal where Mrs. Goncalves was born.

149

To serve 4

1 pound salt cod
4 tablespoons olive oil
1½ cups coarsely chopped onions
1 cup tomato purée
1 cup chicken stock, fresh or canned
1¼ teaspoons salt
Freshly ground black pepper
¼ cup finely chopped parsley
1 pound potatoes, peeled and sliced
    crosswise into ⅛-inch-thick
    rounds
5 tablespoons butter, cut into bits
2 hard-cooked eggs, sliced into
    ¼-inch-thick rounds

Bacalhau à Beira Alta (*Portuguese*)
BAKED SALT COD AND POTATO CASSEROLE

Starting a day ahead, place the salt cod in an enameled, glass or stainless-steel pan or bowl. Pour in enough cold water to cover the salt cod by at least 2 inches, and soak the fish for at least 12 hours, pouring off the water and replacing it with fresh water three or four times.

Drain the cod, rinse under cold running water, place it in a saucepan and add enough cold fresh water to cover the fish by 1 inch. Bring to a boil over high heat, then taste the water. If it seems excessively salty, drain it off, cover the cod with fresh cold water and bring to a boil again. Repeat if necessary.

Lower the heat and simmer the cod, partially covered, for 20 minutes, or until the fish flakes easily when prodded gently with a fork. Drain the cod thoroughly. Remove and discard any skin and bones, and flake the fish into 1-inch pieces with a fork.

Heat the 4 tablespoons of olive oil in a heavy 10- to 12-inch skillet until a light haze forms above it. Add the chopped onions and cook over moderate heat for 5 to 8 minutes, until they are soft and lightly colored. Stir in the cup of tomato purée, the cup of chicken stock, ¾ teaspoon of the salt, ⅛ teaspoon of the black pepper and the chopped parsley. Bring to a boil over high heat, then reduce the heat to low and simmer uncovered for 5 minutes, stirring occasionally. Remove the tomato sauce from the heat and set it aside to cool to room temperature.

Preheat the oven to 350°. Spread one third of the tomato sauce on the bottom of a 2½- to 3-quart casserole. Arrange half of the potatoes on top of the sauce and sprinkle with ¼ teaspoon of the salt and several grindings of black pepper. Top the potatoes with half of the flaked cod, then repeat the layers, sprinkling the remaining ¼ teaspoon of salt and a few grindings of pepper on the potatoes, and ending with a layer of tomato sauce. Scatter the butter bits over the top of the sauce and bake in the center of the oven for 1 hour. Garnish the casserole with the slices of hard-cooked eggs and serve at once.

To make about 4 dozen cookies

1 tablespoon butter, softened
3 egg whites
¾ cup sugar
⅛ teaspoon vanilla extract
½ teaspoon strained fresh lemon
    juice
1 teaspoon grated lemon rind
1 cup slivered blanched almonds

Suspiros (*Portuguese*)
SIGHS

Preheat the oven to 250°. With a pastry brush or paper towel, lightly coat two cookie sheets with the tablespoon of softened butter. Set the cookie sheets aside.

In a large mixing bowl (preferably one of unlined copper), beat the egg whites with a whisk or a rotary or electric beater until they froth. Gradually beat in the sugar and vanilla extract, and continue to beat until the whites are stiff enough to form firm unwavering peaks on the beater when it is lifted out of the bowl. With a rubber spatula, using an over-and-under rather than a stirring motion, gently but thoroughly fold in the lemon juice, lemon rind and almonds.

Drop the meringue by the teaspoon onto the buttered cookie sheets, letting it mound naturally and leaving at least 1 inch between each mound. Bake in the center of the oven for 40 minutes, then transfer the cookies to wire racks to cool to room temperature.

A Portuguese casserole containing layers of salt-cod flakes, potato rounds and tomato sauce is accented by slices of hard-cooked eggs.

Carne de Vinho e Alhos (Portuguese)
GRILLED PORK AND SAUSAGE

To serve 6 to 8

In a large mixing bowl, combine the garlic, paprika, cinnamon, salt, pepper, bay leaf, orange rind, orange slices, wine and water. Add the pieces of pork and toss them in the marinade to coat them thoroughly. Marinate the pork at room temperature for 8 hours or refrigerate it, tightly covered, for 24 hours. Toss the pieces about in the marinade every few hours to keep them well moistened.

Light a layer of coals in a charcoal broiler and burn until a white ash appears on the surface, or preheat your kitchen broiler to its highest point.

Remove the pieces of pork from the marinade and string them on long skewers, pressing them firmly together. Slice the *lingüiça* crosswise into ½-inch rounds and string them on two additional skewers. Set them aside. Broil the marinated pork 4 inches from the source of the heat for 10 minutes, turning the skewers occasionally, and brushing the pork frequently with the marinade. Now add the skewers of sausage, and broil the pork and sausage for 10 minutes. Slide the pork off the skewers onto individual heated plates, then divide the sliced sausages among the servings.

2 teaspoons finely chopped garlic
2 teaspoons sweet Hungarian paprika
1 teaspoon cinnamon
1½ teaspoons salt
½ teaspoon freshly ground black pepper
1 large bay leaf, crumbled
1 teaspoon grated orange rind
1 orange, thinly sliced
½ cup dry white wine
½ cup water
2 pounds boneless pork, cut into 1½-inch pieces
1½ pounds *lingüiça,* or substitute 1½ pounds of any other garlic-seasoned smoked pork sausage

151

From the Isles of Greece to the Shores of Florida

In 1906 the first Greek-American child was born in Tarpon Springs, Florida, northwest of Tampa on the Gulf of Mexico. A Greek Orthodox priest came down from Savannah to baptize the baby, and the Greek men invited all their old-stock American neighbors to the christening feast. Casks of *retsina* and *kokkinelli* (white and red resinated wines, respectively), jars of olives and pickles, and tubs of *feta* (a crumbly white goat cheese packed in brine) had arrived from Greece for the party. The colony roasted lambs, and everyone ate, sang and danced far into the night while the infant guest of honor slept through it all.

The same food and drink still appear at every Greek-American feast in Tarpon Springs—and on almost every other day, as well—but it is not the food alone that links the community to the Old Country. While Greek colonies are scattered throughout the United States, Tarpon is unique. The average Greek-American, like most immigrants, found himself a new trade and a new way of life in America, but the Greeks of Tarpon went on doing a job they had always done superbly—diving for sponges. And they have contrived to retain the calm neighborliness of life in an Aegean village while absorbing the good things of their new home.

Even before the first Greeks arrived in 1905, Americans from Key West had "hooked" sponges at Tarpon Springs by bringing them to the surface impaled on poles. But the Greeks dived right down to the sponge beds, cut the sponges loose and bagged them—a far more efficient method. Sponge diving was difficult and dangerous in the Gulf, as it had been in the Aegean, but in Florida sponge fishermen could earn sums undreamed of at home. By 1908 some 700 divers and boatmen had arrived, and other Greeks came from all over the United States to open shops and cafés and run the business end of sponging. St. Nicholas Greek Orthodox Church was built, and families began to settle down.

Today there are about 3,000 Greek-Americans in Tarpon Springs. The Sponge Exchange holds auctions twice a week, and 40-foot caïques with strings of drying sponges hanging from their masts glide into the Sponge Docks. Tarpon Springs is, in fact, the sponge-fishing center of the U.S., though it no longer depends solely on the trade—the young American-born men can find easier and safer ways to make a living. So new divers still come from Greece to keep the ancient craft alive.

While the Greek-Americans of Tarpon Springs still eat Greek food, they eat much better than their forebears. Almost all are *nisiotes*—"men from the islands." That is, they came from the islands of the Dodecanese, primarily from the one called Kalimnos. These spare, lovely islands produce little food. Until recently there were villages on them

where meat was eaten as seldom as twice a year: roast lamb at Easter, and another meat meal on the feast day of the village's patron saint. Even fish was relatively scarce, for much of the Aegean, after thousands of years of fishing, has been almost emptied of fish.

But Tarpon Springs has all the abundance of the Gulf of Mexico, as well as Florida's plentiful meat and fresh vegetables. The greens Americans think of as essentially Southern—collard, chard, turnip, mustard and beet greens—appeal to the Greek soul too. In Tarpon Springs they boil these greens, then dress them with oil and lemon, and serve them slightly above room temperature—a delicious dish, somewhere between a salad and a vegetable. Friday's fish can be mackerel, pompano, flounder, or black or yellow grouper. Whatever the fish, it is prepared in a Greek way, either broiled over charcoal with olive oil, lemon juice and oregano, or baked in a vegetable-and-tomato sauce *(Recipe Index)*.

Mrs. Catherine Kalariotes, wife of Father Elias, the pastor of St. Nicholas Church, often prepares fish in the latter fashion. She rubs it inside and out with the juice of a whole lemon. Then she sautés onion and garlic in olive oil, and adds parsley, dill, carrot and bell pepper. In a few minutes the onions are golden, and she adds tomato sauce and a little white wine. She pours the sauce over the fish and braises it slowly in the oven. The flavors blend and permeate the fish; drops of olive oil glisten and burst on the surface. This balance of oil and lemon, rich yet refreshingly tart, is the essence of Greek cooking. The lemon juice holds the oil in gen-

Bishop Amilianos of the Greek Orthodox Church blesses Nikitas Manias, 19, who retrieved the gold Epiphany cross flung into the harbor at Tarpon Springs in a yearly ritual. The honor is vigorously sought, and the cross is Nick's to keep.

153

tle check, never allowing it to dominate the dish. All that is needed to complete the meal is some good Greek bread to sop up the sauce.

And crusty, chewy Greek bread is easy to find in Tarpon. Several bakeries turn out oval, round or flat loaves. At Eastertime the National Bakery performs another service: it roasts 50 or more lambs for customers. You choose your lamb on the hoof at Angel's Market, adjoining the bakery. The men at the market slaughter it, and you take it home and stuff it with rice, mint and oregano. On Saturday you bring it back to the National, where it will slowly roast for five hours. On Easter Sunday the bakery warms it up, and you pick it up in the morning. The custom follows an Aegean tradition: because fuel is scarce and costly on the islands, all baking and roasting are done in the baker's oven.

Although Mrs. Kalariotes buys her bread, she does a great deal of baking on her own. When she makes her specialty, Athenian torte *(page 159 and Recipe Index)*, she needs her refrigerator as well. She slightly freezes a lemon-flavored spongecake to stiffen it, so that she can more easily cut it into layers with a thin serrated knife. Even the fanciest Athenian pastry shops rarely attempt more than four layers, but Mrs. Kalariotes once achieved 10. She ices the layers with alternate spreads of chocolate custard and almond custard, and sprinkles each layer with brandy or the anise-flavored Greek liqueur called *ouzo.* She covers the cake with frilled whipped cream and apricot halves. When the cake is about to be presented, sugar cubes dipped in brandy are placed on top and ignited, and the cake comes to the table in a blaze of glory. Not a dessert for every day, but marvelous for such occasions as Epiphany, or Twelfth Night.

The Feast of the Epiphany, which falls on January 6, is the major holiday of the year for Tarpon Springs. All year round the community's social life centers largely around the church: families and friends celebrate their saints' name days as well as birthdays, and weddings and christenings bring rounds of feasting. But on Epiphany, when the Greek Orthodox Church celebrates Christ's baptism, the people of Tarpon Springs regale not only themselves, but anyone else who wants to come.

Tourists come to Tarpon in droves at Epiphany to see the boys of the town dive for the cross. First there are ceremonies at St. Nicholas (the Greeks revere St. Nicholas as the patron of sailors and seafarers), usually led by the Archbishop of North and South America, because Tarpon Springs holds the official Epiphany ceremony for this entire Greek Orthodox archdiocese. Around noon the archbishop or the bishop of the local see leads the clergy and congregation into the churchyard for the "blessing of the waters." A cross is dipped into holy water, commemorating Christ's entry into the River Jordan. A procession winds through streets draped with Greek and American flags down to Spring Bayou, where a gaggle of lithe teen-age boys will vie for the honor of retrieving the cross from the water. No one really knows the origin of this custom, but it may be a Christian reenactment of pagan human sacrifices to appease the menacing sea. The archbishop holds the cross high, and a few overeager lads fall into the water. He casts it far out, symbolizing the Word of God cast into the world. The boys dive in an explosion of water, struggle mightily to find the cross (the Christian symbol here is that of mankind seeking the truth) and the winner surfaces, cross held triumphantly aloft. He kneels, dripping, before the archbishop, and receives a special blessing. The cross and a special gold trophy are his to keep.

With that the religious ceremonies are over, and the *glendi*—the celebration—begins. Many of the visitors are Greeks of Dodecanese descent, but everyone is welcome. In a recent year there were 30,000 visitors, and several thousand of them stayed to dinner. Long tables are set up in the tree-lined courtyard of the Sponge Exchange, and a hungry line snakes past all afternoon. Church members prepare the meal, and charge a small fee for it. The main dish is *kavourma,* the traditional ration of spongemen, developed in a land that had no scientific method of preserving meat. Beef fat and salted beef are cut into inch-and-a-half cubes; then the fat is melted, and the beef cubes braise in the fat for several hours.

For spongers, the meat is lifted out and put in five-gallon cans; the fat is poured over it and, as it cools, forms a seal that will preserve the meat for at least a month. For the *glendi,* 50 pounds of meat at a time are cooked in great iron pots over oak-wood fires. The mayor insists that real expertise is needed: the cubes of meat must not be too small or too large, the fat must not be too hot or too cool; but when a perfect *kavourma* is eaten warm, with a squeeze of lemon—ah! There is also Greek salad, and for anyone with a little room still left, there is pastry—*baklava,* flaky and sticky with honey; or *finikia (Recipe Index),* an equally sticky cookie, flavored with orange juice, cinnamon and walnuts. If you eat these two first, you can use your honey-smeared fingers to snare the crumbs that fall from the *karidopeta,* which are rich, cherry-topped cakes *(Recipe Index).*

The *glendi* comes but once a year, but a number of restaurants in Tarpon serve Greek food all year round. The largest of them is Louis Pappas' Riverside Café, right on the Sponge Docks. The late Louis Pappas emigrated from Sparta in 1904, served as a cook to General Pershing's Wildcat Division in France in World War I, and opened his restaurant in 1925. At the Riverside Café, he created what is called, in simple justice, "Louis Pappas' Famous Greek Salad" *(Recipe Index).*

The salad may be Greek in inspiration, but it is lavishly American in size, design and imagination. It is also peculiarly American in being put together on a kind of assembly line. One of three chefs lines a huge plate with lettuce and places a mound of oniony, oil-drenched potato salad in the center. He skids the plate along to the next man, who scatters the base with shredded lettuce and the dark-green sprigs of a plant called rocket. Known as *roka* in Greek, and *arugula* in Italian, rocket tastes rather like peppery raw spinach. (Ancient Greeks considered it an aphrodisiac, but if you mention this you may have a hard time getting your fair share.) The third and most dazzling member of the assembly team fits tomato, cucumber and avocado wedges around the plate. He places slices of *feta* cheese on top, and strips of green pepper over that. He deftly fits radishes, olives and small, vinegary, not-too-fiery peppers into any empty spaces. And there is more: for each diner, a slice of boiled beet, topped by a fat shrimp, topped by an anchovy at the pinnacle of the creation. Both residents and tourists agree that it is most fun to eat the salad in the friendly Greek way, with everyone digging into a communal platter and mopping up the dressing with garlic-toasted Greek bread. The only problem is that you are left with no incentive to leave Tarpon Springs.

—Lyn Stallworth

The children of Tarpon Springs join in the Epiphany parade with the boys dressed as the *evzones,* or Royal Guards, of Greece.

Festivity and Food in a Greek-American Town on the Gulf Coast

Epiphany, January 6, is the great festival day of Tarpon Springs. A procession marches at noon from the town's Greek Orthodox church to Spring Bayou to see young men dive for a ritual cross *(page 153).* By custom, relatives in the home island of the Old Country send costumes as presents to be worn for the occasion by children as young as the tiny *evzone* shown at left, who may be dreaming of the day he can join the big kids. Tourists come to watch the show—and, of course, to eat. To serve a few of them, waitress Joanna Papakaladoukas *(right),* a tower of strength at Louis Pappas' Riverside Café, proudly carries enough of Pappas' "famous Greek salad" *(Recipe Index)* to feed 17 people.

At an Epiphany dinner, Mrs. Catherine Kalariotes (*above*) serves a platter of stuffed baked shrimp to her husband, Father Elias, priest of St. Nicholas Greek Orthodox Church in Tarpon Springs. The family loves to eat seafood, and along with the shrimp the children will be served Mrs. Kalariotes' red snapper. The fish, shown on the table above and in close-up at right, is baked in a vegetable-based sauce with olive oil and lemon juice, and decorated with carrot rounds (*Recipe Index*). The children— Alexe, Lia and Cub Scout John—drink milk, but their parents have white wine with the meal. Father Elias says his wife is "the best cook I know."

Three-year-old Alexe *(left)* sneaks a wedge of *baklava* from a tray of seven holiday sweets, all baked by Mrs. Kalariotes. Besides the *baklava* (1) there are: (2) cherry-topped *ravani;* (3) *karidopeta (Recipe Index),* chocolate-walnut cakes with cherries and whipped cream; (4) *koulourakia,* twisted butter cookies sprinkled with sesame seeds; (5) *finikia (Recipe Index),* syrupy, nut-coated cookies, flavored with orange juice and cinnamon; (6) *kourabiedes,* sugar-dusted butterballs; and (7) *karidata,* jelly-filled nut cookies. Mrs. Kalariotes' eighth baking wonder, an Athenian torte *(Recipe Index),* is brought to the table by Alexe's big sister Lia *(above),* who has just put a match to the brandy-soaked sugar cubes atop the cake. To make this torte, six thin spongecake layers were alternated with separate fillings of almond and chocolate custard; apricot halves dot the frosting.

159

A handsome red snapper, fresh from the Gulf of Mexico, floats on a vivid sea of Greek vegetable sauce before being baked.

To serve 4 to 6

6 tablespoons vegetable oil
1 cup finely chopped onions
1 teaspoon finely chopped garlic
½ cup finely chopped celery
1 green pepper, halved, deribbed,
   seeded and finely chopped
   (½ cup)
½ cup thinly sliced carrots
2 tablespoons finely chopped dill
1 tablespoon finely chopped parsley
2 one-pound cans solid-pack
   tomatoes and 1 cup of their liquid
1 cup dry white wine
A 5½- to 6-pound red snapper,
   cleaned and scaled but with head
   and tail left on
1 teaspoon salt
¼ cup strained fresh lemon juice
Freshly ground black pepper
1 tablespoon butter, softened

Red Snapper with Vegetable Sauce (Greek)

Heat the oil in a heavy 10- to 12-inch enameled or stainless-steel skillet until a light haze forms above it. Drop in the onions and garlic and, stirring frequently, cook until the onions are soft and translucent. Stir in the celery, green pepper, carrots, dill and parsley, and cook for 3 to 5 minutes more, or until the vegetables are soft. Add the tomatoes, 1 cup of tomato liquid and the wine, and bring to a boil over high heat. Reduce the heat and simmer, partially covered, for 15 minutes. Pour the vegetable sauce into a flameproof baking dish just large enough to hold the fish comfortably, and set it aside.

Preheat the oven to 400°. Wash the fish under cold running water and pat it thoroughly dry with paper towels. Sprinkle the fish inside and out with the salt, lemon juice and several grindings of black pepper. Lay the fish on top of the vegetable sauce. Cut a piece of wax paper just large enough to fit the baking dish and coat it with the softened butter. Set it buttered side down on top of the fish.

Bake the snapper in the center of the oven for 35 to 40 minutes, or until it feels firm when prodded gently with a finger. Transfer the fish to a heated serving platter and place in the turned-off oven to keep warm while you complete the sauce.

Set the flameproof baking dish on top of the stove and bring the sauce to a boil over high heat. Boil briskly, uncovered, until the sauce has thickened to the consistency of heavy cream.

Spoon the sauce over the fish or, if you prefer, serve it separately in a heated bowl or sauceboat.

Louis Pappas' Greek Salad

Louis Pappas' Riverside Café in Tarpon Springs, Florida, is renowned for its colorful and substantial Greek salad. Pappas based his extravaganza on the simple, classic Greek salad of roka (arugula), feta cheese and black olives. Surrounded, however, by a wealth of fresh ingredients from the gardens of the American South, he constructed an elaborate and delicious montage of Greek and American foods. The recipe below follows Pappas' style in assembling the salad, but the manner in which the ingredients are assembled—and even the proportions of the ingredients themselves—may be varied to suit your own taste.

POTATO SALAD: Bring the water to a boil in a 3- to 4-quart saucepan and drop in the potatoes. Boil uncovered for 30 minutes, or until they offer no resistance when pierced with the tip of a sharp knife. Drain the potatoes and let them cool to room temperature, then peel and cut them crosswise into ¼-inch-thick rounds.

Place the rounds of potatoes in a large mixing bowl, drop in the chopped onions, sliced scallions and chopped parsley and, with a rubber spatula, toss together lightly but thoroughly.

Pour the red wine vinegar into a small mixing bowl and, a tablespoon at a time, beat in the cup of olive oil. When it is well incorporated, beat in the salt and freshly ground black pepper, and pour the dressing over the potatoes. With a rubber spatula, toss the salad lightly until the dressing is evenly distributed.

GREEK SALAD: Drop the shrimp into 1 quart of boiling water and let them boil briskly for 3 minutes. Drain and peel the shrimp, then devein them by making a shallow incision along their backs with a small sharp knife by lifting out the black or white intestinal vein with the tip of the knife. Set them aside.

Separate the head of romaine lettuce into individual leaves and wash the leaves thoroughly under cold running water. Spread the leaves out on paper towels, and pat them completely dry with additional towels. Line a large serving platter with the largest of the lettuce leaves, and mound the potato salad in the center. With a sharp heavy knife, cut the remaining lettuce leaves into shreds, and strew them and the sprigs of *roka* or watercress over and around the potato salad.

Surround the potato salad with alternating pieces of the tomatoes, cucumber, avocado, scallions and radishes. Lay the slices of *feta* cheese over the top of the potato salad and top them with the rings of green pepper. Set the beet slices on top of the green pepper rings and on each beet place a shrimp draped with an anchovy fillet. Scatter the olives over and around the salad, and sprinkle the whole with oregano. Chill the salad until ready to serve.

DRESSING: Just before serving, place the distilled white vinegar in a small bowl. Whisking constantly, pour in the olive-and-vegetable-oil mixture in a slow, thin stream. When it is well incorporated, pour the dressing over the salad and serve at once.

Greek salad may be served as a light luncheon or supper dish, accompanied by Greek bread or, if you like, by a loaf of Armenian *peda* (*Recipe Index*).

To serve 4 to 6

POTATO SALAD
2 quarts water
2 pounds boiling potatoes (6 to 8)
2 medium-sized onions, finely chopped (¾ cup)
½ cup thinly sliced scallions
⅓ cup finely chopped parsley
6 tablespoons red wine vinegar
1 cup olive oil
2 teaspoons salt
1½ teaspoons freshly ground black pepper

GREEK SALAD
1 quart boiling water
6 medium-sized shrimp
1 large head romaine lettuce
12 leaves *roka (arugula),* or substitute 12 sprigs watercress
2 firm ripe tomatoes, each cut into 6 wedges
1 medium-sized cucumber, peeled and cut lengthwise into 6 strips
1 avocado, peeled and cut into 6 wedges
6 scallions, washed and trimmed
6 radishes, washed and trimmed
6 ounces *feta* cheese, cut into 4-by-4-by-½-inch slices
1 green pepper, cored, seeded and cut crosswise into ¼-inch-thick rings
6 slices canned beets
6 flat anchovy fillets, washed
12 black olives, preferably the Mediterranean variety
1 teaspoon oregano, crumbled

DRESSING
½ cup distilled white vinegar
¼ cup olive oil combined with ¼ cup vegetable oil

The Exotic Becomes Familiar
in Oriental Restaurants

As a rule Americans have been readier to accept new immigrants personally and culturally than to eat their foods. A Polish-American steelworker in Gary drinks beer with Irish-Americans who would be baffled by *kiełbasa;* a Puerto Rican boy in New York plays stickball with blacks who would just as soon not go near a *cuchifrito.* The marked exception to this rule has been the national acceptance of the Chinese cuisine—an acceptance that is now being repeated to some extent with the Japanese. Personally and culturally, Oriental-Americans are still a bit of a mystery to most of their fellow Americans of other ancestry. But their food! In almost every city, Americans have eaten and enjoyed "Chinese" food, and an increasing number of them are coming to know Japanese cooking.

There are good historic reasons for this paradox. The first groups of Chinese arrived in California in the early 1850s on the heels of the forty-niners, right after the discovery of gold in Captain Sutter's millrace. Lured by dreams of wealth from their villages along the Pearl River estuary, which lies in southeastern China between the great ports of Canton and Hong Kong, they disembarked seeking gold like everyone else. But as the Chinese scattered through the mining camps, a pattern of discrimination emerged that would dog them for generations. The white men forcibly prevented the Chinese from working their own claims. They had to take work as laborers—and often as cooks.

During and after the Civil War, when the Central Pacific Railroad was being pushed eastward across the High Sierra, thousands of Chinese arrived as indentured laborers. They, too, came from that same small area on the China coast. Nearly all of them dreamed of earning a fortune with which they could return home in triumph. As it turned out, few realized the dream. When the railroad was finished the pigtailed coolies in their somber black pajama-suits dispersed to find jobs wherever they could. Many wound up back in San Francisco, where the nation's first Chinatown came into existence; others worked on farms and in vineyards, in lumber mills and factories up and down the Pacific Coast. Gradually, however, racial prejudice forced the Chinese to limit their modest ambitions yet again. By custom and by law, they were excluded from all but a few jobs. One of these was laundryman. Another was restaurant-keeper.

These people from South China were poor village folk; their cooking was utilitarian, designed to make the most of simple, cheap ingredients. Isolated by language and working conditions, they preserved their own ways of eating even on the railroad gangs. Most companies furnished food to the workmen as a part of their wages, and some companies that employed large numbers of Chinese even imported supplies of dried fish,

squid, oysters, bamboo shoots, mushrooms and other staples, with which the workmen prepared their own Oriental-style meals. Thus an ancient, thoroughly alien style of cooking was implanted in the United States. And by the time Chinese restaurants began cropping up in the 1880s and 1890s, a network of suppliers and middlemen had become available to make sure the bean paste never ran out.

At first most of the customers were other displaced Chinese, but once the word got around that one could eat substantially and well for very little money—and get a free pot of tea in the bargain—the rush was on. Titillated by stories of tong wars and opium dens, slummers ventured hesitantly into the lantern-hung twilight of Chinatowns in San Francisco and New York, in Seattle and Los Angeles. Home folks in small Midwestern towns tried out the local equivalent, usually unassuming and likely to include fried eggs on the menu along with the egg foo yung.

As Chinese food took hold, certain dishes became predictable standards. One was chop suey *(Recipe Index)*—a name that in Cantonese means "miscellaneous fragments." While it would not be recognized in China, chop suey is closely related to a number of commonplace Chinese dishes involving a little pork and a lot of vegetables, all sautéed together. At its best, with the crispness and stringiness of celery dispersed through a rich gravy and the whole ladled steaming over a bed of white rice, it can be a roundly satisfying one-course meal. The same can be said for egg foo yung, shrimp chow mein *(Recipe Index)*, fried rice—each has its Ori-

Demon-dispelling lions, with heads of papier-mâché and bodies of silk, cavort in San Francisco's Chinatown amid the din of drums, cymbals and firecrackers. Their parade is the climax to a week of celebration that marks the Chinese New Year.

163

At the ready-cooked food counter of a San Francisco supermarket, clerk Leung Liu fills an order of chicken and snow peas from an array of Chinese-American favorites. The kinship of Chinese-style food to other ethnic dishes is evident in the tray at far right, which contains Chinese versions of tamales—bamboo leaves stuffed with bits of shrimp, sausage, barbecued pork and rice.

ental antecedent, yet each underwent a sea change during the long Pacific crossing into something that, if not precisely exotic, is somewhat more Chinese than American.

As with so much else in American life, World War II brought an end to innocence about Chinese food. By that time a class of professional chefs skilled in a variety of Chinese regional cuisines had arrived in this country, many of them brought over by wealthy Chinese diplomats or businessmen to ornament their own kitchens. Established later in restaurants, these chefs demonstrated for a growing public that there was much more to China than Canton—and, for that matter, much more even to Cantonese cooking than most Americans had suspected. Restaurateurs branched out into such arcane culinary concepts as the lively Szechwan cooking (full of fiery pepper sauces), Peking duck (several dishes in one, all based on duck, starting with the crisp skin and ending with pancake-wrapped slices of the meat) and Mongolian fire pot (a round cooking vessel in which each diner cooks his own meat and vegetables). And where the seeker of authentic dishes once had to go underground into basement dens on Mott or Doyer Streets in New York, or climb a flight or two above Grant Street in San Francisco, he could now enjoy premises as convenient (and often as plush and expensive) as those of any first-rate European restaurant. If he was a real buff he could even enroll in a cooking school, buy himself a *wok,* and learn how to "cook Chinese" in his own home, and in the past two decades thousands have.

Not that most Americans, even today, have a clear and complete idea of the fine points of Chinese cooking. They consume staggering quantities of pseudo-Chinese food, particularly in the form of the canned and frozen egg foo yung, egg rolls, chow mein and chop suey that are in almost every supermarket. But to a greater degree than any other cuisine in this book—except perhaps the Japanese—authentic Chinese food in the U.S. is still primarily restaurant food. The Chinese themselves, in Hong Kong no less than in New York, depend on restaurant feasts to mark most major events, from weddings to birthdays. And for a family with children there is no better place to eat than a Chinese restaurant.

In the view of many serious gastronomes there are only two truly superlative cuisines in the world: the classic French and the Chinese. The real key to an appreciation of either one must be a meal in a fine restaurant. Unfortunately there are few places where the French *grande cuisine* can be encountered at its unsurpassable best, and those few that exist are expensive. But luckily there are many places where the older (and probably healthier, being less rich) cooking styles of China can be enjoyed. A splendid way to enjoy is to partake of a meal arranged by a Chinese food connoisseur. Not long ago an appreciative group of diners experienced such a meal at a Cantonese-accented restaurant in midtown New York with Florence Lin, a native of Ningpo who for more than a decade has been teaching Americans how to cook Chinese food.

The six diners sat around one table, the standard six-foot-diameter

For those who prefer meals prepared at home to the cooked food packaged by Leung Liu, a nearby Chinatown shop sells all traditional utensils of the Chinese kitchen. On the middle shelf are *woks,* indispensable cooking vessels that do double duty as frying pans and covered pots; below them are brass ladles, brass strainers and the bamboo brushes that are used for scrubbing kitchen equipment.

Ten-year-old Michelle Lim raptly sips clear chicken broth flavored with winter melon.

An Intermingling of Customs

At the sumptuous Empress of China restaurant overlooking San Francisco Bay, three generations of a Chinese-American family, the H. M. Frank Lims, greet the Chinese New Year—the most important holiday in the Chinese calendar, and a time for feasts and family reunions. The course being served at left, pressed duck with kumquats, is a Chinese delicacy, but the service, typical of a banquet meal, resembles the American style. Each diner receives an individual portion rather than filling his dish from common bowls and platters.

True to Chinese custom, the elaborate dinner eaten by the Lim family consisted of nearly a dozen courses, one of which is shown above—a platter of garden-fresh asparagus smothered with luscious Chinese mushrooms, and garnished with cucumber and tomato slices. At left, Christopher Lim, Michelle's brother, exhibits a firm grip on his chopsticks as he tackles a two-treat plate: chicken with cubed pineapple, and lobster cooked with a variety of Chinese vegetables.

167

round table that is the basic seating unit of Chinese banqueting. They began their meal with a cellophane-noodle soup based (as most Chinese soups are) on chicken stock. In this case the stock retained its light, fragrant clarity even after the addition of thin transparent "cellophane" noodles made from mung-bean starch paste, meatballs of ground pork flavored with ginger, crisp slices of water chestnuts and equally crisp snow peas, and lotus root. All these tastes and textures contended vigorously on the tongue, leaving behind a sense of brisk freshness and an appetite for the contents of the covered serving dishes that were beginning to crowd the center of the table.

The soup dishes were cleared away, each diner was given a substantial bowl of white rice and a tiny saucer of soy sauce, and the eating began in earnest. Mrs. Lin had chosen dishes that balanced strong-flavored with bland, crisp with soft, rich with light. Morsels of steamed pressed duck, deep-fried and served in a sauce composed of natural juices, sherry and soy sauce, elegantly complemented lobster Cantonese—chunks of Maine lobster briefly stir-fried in a sauce of crushed fermented black beans, ground pork, garlic, scallions and soy sauce, then simmered to perfection with added chicken stock. A filet mignon, cubed and deep-fried in the Cantonese style, came to the table bathed in mushroom sauce with tender green snow-pea pods. Asparagus with mushroom sauce *(Recipe Index)* combined the crunchy freshness of the barely cooked vegetable with the complexity of a long-simmered sauce made from dried mushrooms, chicken stock, oyster sauce, soy sauce and sugar. Pieces of white chicken meat were stir-fried with delicate bean sprouts to emphasize the mild flavor of the fowl. There was a magnificent union of succulent ivory king-crab meat and flowerets of broccoli, again cooked minimally.

When everyone was thoroughly sated, there were small steaming cups of fragrant jasmine tea to conclude the meal, and hot damp washcloths with which to freshen one's face and hands. No dessert, though there might have been some fruit; the Chinese prefer to save sweets for ceremonial occasions or for snacks. In any case most Chinese desserts are not sweet enough for Americans, which is why Chinese restaurants tend to offer ice cream, preserved kumquats, litchee nuts, pineapple or the ubiquitous fortune cookie, the last an invention of the mysterious Occident.

Compared to the familiar chop suey, Japanese food still strikes many Americans as exotic. It is, of course, a newcomer; only a handful of Japanese restaurants existed here before the late 1950s. But in the past few years, encouraged by many Japanese businessmen and their families in residence in American cities, Japanese restaurants have been opening at a more rapid rate than those serving any other foreign-style food. As a result, more Americans are eating such things as *sashimi* (sliced raw fish), *yakitori* (grilled chicken), *tendon* (rice with deep-fried shrimp) and *misoshiru* (soybean-paste soup). And *tempura* (batter-coated shrimp and vegetables, *Recipe Index)* and *sukiyaki* (simmered beef and vegetables) are well on their way to being as "American" as herring in sour cream.

Like their cuisine, the Japanese were slow in reaching the U.S. By 1870, when some 63,000 Chinese had come to America, only 186 Japanese had disembarked on the West Coast. Not until the turn of the century did Japanese come in substantial numbers, and even then few of them ventured to open restaurants. In their own homes they cooked and ate as they always had, but among their children there was a tendency to reject the old ways, or at any rate to mix them with the new. One New England-born Nisei (second-generation Japanese-American), writing in the 1930s, told how as a boy he "sat down to American breakfasts and Japanese luncheons. My palate developed a fondness for rice along with corned beef and cabbage. I became equally adept with knife and fork and with chopsticks . . . I hung my stocking over the fireplace at Christmas, and toasted *mochi* [rice cakes] at Japanese New Year."

Partly as a result of Japanese diffidence, a profound ignorance about Japanese food persisted among most Americans until the end of World War II. The American occupation of Japan, and later the Korean War, took thousands of soldiers across the Pacific and gave them a chance to scout the virtues of Japanese cuisine for themselves. What they found they liked, partly for its taste and partly because it was so beautifully presented. There were some difficult delicacies—*sushi* (vinegared rice, usually with raw fish) and bean curd and seaweed—but there were also savory grills of meat and fowl, steaming bowls of soup and noodles to be sipped on street corners, and a spectrum of incredibly lovely seafood that ranged from salt-broiled, troutlike *ayu* to deep-fried shrimp.

It was a strange and alluring mixture, a combination of the wholly unknown with the transformed familiar, and its inherent virtuosity explains the surprising variety to be found among the Japanese restaurants that have been springing up in this country. A Japanese meal in New York today may mean a multicourse *teishoku,* or fixed-menu dinner, to be consumed with the warming *sake,* rice wine, in the straw-matted private rooms of a traditional-style Japanese restaurant. Or it may mean a visit to a *tempura* bar, where a cook prepares deep-fried, batter-dipped shrimp, fish and vegetables before your eyes. Or it may mean a Japanese steakhouse, a relatively new restaurant phenomenon where guests are seated at a large square table around an expanse of hot metal on which sizzles steak, shrimp or chicken, plus vegetables.

In such a steakhouse the American may think he is eating Japanese food, while an Osaka businessman eating in a similar establishment in his own city thinks he is eating in the American style. Yet does it really matter? Japan has been borrowing foreign ideas throughout her history. It was the Portuguese who, in the 16th Century, imported both Christianity and *tempura* to Nagasaki; the *tempura* survived. It seems the Dutch brought *sukiyaki;* that survived, too. Now the time has come for export. On an evening in San Francisco or New York, one Japanese restaurant cook may be preparing an authentic national specialty, such as a small, beautiful tray of *sushi,* its flavor heightened by *wasabi* (horseradish paste). Another may be assembling a basket of airy *tempura,* and still another may be grilling a juicy cut of Kobe beef (one of the world's best). Whatever they are doing, these Japanese cooks do it with an authoritative artistry of touch. The manner, if not always the substance, is unique, and it is this esthetic characteristic that makes this cuisine at once the least assimilated and most fascinating element in America's Melting Pot.

—Charles Elliott

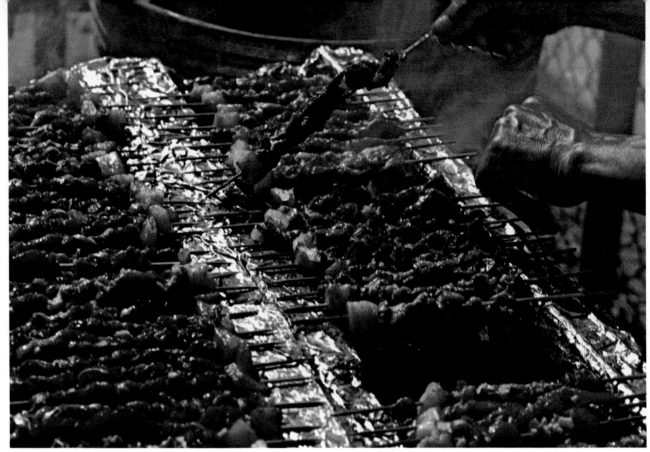

At a festival booth a cook turns skewers of beef *teriyaki*—slices of sirloin grilled with pineapple. *Below:* An intent fairgoer addresses herself to this Nisei classic.

Far Eastern Folkways in American Settings

At a number of annual outdoor summer festivals, the Japanese-Americans of California blend the cultural heritage of Japan with typically American pageantry. The Nisei Week Festival shown on these pages, which takes place in the part of Los Angeles known as Little Tokyo, includes a number of American features: a beauty queen, fashion and baby shows, and a grand parade complete with motorized floats. But many of the festival's events reflect uniquely Japanese customs. There are exhibitions of Japanese folk music and dancing, demonstrations of the courtly, centuries-old etiquette of the tea ceremony, and booths offering the traditional Japanese foods that are now being discovered and appreciated by Americans at large.

Joanne Uyemura and Sally Okizaki dig into boxes of *sushi*, a rice-and-raw-fish delicacy that is as Japanese as their kimonos.

Less flamboyant than the Nisei Week Festival is a chicken *teriyaki* feast organized by Japanese-Americans at Sebastopol, north of San Francisco. At one of the few Buddhist temples in the United States *(above)*, some 3,500 chickens are barbecued American-style over charcoal pits, sprayed with a Japanese-inspired soy-and-sake sauce, and served with rice and potato salad.

Fingers or chopsticks, hair bow or ten-gallon hat—anything goes in table manners and dress at the chicken barbecue.

Crisply brown and richly glazed with soy-seasoned sauce, a heaping panful of chicken *teriyaki* is ready to be served.

To serve 4

6 tablespoons peanut or other
   vegetable oil
2 pounds shrimp, shelled and
   deveined (see pollo vascongado,
   page 122), then split in half
   lengthwise and cut lengthwise
   into ¼-inch-wide strips
2 teaspoons finely chopped garlic
1 medium-sized onion, cut in half
   lengthwise, then crosswise into
   ¼-inch-wide semicircles (1 cup)
2 stalks celery, cut crosswise into
   4-inch lengths, then cut
   lengthwise into ⅛-inch-wide
   strips (1 cup)
1 cup finely shredded bok choy
   (Chinese cabbage) or white cabbage
1 cup snow peas, thoroughly
   defrosted if frozen, and cut in
   half diagonally
½ cup canned water chestnuts,
   drained and thinly sliced
½ pound fresh mushrooms, cut
   lengthwise into ⅛-inch-wide
   slices (2 cups)
1½ cups canned bean sprouts,
   drained
1 teaspoon salt
3 tablespoons soy sauce
1¾ cups chicken stock, fresh or
   canned
2 tablespoons cornstarch
½ cup toasted slivered almonds

To serve 4

2 ounces dried Chinese mushrooms
2 cups chicken stock, fresh or
   canned
¼ cup Chinese oyster sauce (see
   Glossary)
2 tablespoons imported Chinese or
   Japanese soy sauce
4 teaspoons sugar
2 tablespoons cornstarch combined
   with ¼ cup cold water
2 pounds firm fresh asparagus, or
   two 10-ounce packages frozen
   asparagus, thoroughly defrosted

Shrimp Chow Mein (Chinese)
SHRIMP WITH CHINESE VEGETABLES

Chow mein, with shrimp or chicken, is one of the most popular Chinese-American restaurant dishes. It is readily adaptable to home cooking, since it calls for easily obtainable fresh ingredients and widely distributed canned or frozen Chinese vegetables. As in all Chinese dishes, the ingredients can be cut and measured in advance.

Heat the oil in a 12-inch *wok* or in a 10- to 12-inch heavy skillet until it is very hot but not smoking. Add the shrimp and toss them over moderately high heat for 1 minute, or until they turn pink. Transfer the shrimp to a plate and add the garlic, onion, celery, cabbage, snow peas, water chestnuts, mushrooms and bean sprouts to the skillet. Stirring constantly, cook the vegetables for 2 or 3 minutes, then sprinkle with the salt, pour in the soy sauce and 1¼ cups of the chicken stock, and cover the pan. Cook over moderate heat for 6 to 8 minutes, or until the vegetables are tender but still slightly resistant to the bite.

Replace the shrimp in the skillet and, in a small mixing bowl, combine the cornstarch and the remaining ½ cup of chicken stock. Stir to dissolve the cornstarch, then pour into the chow mein. When the sauce has thickened and become clear—about 30 seconds—remove the pan from the heat. Transfer the chow mein to a heated platter and sprinkle with the almonds. Serve at once, with Chinese noodles or boiled rice.

Asparagus Tips with Chinese-Mushroom Sauce (Chinese)

Place the mushrooms in a small bowl, pour in enough warm water to cover them by at least 1 inch and let them soak for 30 minutes. Drain the mushrooms in a sieve and discard the water. Cut off and discard the mushroom stems, and cut each cap into eight pieces.

Combine the mushrooms, chicken stock, oyster sauce, soy sauce and sugar in a 12-inch *wok* or heavy 8- to 10-inch skillet and, stirring constantly, bring to a boil over high heat. Reduce the heat to low, cover partially and simmer for about 45 minutes, or until the mushrooms are tender. Give the cornstarch-and-water mixture a quick stir to recombine it and, stirring constantly, pour it into the mushroom sauce in a slow, thin stream. Stir over moderate heat until the sauce comes to a boil, thickens lightly and is clear. Taste for seasoning.

Meanwhile, with a sharp knife, cut off the top 2 inches of each asparagus spear. Reserving the remaining pieces of asparagus for another use, drop the tips into enough lightly salted boiling water to cover them by at least 2 inches. Cook briskly, uncovered, for about 5 minutes, or until the tips are barely tender and show only slight resistance when pierced with the point of a small sharp knife.

Drain the asparagus tips in a colander, then transfer them to a heated bowl. Pour the mushroom sauce over the asparagus and serve at once.

Tender tips of pale-green asparagus glisten under a silky coating of Chinese-mushroom sauce, which in turn has been sharpened with soy and oyster sauces.

Tempura (Japanese)
DEEP-FRIED SHRIMP AND VEGETABLES

This recipe for tempura lists only a few of the many ingredients that the Japanese dip in batter and deep-fry. Substitutions or additions might include 1-inch pieces of scallions, snow peas, ¼-inch-thick rounds of peeled sweet potatoes or ¼-inch-thick slices of fish fillets.

Since tempura must be served hot, one practical way to cook enough for several people is to fry a complete serving—several shrimp, string beans, eggplant slices and mushrooms—and keep it warm in a low oven while the remaining portions are being fried.

DIPPING SAUCE: Heat the sherry in a small skillet over moderate heat until it is lukewarm. Ignite the sherry with a match, turn off the heat and shake the pan gently until the flames die out. Add the soy sauce and chicken stock, and bring to a boil over high heat. Pour the sauce into four small bowls and cool to room temperature.

SHRIMP AND VEGETABLES: Butterfly the shrimp by cutting them three quarters of the way through along their inner curves and gently spreading them open. Flatten them slightly with the side of a knife.

Divide the shrimp, string beans, eggplant and mushrooms into four individual portions, and place them near the stove on separate dishes or sheets of wax paper.

BATTER: Place the 2 cups of flour in a large mixing bowl and make a well in the center. Drop in the egg and 2 cups of the ice water. With a large wooden spoon, gradually stir the flour into the liquid. Continue to stir vigorously until the batter is very smooth, using up to ½ cup of the traditional ice water if necessary to make a somewhat thin batter that will coat a spoon lightly.

Preheat the oven to 250°. Pour vegetable oil into a deep-fat fryer or heavy 3- to 4-quart saucepan to a depth of 3 inches. Heat the oil until it registers 375° on a deep-fat thermometer.

Dip the shrimp and pieces of vegetable one at a time in the batter, twirling each piece around to coat it evenly, then drop it into the hot oil. Fry six or eight pieces at a time for 3 to 4 minutes, or until they are a light gold. Drain on paper towels, arrange a serving of food on an individual plate or in a basket and keep warm in the oven.

With a mesh skimmer or slotted metal spoon or spatula, skim any food particles from the surface of the oil. Check the temperature of the oil to make sure that it remains at 375° and fry the remaining portions as described above.

Serve each portion of *tempura* with its own bowl of dipping sauce.

Fish Teriyaki (Japanese)
BROILED FISH FILLETS WITH SWEET SOY-SEASONED GLAZE

Preheat the broiler to its highest setting. In a small bowl, mix the powdered mustard with just enough hot water to make a thick paste. Set aside for 15 minutes.

Combine the soy sauce, sherry, chicken stock and sugar in a small saucepan, and bring to a simmer over moderate heat. Stir the combined

Draining on the rack of a Japanese deep fryer are shrimp, eggplant, mushrooms and string beans, veiled in *tempura* batter.

cornstarch and water into the sauce, and cook over low heat, stirring constantly, until the mixture thickens to a clear syrupy glaze. Immediately pour into a dish and set aside.

Pat the fish fillets completely dry with paper towels. With a pastry brush, spread the tablespoon of oil over the rack of the broiler pan. Place the fillets on the rack, skin side down, and brush them with about 2 tablespoons of the glaze. Broil 4 inches from the heat for 6 to 8 minutes, brushing the fillets three or four times with the remaining glaze, until the fish feels firm when prodded gently with a finger.

Mix the reserved mustard paste into the remaining glaze and spoon a little over each serving of fish. Garnish each fish fillet with a sprig of parsley and serve at once.

NOTE: *Teriyaki* glaze is easily adaptable to broiled steak or chicken. For steak, slice 1 pound of lean boneless beef (preferably tenderloin or sirloin) into ¼-inch-thick slices, or cut the meat into ½-inch cubes and string the cubes on skewers. Broil 2 inches from the heat for 1 or 2 minutes on each side. For chicken, use four whole chicken breasts, boned but with their skin intact; or cut the boned chicken breasts into 1-inch pieces and alternate them on skewers with 1-inch lengths of scallions. Broil 3 inches from the heat for 3 to 4 minutes on each side.

VII

by PETER WOOD

A staff writer for TIME-LIFE BOOKS, Mr. Wood has also worked as a freelance photographer and contributed stories to *The New Yorker*. For the past four years he has lived near Manhattan's Puerto Rican Barrio, becoming a lover of Latin cookery.

A Movable Feast from the Caribbean

In one of several hundred civic and social clubs enjoyed by New York's Puerto Rican community, Librada Cruz peels a green plantain—a first step in making the steamed pork-filled Puerto Rican specialty called *pasteles (Recipe Index)*. The clubroom, adorned with candles and religious statuary, is used by immigrants from Arroyo, a town in southeastern Puerto Rico. But the *pasteles* will be offered to the public at large at La Fiesta Folklórica Puertorriqueña, an annual event held in Central Park *(pages 182-183)*.

I am playing a game I sometimes play. It goes like this: I snap my fingers and disorient myself, assuming a state of partial amnesia. The point of the game is to figure out where I am—not by remembering how I got here, but by studying the clues around me.

Right now I can tell I am in a luncheonette, contemporary American style. That much is obvious from the Formica décor, the martial row of red Naugahyde-capped stools at the U-shaped counter, and the chrome platters displaying Danish pastries, doughnuts and English muffins under plastic domes. A jukebox throbs with soul music. Ads for Salem and Winston cigarettes are pasted on the back of the cash register. Across the counter from me, a girl with lustrous black hair and small gold loops in her ears is sipping a Coke and eating a cheeseburger doused with ketchup.

But what about the truck driver next to her, with the Afro haircut and granny glasses? He has just added a liberal squirt of Red Devil pepper sauce to an orange-colored chicken-noodle soup. That soup never came out of a can—not with a whole chicken drumstick floating in it. And what about my own plate, heaped with a longshoreman's portion of plantain, the starchy Caribbean staple that is big brother to the common banana? This is no common luncheonette. Most of the clientele, I now notice, are speaking Spanish with the rapid, clipped accent of Puerto Rico. My plantain—*plátano*, in Spanish—has been deep-fried (even well-ripened *plátano* must be cooked before being eaten), mashed together with crisp niblets of pork crackling and doused with a thick orange gravy. It is the Puerto Rican dish called *mofongo*, unless I miss my guess.

179

To go with my *mofongo,* the counterman sets before me a *batida de tamarindo,* a lemony-tasting milk shake flavored with tamarind pulp. And at this moment a crucial clue in my game turns up: through the plate-glass window of the luncheonette I espy its name, the Jaragua, and the words *comidas criollas* (literally, "domestic food") blazoned in white letters on the red awning above the entrance. These words, I have come to learn, are the flag that Puerto Rican kitchens raise to advertise real home cooking—or rather, cooking as it is done on the home island. But in Puerto Rico proper, the phrase *comidas criollas* would be redundant, and so I am on the mainland of the United States. And since I have done some research on the subject, I know that about two thirds of the 1.5 million Puerto Ricans now on the mainland live in New York City; the others are congregated in such cities as Chicago, Newark and Boston. As a betting man, then, I pick New York City as the place where I must now be.

The odds favor the part of New York called Spanish Harlem, a 125-block area of northeast Manhattan so distinctively Puerto Rican that it is known as El Barrio (the neighborhood). But I might also be in one of several other burgeoning Puerto Rican neighborhoods—the South Bronx, perhaps, or the Lower East Side, where Puerto Ricans are rapidly replacing the Jews who dominated the area for decades. And now a final clue appears. Up the street I see a battered old sign reading "Goldberg's Shoe Store" with the addition of the Spanish word *zapatos,* or shoes, in fresh white paint. A buzzer sounds in my head: I am indeed on New York's Lower East Side, in the very vortex of the Melting Pot. And I award myself the prize in my little game, which in this case is the most typical of all Puerto Rican luncheonette desserts: a rich yellow *flan,* coated with a thick layer of dark brown syrup—a custard sweet as a drugstore sundae and every bit as gaudy. The French *crème caramel* is a pale northern maiden compared to this lusty Latin gypsy of a dessert.

Emerging from the Jaragua that first warm day of spring, I found myself at the corner of Clinton and Rivington Streets—named for Englishmen of colonial days, when the Lower East Side was a rustic suburb of a very un-Latin city. James Rivington allegedly spied for Washington against the Crown; Charles Clinton fathered the first American governor of New York State and grandfathered (if that be the verb) DeWitt Clinton. But the Clintons and Rivingtons moved away long ago, abandoning the Lower East Side to the periodic tides of European immigration that reached their flood at the turn of the century. By the 1920s, when quotas were imposed, immigration had dwindled to a trickle. But now, still another wave of foreign-speaking people is flowing into the Port of New York —not from Europe but from the Commonwealth of Puerto Rico. Because they are American citizens by birth, Puerto Ricans need no passports or visas to come to the States—only the airplane fare from San Juan. Yet in almost every other respect they confront the same problems of jobs, housing, schools, language and generation gaps as did the waves of Germans, Italians and Jews who preceded them. And like their predecessors, they have brought their eating habits and their special foods with them.

If you had a parent, grandparent or great-grandparent who came to this country in steerage, and if you would like to see what his first years in an American city were like, visit El Barrio or the Lower East Side in New York or the Puerto Rican neighborhood of any large city. Above all, sample the food, which will be all around you—in luncheonettes like the Jaragua, where for a dollar or two you can eat enough to last you all day; in the small stands crammed with *frituras* (literally, "fried things"), those deep-fried snacks that are the Puerto Rican counterparts of hot dogs, pizza slices and knishes; in the *bodegas,* or local grocery stores, stocked with all manner of exotic foods; and in the big markets, where a broad spectrum of tropical fruits and roots is spread out for you to poke, pinch, fondle and sniff. This is how it is to be in America, but not yet to be an American. And *¡Viva la diferencia!*

It was just such an investigation that took me to the Jaragua—and to some equally interesting corners of New York.

Mrs. Cecilia Hernandez and her family live in a tenement on the edge of El Barrio in a block that looks bombed out. Mr. Hernandez is employed at present, but he has a bad heart that kept him in an upstate New York hospital for five years, and now he must go easy; the family needs and gets welfare assistance. He and his wife have raised eight children in El Barrio, and in the process Mrs. Hernandez, who left San Juan for New York some 20 years ago, has learned to cope. One way she makes extra money is to cook *frituras* and other delicacies to sell to her neighbors. Her reputation as a cook is such that I heard about her from a friend of mine who lives in the next block, and I went to ask if I could watch her cook. "Sure," she said. "Sit."

I grew up in a part of Manhattan known as Little Italy, a few blocks west of where the Jaragua luncheonette is now located, and though I had no ethnic ties with the Neapolitan and Sicilian immigrants who lived around me, they and their way of life were an integral part of my childhood. And so I had a comfortable feeling of homecoming when Mrs. Hernandez swept a copy of *El Diario,* one of New York's Spanish-language newspapers, off the only chair in her kitchen and bade me "sit." To begin with, the spotless kitchen reminded me of the kitchens of my childhood. Even more reminiscent were the dimensions, complexion and manner of Mrs. Hernandez herself. She is a great mountain of a Latin woman with arms as big around as my legs, with glossy black hair, warm dark eyes and an unforgettable voice—mellifluous in conversation, gorgonlike when ordering a reluctant child to run to the store and, though always comprehensible, totally oblivious to English syntax. Not a flattering picture, in the conventional sense, but Mrs. Hernandez is a woman who, in her role of earth mother in a crumbling brick and concrete world, has a beauty and a grace that quite transcends our modern, *Vogue*-inspired concept of how a woman should look and act.

On the morning I met her, Mrs. Hernandez was making *pastelillos* (little pies), not to sell but because she had guests coming to lunch. In the Recipe Booklet you will see a recipe for *pastelillos* that has been tried and found good. It will enable you to prepare a deep-fried pork turnover that is one of the brighter stars in the *fritura* constellation. Mrs. Hernandez, though, made her own version with ground chuck steak. Our recipe calls for a flour dough that includes baking soda, butter and egg yolks. Mrs.

Hernandez made hers with flour, water and some fat skimmed off the top of the simmering meat. She rolled her dough not on a floured board but on a plastic mat set on top of her washing machine, and she used the scalloped edge of a saucer to cut pastry rounds that were twice the size called for in our recipe. She fried the *pastelillos* not in oil but in lard, as she does all her fried foods. And they were delicious—as light and crisp as fresh cookies, but with a hearty, meaty flavor.

I bring up Mrs. Hernandez' variations not to cast doubt on the classic *pastelillo* recipe, but to illustrate the point that in cooking, as in taxidermy, there is more than one way to skin a cat. If Mrs. Hernandez had been in the habit of cooking with butter and egg yolks, and if there had not been a special on chuck steak at her local A&P the day before, and if baking soda were a regular ingredient in her kitchen, she might have followed the standard recipe verbatim. But I doubt it; some good cooks never follow standard recipes.

In the week that followed my initial meeting with Mrs. Hernandez, I learned a lot about her cooking. But first, a word of explanation. While I must report on one dish at a time, you must imagine that Mrs. Hernandez has three or four other dishes simultaneously in progress. For instance, suppose that her daughter, 14-year-old Juanita (who prefers to be called Janet), and I are grating green bananas and green plantains for the crisp yet chewy outer coating of an *alcapurria,* a meat-filled fritter. (Mrs. Her-

At La Fiesta Folklórica Puertorriqueña in New York's Central Park, ladies in bright blouses and peasant skirts pick up the mambo beat of music welling up around them. The late-summer festival manages to combine a celebration of Puerto Rican customs and traditions with a jamboree of dancing, music, food and drink.

nandez sells them for 25 cents each, undercutting the street stands by a nickel.) At the same time, Mrs. Hernandez may be bending her solid frame over the oven as she pares the fat from two enormous roast fresh hams, or she may be adding a can of tomato paste ("look at that beautiful color!") to a cauldron of *gandinga,* a stew made from pork innards.

Moreover, between every step in her cooking there is likely to be an interruption. Mrs. Hernandez' youngest son comes home from school, grabs a *pastelillo* from the sieve on the stove where it is draining, disappears into the back room, reappears pounding his fist into a baseball mitt, grabs another *pastelillo* and exits to the street. A little girl comes to the door with a nickel and a note from her mother asking if Mrs. Hernandez will add the necessary change to buy a quart of milk; Mrs. Hernandez takes the coins out of a teacup in the cupboard. Mrs. Hernandez' mother, who lives next door, comes with a can of coffee; she needs help to open it. Several neighbors want to know when Mrs. Hernandez will next have *pastelillos* for sale, and each must knock at her door to ask, because there is no telephone. Another school-age son comes in and, scorning the *pastelillos,* pops a frozen waffle into the toaster. Manuel, who sells numbers (the popular though quite illegal New York City version of a daily lottery), drops in, and Mrs. Hernandez goes to the teacup again. I bet a quarter on number 031 and forget to look in the newspaper next day to see whether I win. And so on and on and on.

On Monday mornings Mrs. Hernandez makes *sofrito (Recipe Index),* a garlicky, herby blend of vegetables, fat and ham that forms the cornerstone of many Puerto Rican dishes. She makes a lot of it—enough to fill three or four large mayonnaise jars—using an electric blender.

A second element of Puerto Rican cooking is an *adobo,* a spicy dressing or marinade used to flavor meats and poultry. At *adobo*-making time in Mrs. Hernandez' house, she grabs her heavy *pilón* and *maceta* (mortar and pestle—available in any *bodega)* and a whole bulb of garlic and goes to work. She deftly peels each clove, pops it into the mortar and mashes it and its brothers with a blend of oregano, salt, black pepper and capers. Then she stirs in olive oil and vinegar. Her mixture may be rubbed into meat or chicken and left overnight in the refrigerator, or it may go directly onto slices of roast pork. Either way, it adds interest to the meat —and you can be sure the garlic content will make the person next to you on the subway going home sit up and take notice.

The third basic ingredient of Mrs. Hernandez' kitchen is *manteca de achiote,* the agent that gives many Puerto Rican dishes a characteristic orange-yellow color. You can buy this readymade too, but making it yourself is simple: just simmer a handful of the little red seeds of the annatto tree in lard until they give up their color. Strain the mixture and use the orange-tinted lard whenever a little cooking fat is called for. The attractive color of *achiote* adds visual zest to a cuisine based largely on such foods as tropical roots, collectively called *viandas,* that by themselves cook up to an uninteresting gray. Indeed, I suspect that if it were not for their color the little red annatto seeds would soon be forgotten. Mrs. Hernandez herself, as a matter of fact, is not partial to *achiote.* She says it gives her indigestion, and she often uses tomato paste in its place.

At one of many festival tables, Iliana Gomez *(yellow blouse)* slices an orange while Crucita Rosado squeezes another into a crystal punch bowl. In the *ponche de frutas* they are preparing, almost any fruit juice is welcome; other ingredients include coconut milk and a commercial punch that gives the drink a characteristic pink color.

Of all the foods in the Puerto Ricans' repertoire, probably none is more dear to their hearts than the parchment-wrapped meat-and-starch mixtures called *pasteles (Recipe Index)*—and short of roasting a whole pig none takes more work to prepare. (Perhaps that is why Mrs. Hernandez charges 50 cents apiece for hers.) No Puerto Rican Christmas would be complete without *pasteles,* but they are in demand the rest of the year as well; during the week I spent in her company Mrs. Hernandez had a backlog of 300 orders. So on Thursday afternoon, I offered to drive her to the Marqueta, in the heart of El Barrio, where she could buy *pasteles* ingredients for much less than she would have to pay at her local *bodega.* The Marqueta is a Caribbean marketplace transplanted to New York. Stretching from 111th to 116th Street on Park Avenue, it consists of nearly 500 stands enclosed underneath the elevated Penn Central railroad tracks that connect New York with the suburbs of Westchester County and Connecticut. Overhead, the trains carry the organization men to and from Greenwich and Darien, Bronxville and Brewster. Down below, Barrio dwellers jam the aisles of the Marqueta, sizing up the wherewithal of Puerto Rican gastronomy. If you want to grasp the gamut of the Puerto Rican larder, this is a good place to start.

Having bought a crate of green bananas and another of green plantains from a wholesale distributor and deposited them in the back of my car, Mrs. Hernandez, Juanita and I plunged into the 111th Street entrance to the Marqueta. Some of the stall owners spoke Spanish with a Jewish or Italian accent, but in every other respect we might have been transported directly to the Caribbean. There was much that was new to me, such as whole split chickens; in their pale pink bodies they cradled forlorn rows of yolk-orange unlaid eggs. There were paper-clad rolls of wine-red beef unflecked by fat; bins of beans of every hue and shape; and, in open gunnysacks, varieties of rice ranging in color from pearl white to tan, and in shape from long-grain to nearly round. Most plentiful of all were the mounds of *viandas,* coarse hairy vegetables broken in half so buyers could inspect their firm interiors, and the jungle-green plantains that, together with the *viandas,* are the pasta and potatoes of the Caribbean.

Mrs. Hernandez was looking for a properly ripe plantain so that she could later show me the true taste of a *relleno de amarillo* (a deep-fried ball of boiled ripe plantain and chopped pork). After surveying several stands, she finally pinched and sniffed her way to a plantain as black as an old stick, for which she paid a five-cent premium. With the plantain, Mrs. Hernandez bought 15 cents' worth of *recao,* which, like *achiote,* is responsible for the particular savor of much Puerto Rican fare. *Recao* is a blend of three vegetables: *culantrillo,* or fresh coriander, a leaf like that of flat parsley, with an exotic, pungent taste; *culantro* (there is no equivalent in English), a larger, spiky leaf that mimics the taste and smell of *culantrillo* but is even stronger; and *ají dulce,* a tiny, sweet pepper. Ask a Puerto Rican greengrocer for *recao* and you will get roughly equal amounts of all three. You use them, most often in a *sofrito,* to supercharge the basic taste of meat or sauce or soup without adding the killing kick of hot pepper, which good Puerto Rican cooks use sparingly.

From the same vendor Mrs. Hernandez bought sheets of parchment paper to wrap the *pasteles* in, and a ball of butcher's string to tie them up. She did not buy any *yautía,* one of the *viandas* on display, because it was too expensive that day, but she did get a five-pound wedge of *calabaza,* a green-skinned pumpkin with firm orange-colored flesh.

On Friday morning, back in the Hernandez kitchen, work began in earnest. The night before, Mrs. Hernandez had diced and stewed 20 pounds of pork loin in her largest pot along with *achiote* lard, *sofrito* and tomato paste. But the real work was still to come. What takes the most time in making *pasteles* is peeling and grating the plantains, the bananas and the *yautía,* or whatever substitute for it suits the cook's fancy and purse.

It was midmorning before the peeling and grating were done—and it would have taken much longer if Juanita had not stayed home from school and if half the job had not been farmed out to Mrs. Hernandez' aunt next door. Then the three pastel-hued heaps—orange pumpkin, tan plantain and cream-colored banana—were blended into one viscous mass with *achiote* lard, milk and some of the water in which the pork bones had boiled. Bowls of cooked chick-peas, raisins and green olives were laid out on the dining-room table, the sheets of parchment and the ball of string were made ready, and production began. A spoonful of the vegetable "dough" was spread over the center of a parchment-paper sheet, followed by chopped pork filling, a couple of olives, a couple of raisins and a few chick-peas; a decisive fold was made down the center of the paper, and this step was followed by a deft packaging maneuver, creasing the top edges of the paper in several overlapping folds, turning the ends in, tying the whole package with string; and then on to the next *pastel.*

For my delectation, a *pastel* was taken from the boiling salt water in which it had cooked for half an hour, the steaming package was impatiently unwrapped (not without a scalded finger or two) and the concoction was turned out onto a plate. Somehow, the banana and plantain and pumpkin had been transformed into a single savory, somewhat glutinous substance that reminded me of banana-flavored whole wheat, permeated with the tropical flavor of the combined *sofrito* and pork; and the chunks of pork, the raisins, olives and chick-peas were special, toothsome surprises. This was no *fritura* snack; a *pastel* is a one-course meal.

When I left Mrs. Hernandez on Friday afternoon, the first of her neighbors had already gone off with a dozen *pasteles,* and six dollars were added to Mrs. Hernandez' purse beside the teacup in the cupboard.

I had watched a great deal of food being made in the Hernandez kitchen, and I had consumed a good deal of it myself, but I never did sit down to an entire meal there, for I did not wish to impose myself upon an already crowded dinner table. The pleasure of a complete home-cooked Puerto Rican repast was reserved for another day, when my wife and I had a late-afternoon meal with my friend Willie Marrero and his wife Mercedes, who live in the Bronx. Willie has lived in New York since 1948, when he was 14 and his family sold their 15-acre farm in Puerto Rico and moved, all 10 of them, to the mainland. Formerly a semiprofessional baseball player—half the able-bodied Puerto Rican men I have met either play semipro baseball or used to—Willie now works in the gymnasium of a New York men's club. Mercedes is a nurse, and because she was on

At the heart of the Puerto Rican community in New York's Spanish Harlem is the Marqueta, a five-block-long string of stalls on upper Park Avenue. There are no supermarket frills or fancy boxes at the Marqueta, no adman's come-ons or brand-name displays. A shopper can pick a ripe mango from a box just arrived from the tropics *(left)* or, like the lady shown below, buy pumpkin by the chunk at Meyer Mazza's stall. Mazza set up shop in the neighborhood back in 1925, selling broccoli to Italians and fresh horseradish to Jews from a pushcart; he now boasts a smattering of Spanish, and is an expert on the roots and tubers Puerto Ricans favor.

Dried salt cod *(below)*, which needs no refrigeration, is sold in open stalls alongside beans and vegetables. Its ease of keeping and low price have made the fish one of the prime ingredients of Puerto Rican cooking.

Among the few traces of modern packaging at the Marqueta are beans *(above)* in plastic bags and tropical vegetables *(below)* in cans. (The canning, incidentally, was done in Jamaica.) The galaxy of fruits and vegetables at right include green and ripe plantains (15 cents each, two for 25 cents); snow-white yuca, a starchy tuber; and, in the foreground, coconuts and pumpkin.

call and had to stay near the telephone, Willie and I did the shopping that Saturday morning. While we were out, she put together the delicious rice and coconut pudding called *arroz con coco (Recipe Index)*. I can reveal that she used a can of coconut cream rather than personally extracting the milk from a ripe coconut. It was neither as authentic nor as good, but since it took her about one tenth the time, it was more in keeping with the tempo of a busy New York nurse and mother. For the rest of the meal, no corners were cut.

A block from the Marreros' apartment is the outdoor Simpson Street Market. At the Marqueta de Simpson, produce fills the sidewalk and the buyers walk in the street, past washtubs afloat with melon-sized green *panapenes,* or breadfruit—the fruit, used mainly as a vegetable, that led to the mutiny on H.M.S. *Bounty.* Our first purchase was a *chayote*—a small pear-shaped squash, by itself so bland that Puerto Ricans call it, with a wink, *mujer propia,* "your own wife." Next we bought a slab of *bacalao,* or dried salt cod, an inexpensive protein staple of the island that keeps without refrigeration and has been adapted to a myriad of dishes. Our third purchase was a *longaniza,* a lengthy *achiote*-tinted pork sausage.

With these in hand we rejoined Mercedes and started cooking. My wife joined us later in the afternoon and missed a platter of light, crisp *bacalaitos,* or cod fritters *(Recipe Index),* that helped Willie and me polish off a six-pack of beer while the dinner was made ready. The four of us sat around a tiny table in the kitchen, which the Marreros assured us had often seated 10; before we started to eat, Willie stood up on a stool and took a picture. If it comes out, it may show a great heaping bowl of *serenata (Recipe Index),* a salad based on boiled codfish, hard-cooked egg and potato that accounted for both the *chayote* and the remainder of the salt cod. Boiled and served cold, the *chayote* made a perfect textural foil to the potatoes in the salad. As at every decent Puerto Rican meal there were also a bowl each of rice and beans—the rice cooked with *achiote* lard, *sofrito* and the *longaniza* sausage; the beans with lean salt pork and a tomato sauce. The picture may also show a blurred flurry of hands, for there is no waiting on ceremony at a Puerto Rican table; everyone serves himself, and all the food, including the salad, goes on the plate together. A fourth serving bowl on the table contained *pegao,* the crunchy, dark-brown crust of rice and *longaniza* scraped from the bottom of the pot, so esteemed that it is served as a special dish.

Willie announced that everything had turned out just right; Mercedes, who did all the cooking, smiled demurely. I reported to them both that I found the beans more gooey than I had expected and the rice drier, but since the beans were mixed with the rice, the overall consistency was about what an American palate would expect, while the contrast in textures and flavors of these two staples made the combination perfect.

I learned more at the Marreros' that day. Here, at random, are a few of the culinary tips I acquired. Item: I can eat eight *bacalaitos* in a half hour, if the beer holds out. Item: the onions for a *serenata* should be put into vinegar for a good half hour before they are added to the salad; this gives the vinegar a good oniony flavor and takes the harsh bite out of the raw onion. Items (both from Mercedes): "Olive oil is the main attraction when you are dealing with fish,'' and ''Fingers are very handy in eating Puerto Rican food.'' Item: three huge helpings of beans and rice are no impediment to downing a huge portion of *arroz con coco* for dessert. Item: *serenata* deserves its name, for like a serenade, it wooed me and put me to sleep at one and the same time.

It remains for me to mention, now that I have come to the end of this chapter and this book, the very first Puerto Rican dish I ever tasted. It was cooked for me by Olga Gandara, under whose guidance the recipe section of this chapter was compiled, and it is so typical of the friendly simplicity of Puerto Rican cooking that it has the informal name of *sopa casera,* or soup of the house—which means that whatever comes to hand goes into it. On this occasion, Olga's *sopa casera* was actually a *sopa de fideos (Recipe Index),* or vermicelli soup, a thick blend of vegetables and oxtail, heavily laden with the thin pasta. The two ingredients that made it most memorable to me were one-inch rounds of fresh corn and big chunks of *calabaza,* the same type of pumpkin that went into Mrs. Hernandez' *pasteles.* As I have said, it was spring when I began my investigation of *las comidas criollas,* but this soup—and particularly the taste of the pumpkin and corn, blended with the rich oxtail broth—transported me halfway around the year to autumn. I could almost smell burning leaves and see jack-o'-lanterns grinning at me in the dark. And it may have been the sudden evocation of a childhood memory of Halloween that fixed the taste of this *sopa casera* so firmly in my mind.

But my real reason for mentioning *sopa casera* is that, in watching Olga prepare it, I was reminded of a childhood misconception about the Melting Pot. Technically, I suppose, the image behind the phrase is that of a crucible in which metals are fused and changed to become an alloy. In my imagination, though, the Melting Pot had always taken the form of a big kitchen cauldron of just the sort Olga was using. She put in the halved onions (call them, say, the Irish), the halved peppers (call them the Italians), the pieces of pumpkin (the English), the corn (the Jews), the this and the that, and stewed the whole for an hour or so. Then she lifted out the softened hulks, except for the oxtail and the corncobs, and put them into the blender; the resulting purée was put back into the pot. This, to me, was a true Melting Pot. America may indeed gain strength through the amalgamation of nationalities and races, but I prefer my first image, that of the blending of many foods, from which the country has continuously drawn nourishment and strength.

At Levy's lunch stand on the Lower East Side, only a few blocks from the Jaragua, there is a series of signs along the wall that together say it all. They go something like this: ''Tasty Pizza,'' ''Tempting Knishes,'' ''All-Beef Frankfurters,'' ''French Fries''—and finally, hand-lettered on a scrap of paper, *''Pastellios* 25 cents.'' In a few more years, if Levy hasn't moved to the suburbs, it is likely that he will learn to spell *pastelillos* and have a proper sign printed—but by then some twist of world politics may have thrown a new ingredient into the pot. Another nationality will then be low man on the totem pole, shopping under the tracks, while the sons and grandsons of the Puerto Ricans ride the trains above—and the soup of this American house of ours will be that much richer.

Overleaf: At first glance, *sancocho* looks like an ordinary meat-and-vegetable stew—but some of its ingredients are very far from ordinary. Along with such conventional items as onions, tomatoes, green and red bell peppers and garlic, there are corn, pumpkin, plantain and *(at bottom, center)* the knobby Puerto Rican root vegetable called *yautía.*

To make about 4 dozen hors
   d'oeuvre

½ pound salt cod
1½ cups all-purpose flour
1 teaspoon double-acting baking
   powder
1½ cups cold water
1 large clove garlic
¼ teaspoon freshly ground black
   pepper
Lard or vegetable oil for deep
   frying

Bacalaitos (*Puerto Rican*)
DEEP-FRIED COD FRITTERS

Starting a day ahead, place the cod in a glass, enameled or stainless-steel
pan or bowl, cover it with cold water, and soak for at least 12 hours,
changing the water three or four times. Drain the cod, rinse it under cold
running water, place it in a saucepan and add enough fresh cold water to
cover the fish by 1 inch. Bring to a boil over high heat. Taste the water; if
it seems excessively salty, drain, cover the cod with fresh water and bring
to a boil again. Reduce the heat to low and simmer uncovered for about
20 minutes, or until the fish flakes easily when prodded gently with a
fork. Drain thoroughly. With a small knife, remove and discard any skin
and bones and separate the fish into fine flakes.

In a large mixing bowl, combine the flour and baking powder. Make a
well in the center and pour in the 1½ cups of cold water. With a large
wooden spoon, gradually incorporate the flour into the water, then stir

In *asopao,* a hearty Puerto Rican soup eaten as a main course, shrimp dominate but ham, peas, pimientos and olives also figure.

until the mixture is smooth. Place the garlic and pepper in a mortar and, with a pestle, pound and mash them to a paste. Stir the paste into the flour-and-water mixture, then stir in the cod flakes.

Place the lard or oil in a deep fryer or a large heavy saucepan to a depth of 2 or 3 inches and heat the oil until it reaches a temperature of 350° on a deep-fat thermometer.

To form each fish ball, scoop up about 1 tablespoon of the fish mixture and shape it into a round ball about 1 to 1½ inches in diameter. Fry the fish balls four or five at a time for about 10 minutes, turning them frequently with a slotted spoon. As they brown, transfer them to paper towels to drain and keep them warm in a low oven while you fry the remaining fish balls. Serve the *bacalaitos* while they are still warm, as a first course or as an accompaniment to drinks.

Asopao de Camarones *(Puerto Rican)*
SHRIMP-AND-RICE SOUP

Heat the lard in a heavy 2½- to 3-quart casserole and, when it is very hot but not smoking, stir in the diced ham. Tossing the dice constantly, cook them over moderate heat until they are evenly browned, then stir in the onions, green pepper, tomatoes and garlic. Cook for 6 to 8 minutes, stirring frequently, until the vegetables are soft, then stir in the tomato purée, rice, water or stock, and salt. Bring to a boil over high heat, then cover the casserole, lower the heat, and simmer for 20 minutes, or until the rice is tender; the mixture should still be soupy by the time the rice is cooked. Add the shrimp and peas to the casserole, cover it again, and cook for another 5 minutes, or until the shrimp are pink.

Stir in the capers, olives and pimientos, cover and simmer for 1 or 2 minutes more. Taste for seasoning and ladle the *asopao* into a large heated tureen or individual soup plates.

To serve 4 to 6

4 tablespoons lard
¼ pound smoked ham, cut into ¼-inch dice (½ cup)
1½ cups finely chopped onions
1 cup finely chopped green pepper
3 medium-sized tomatoes, finely chopped (2 cups)
1 tablespoon finely chopped garlic
½ cup tomato purée
2 cups long-grain unconverted white rice
2 quarts water or 2 quarts chicken stock, fresh or canned
2 tablespoons salt
2 pounds shrimp, peeled and deveined *(see pollo vascongado, page 122)*
1 pound green peas, shelled
1 tablespoon capers
½ cup pitted olives
¼ cup pimientos, finely chopped

Arroz con Coco *(Puerto Rican)*
COCONUT RICE PUDDING WITH RAISINS

In a 1- to 1½-quart saucepan, combine the milk, cinnamon sticks, cloves and ginger. Bring to a boil over high heat, then lower the heat and simmer the milk uncovered for 5 minutes. Remove the pan from the heat and set it aside for at least 1 hour.

Strain the milk through a fine sieve set over a measuring cup; if there is less than 2 cups of milk, add enough cold milk to make 2 cups. Discard the cinnamon, cloves and ginger.

Bring the quart of water to a boil and drop in the rice. Cook uncovered for 5 minutes, then drain the rice in a sieve and wash it under cold water.

In a 2- to 2½-quart saucepan, combine the coconut milk, strained spiced milk, sugar and salt. Bring to a boil over high heat, then stir in the rice, cover the pan, and reduce the heat. Simmer for 30 minutes, then stir in the raisins, re-cover the pan and cook for 10 minutes longer, or until the liquid is completely absorbed and the rice is tender. Transfer the *arroz con coco* to a serving bowl or individual bowls, sprinkle with ground cinnamon, and serve at room temperature.

To serve 4 to 6

2 cups milk
6 sticks cinnamon
1 teaspoon whole cloves
A 3-inch piece of fresh ginger, peeled and crushed with the side of a knife
1 quart water
1 cup long-grain unconverted rice
2 cups coconut milk, made from 2 cups coarsely chopped fresh coconut and 2 cups hot milk *(Recipe Booklet)*
½ cup sugar
1 teaspoon salt
½ cup seedless raisins
Ground cinnamon

To serve 4

FILLING

3 tablespoons annatto oil *(below)*
1 pound ground pork
½ cup finely chopped onions
¼ cup finely chopped green pepper
1 teaspoon finely chopped garlic
1½ teaspoons salt
Freshly ground black pepper
3 medium-sized firm ripe tomatoes,
    peeled, seeded and finely chopped
    (see note)
3 large pimiento-stuffed green
    olives, thoroughly drained and
    finely chopped
1 tablespoon capers, finely chopped
2 tablespoons cider or malt vinegar

PLANTAIN RINGS

2 large ripe plantains, about
    1 pound each
2 tablespoons lard or vegetable oil

Vegetable oil
4 eggs, beaten

To make about 1 cup

½ pound (1 cup) lard
½ cup annatto *(achiote)* seeds

Pionones *(Puerto Rican)*
DEEP-FRIED PLANTAIN RINGS WITH PORK FILLING

FILLING: Heat the annatto oil in a heavy 10- to 12-inch skillet until a light haze forms above it. Add the ground pork and, mashing it constantly with the back of a spoon to break up any lumps, cook until all traces of pink disappear. Add the finely chopped onions, green pepper and garlic and, stirring frequently, cook for 4 to 6 minutes, until the vegetables are soft but not brown. Stir in the salt, a few grindings of black pepper and the finely chopped tomatoes. Stirring occasionally, simmer until all of the liquid in the pan evaporates and the mixture thickens enough to hold its shape lightly in the spoon.

Remove the pan from the heat, stir in the green olives, capers and vinegar, and taste for seasoning. Scrape the contents of the skillet into a large mixing bowl and refrigerate for at least 30 minutes, or until it is thoroughly chilled.

PLANTAIN RINGS: Meanwhile, peel the plantains, following the directions in the drawing in the Recipe Booklet, and cut each plantain lengthwise into four thick strips. Heat the 2 tablespoons of lard or oil in a heavy 10- to 12-inch skillet until a light haze forms above it. Add the sliced plantains and, turning the strips with tongs or a slotted spatula, cook them for about 5 minutes on each side. As they turn golden brown, transfer the strips to paper towels to drain and cool.

To assemble the *pionones,* shape each strip of plantain into a 1-inch-wide ring, overlapping the ends by about ½ inch and securing them with a wooden toothpick inserted crosswise. Lay the rings side by side on a sheet of wax paper and spoon the chilled pork mixture evenly into the center of each one. Pat the meat into place and gently press the top flat.

Pour vegetable oil into the heavy 10- to 12-inch skillet to a depth of 1 inch, and set over high heat until the oil is very hot but not smoking. One at a time, place the *pionones* on a slotted metal spatula and dip them into the beaten eggs, coating them completely.

Slide the rings into the hot oil and fry, four at a time, for about 3 minutes on each side, turning them gently with the spatula or a metal spoon. When the *pionones* are golden brown, transfer them to paper towels to drain. Serve at once, accompanied if you like by stewed red beans and rice *(opposite).*

NOTE: To prepare the tomatoes, drop them into a pan of boiling water for 15 seconds. Place them under cold running water, then peel them with a small sharp knife. Cut out the stem of each tomato and slice the tomato in half crosswise. Squeeze all the halves gently to remove the seeds and juice, then chop the tomatoes.

Annatto Oil *(Puerto Rican)*

Melt the lard in a small saucepan or skillet and stir in the annatto seeds. Simmer the seeds over low heat for 10 minutes, stirring frequently to prevent them from sticking to the pan.

Strain the annatto oil through a fine sieve set over a heatproof jar. Discard the annatto seeds. Tightly covered and refrigerated, annatto oil can be kept for 2 or 3 months.

Arroz con Habichuelas *(Puerto Rican)*
STEWED RED BEANS AND RICE

In a large sieve or colander, wash the beans under cold running water until the draining water runs clear. Transfer them to a heavy 3- to 4-quart saucepan, add ½ teaspoon of the salt, and pour in the water. Bring to a boil over high heat, reduce the heat to low, and simmer partially covered for about 1½ hours, or until the beans are tender but still intact. Drain the beans in a sieve set over a large bowl and set them aside. Measure the cooking liquid and set aside 4 cups, adding more cold water if necessary.

In a heavy 2½- to 3-quart saucepan, melt the lard over moderate heat. Stir in the *sofrito,* the rice, the remaining teaspoon of salt and the 4 cups of bean liquid. Cover the pan tightly and bring to a boil, then reduce the heat to low and simmer undisturbed for about 20 minutes, or until the rice is tender and has absorbed all the liquid. Stir in the cooked beans, taste for seasoning, and serve at once.

To serve 6 to 8

1 pound dried red pinto beans
1½ teaspoons salt
6 cups water
2 tablespoons lard
½ cup *sofrito (below)*
2 cups long-grain unconverted white rice

Sofrito *(Puerto Rican)*
SPICY TOMATO SAUCE

In a heavy 10- to 12-inch skillet, fry the ½ pound of salt-pork dice over moderate heat, turning them about with a spoon until they are crisp and brown and have rendered all their fat. With a slotted spoon, remove and discard the dice, and add the annatto oil to the pork fat in the skillet.

Stir in the onions and garlic and, stirring frequently, cook for 6 to 8 minutes, or until they are soft but not brown. Stir in the smoked ham, the green peppers, tomatoes, salt, coriander, oregano and a few grindings of black pepper. Reduce the heat to low and simmer the sauce for 10 minutes, stirring the mixture from time to time to prevent the vegetables from sticking to the bottom of the skillet.

The *sofrito* can be stored, tightly covered and refrigerated, for 1 or 2 weeks; it can be stored frozen for several months.

To make about 2 cups

½ pound salt pork, finely diced
2 tablespoons annatto oil *(opposite)*
3 cups finely chopped onions
1 tablespoon finely chopped garlic
½ pound smoked ham, cut into ½-inch dice (about 1 cup)
2 medium-sized green peppers, seeded, deribbed, and finely chopped
4 large firm ripe tomatoes, peeled, seeded and coarsely chopped *(see pionones, opposite),* or substitute 3 cups coarsely chopped drained canned tomatoes
2 teaspoons salt
2 teaspoons finely chopped fresh coriander *(cilantro)*
½ teaspoon crumbled dried oregano
Freshly ground black pepper

Plátanos Maduros al Sartén *(Puerto Rican)*
RIPE PLANTAINS IN SYRUP

Melt the butter in a heavy 10- to 12-inch skillet over moderate heat. Add the plantains and cook for 10 to 15 minutes, turning them frequently with a spatula or tongs and adjusting the heat if necessary to prevent them from burning. When they are a deep golden brown, remove from the pan and set aside.

Combine the sugar, water and cinnamon stick in the skillet and, stirring frequently, bring to a boil over high heat. Replace the plantains in the skillet, cover it tightly, and boil briskly for 15 minutes, or until the plantains are tender and show no resistance when pierced with the tip of a small sharp knife. Uncover the skillet, reduce the heat to moderate, and cook for 15 to 20 minutes longer, until the syrup has thickened enough to coat a spoon heavily. Transfer the plantains to a serving dish, discard the cinnamon stick and pour the syrup over the plantains. Serve the plantains whole or sliced, as an accompaniment to meat or eggs.

To serve 2 to 4

1 tablespoon butter
2 very ripe plantains, peeled and left whole
1 cup sugar
1 cup water
1 stick cinnamon

To serve 6 to 8

1½ pounds flank steak, cut into
    1-inch cubes
½ pound boneless pork shoulder,
    cut into 1-inch cubes
¼ pound smoked ham, cut into
    ½-inch cubes (½ cup)
1 tablespoon salt
1 sprig coriander (cilantro)
1 bay leaf
1 teaspoon marjoram
1 tablespoon finely chopped garlic
2 cups finely chopped onions
3 medium-sized tomatoes, coarsely
    chopped (2 cups)
1 medium-sized green bell pepper,
    seeded, deribbed and finely
    chopped
2 medium-sized red bell peppers,
    seeded, deribbed and finely
    chopped
½ pound yautía (see Glossary),
    peeled and cut into 1½-inch
    chunks
½ pound potatoes, peeled and cut
    into 1½-inch chunks
½ pound yam, peeled and cut into
    1½-inch chunks
1 green plantain, peeled and cut
    into ½-inch-wide rounds
1 ripe plantain, peeled and cut into
    ½-inch-wide rounds
2 ears fresh corn, husked and cut
    crosswise into 1-inch-wide rounds
½ pound pumpkin, peeled and cut
    into 1½-inch chunks

To serve 8 to 10

3½ cups sugar
Two 13-ounce cans evaporated milk
½ teaspoon salt
1 tablespoon vanilla extract
8 eggs

Sancocho (Puerto Rican)
BEEF AND VEGETABLE STEW

In a 4- to 6-quart casserole, combine the flank steak, pork, ham, salt, coriander, bay leaf, marjoram, garlic, onions, tomatoes, green pepper and red pepper. Pour in enough cold water to cover the meat and vegetables by 1 to 2 inches. Bring to a boil over high heat, meanwhile skimming the liquid of any scum that rises to the surface. Partially cover the casserole and simmer over low heat for 1 hour.

Add the *yautía,* potatoes, yam and green plantain, and continue to cook, partially covered, for 45 minutes, or until the meat and vegetables are tender and offer no resistance when they are pierced with the tip of a small sharp knife.

Add the ripe plantain, corn and pumpkin, and cook partially covered for 15 minutes longer. Taste for seasoning and ladle the soup into a large heated tureen or individual soup plates.

Olga's Flan (Puerto Rican)
CARAMEL CUSTARD

To line an ovenproof mold—which should hold 2 to 2½ quarts and be at least 2 inches deep—with caramel, it is necessary to work very quickly, or the caramel will harden. Because the temperature of the hot caramel will be over 300°, handle the mold with extreme caution.

Place 1½ cups of the sugar in a small heavy saucepan or skillet and set over high heat. Stir constantly until the sugar completely dissolves, then reduce the heat to moderate and cook briskly without stirring for about 10 minutes, or until the syrup turns a rich golden tealike brown. As soon as the syrup reaches this color, remove the pan from the heat and carefully pour the caramel syrup in a thin stream into the mold. Tip and swirl the mold from side to side to coat the bottom as evenly as possible. Set the mold aside.

Preheat the oven to 325°. In a 1- to 1½-quart saucepan, bring the evaporated milk almost to a boil over moderate heat. Remove from the heat and stir in the salt and vanilla extract.

With a wire whisk or a rotary or electric beater, beat the eggs together in a large mixing bowl until well blended, then add the remaining 2 cups of sugar gradually. Continue to beat until the mixture is thick and pale yellow. Stirring constantly, pour in the hot milk mixture in a slow, thin stream. Then strain the contents of the bowl through a fine sieve directly into the caramel-lined mold.

Place the mold in a large shallow baking pan, and set the pan on the middle shelf of the oven. Pour enough boiling water into the baking pan to come halfway up the sides of the mold. Bake the custard—lowering the oven temperature if the water in the pan begins to simmer—for 1½ hours, or until a thin knife inserted in the center of the custard comes out dry and clean. Remove the mold from the pan, cool to room temperature, then refrigerate the custard in the mold for at least 2 hours, or until it is thoroughly chilled.

To unmold the custard, run a sharp knife around the sides and dip the bottom of the mold briefly in hot water. Wipe the outside of the mold dry, place a chilled serving plate upside down over the mold and, grasping both the plate and mold firmly together with both hands, quickly turn them over. Rap the plate on a table and the custard should slide easily out of the mold. Serve cold.

Almojábanas *(Puerto Rican)*
RICE CRULLERS

In a heavy 2- to 2½-quart saucepan, bring the milk, salt and butter to a boil over moderate heat, stirring occasionally. As soon as the butter has completely melted, remove the pan from the heat and pour in the rice flour. Beat the mixture vigorously with a wooden spoon until it is well blended, then return the pan to moderate heat and cook, still beating vigorously, for 1 or 2 minutes, or until the mixture forms a paste that leaves the sides of the pan and moves freely with the spoon.

Immediately remove the pan from the heat and use the spoon to make a well in the center of the paste. Break 1 egg into the well and beat it into the paste. When the egg has been absorbed, beat in the remaining 2 eggs, 1 at a time, beating well after each addition. The finished paste should be thick, smooth and shiny. Set aside to cool to room temperature, then beat in both the cheeses and the cayenne.

Pour oil into a deep fryer or large heavy saucepan to a depth of 3 inches and place over moderate heat until it reaches a temperature of 350°. Drop the mixture by the tablespoonful into the hot oil and fry the crullers, six or eight at a time, for 4 minutes, or until they are golden brown. Serve the *almojábanas* warm, as "bread" accompanying a meal, or as an accompaniment to drinks.

To make about 2 dozen

1 cup milk
1½ teaspoons salt
5 tablespoons butter, cut into bits
1½ cups rice flour *(see Glossary)*
3 eggs
1 cup grated Queso del País *(see Glossary),* or substitute 1 cup grated sharp Cheddar cheese
¼ cup grated Parmesan cheese
½ teaspoon ground hot red pepper (cayenne)
Vegetable oil or lard

Sopa de Fideos *(Puerto Rican)*
PURÉED VEGETABLE SOUP WITH VERMICELLI

Combine the 2 quarts of water, rounds of oxtail, corn, onion, tomato, green pepper, garlic, coriander leaves and pumpkin in a 6- to 8-quart casserole, and bring to a boil over high heat. Cover the casserole, lower the heat, and simmer undisturbed for about 1½ hours, until the oxtail and the vegetables are tender and offer no resistance when pierced with the tip of a small sharp knife.

With a slotted spoon, transfer the quartered onion, tomato, green pepper, garlic, coriander leaves and pieces of pumpkin to the container of an electric blender and pour in ½ cup of the cooking liquid. Purée the vegetables at high speed for about 30 seconds, then pour the purée back into the casserole.

Lacking an electric blender, purée the vegetables in a food mill set over a large bowl, or push them through a fine sieve with the back of a large wooden spoon.

Stir the tomato purée and salt into the soup and taste for seasoning. Bring to a boil over high heat, then drop in the vermicelli. Lower the heat to moderate and cook for 6 to 8 minutes, until the vermicelli is tender. Transfer the *sopa de fideos* to a large heated tureen or individual heated soup plates, and serve hot.

To serve 8

2 quarts water
2 pounds oxtail, trimmed of excess fat and chopped by the butcher into 2½-inch rounds
2 ears corn, shucked and cut crosswise into 1-inch-wide rounds
1 large onion, peeled and quartered
1 large tomato, quartered
1 small green bell pepper, quartered, deribbed and seeded
2 whole cloves garlic, peeled
¼ cup coriander leaves *(cilantro)*
½ pound pumpkin, peeled and cut into 2-inch pieces, or substitute ½ pound yellow squash, peeled and cut into 1-inch pieces
⅓ cup tomato purée
2 tablespoons salt
2 ounces vermicelli

Glossary

ACHIOTE. *See* Annatto oil.

AL DENTE (Italian): Literally, "to the tooth," term used to describe the point at which pasta is tender but still slightly resistant.

ANNATTO OIL (Puerto Rican): Cooking oil made from lard and annatto (*achiote*) seeds.

ANTIPASTO (Italian): Literally, "before the meal," an hors d'oeuvre or first course.

BAGEL (Jewish): A crusty, chewy ring of dough, boiled briefly, then baked.

BAKLAVA (Greek, Armenian): Sweet pastry, made from layers of *filo* pastry with nut and spice filling and steeped in syrup.

BAMBOO SHOOTS (Chinese): Ivory-colored, conical shoots of tropical bamboo. Available canned, in wedges (in Oriental specialty stores) or slices (in many supermarkets or gourmet shops).

BEAN SPROUTS (Chinese): Young sprouts of the mung bean, sold fresh in Oriental stores and canned in supermarkets and gourmet stores.

BOEREK (Armenian), **BUREK** (Serbian): Fried or baked dish consisting of thin layers of *filo* or similar pastry filled with cheese or seasoned meat; a sweet version contains a nut filling.

BULGHUR (Armenian), **BURGHUL** (Arabic): Cereal made from whole grains of wheat that are boiled and dried. The kernel is then cracked. Available in fine-, medium- or coarse-grain sizes in some gourmet shops and health food stores.

CACCIATORA, ALLA (Italian): "Hunter's style"; meat, poultry or fish cooked in a sauce that usually includes mushrooms, tomatoes and wine.

CELLOPHANE NOODLES (Chinese or Japanese): Also called bean thread (Chinese), *harusame* (Japanese), or transparent noodles. Made from ground mung beans, the dried noodles are available in Oriental stores.

CHICK-PEAS: Round dried peas called *garbanzos* in Spanish, they are also available cooked, in cans.

CHINESE MUSHROOMS: Available dried in packages in Oriental markets. They are usually reconstituted by soaking in water for at least 30 minutes.

CHORIZO (Spanish): Garlic-flavored pork sausage.

CILANTRO: Spanish name for coriander; also called Chinese parsley or *culantrillo* (Puerto Rican). Herb with flat leaves, sold fresh in Chinese, Italian and Latin American markets and in some vegetable stores.

CIORBA (Romanian): Sour soup.

CITRIC (SOUR) SALT: A crystalline extract from lemons and limes that imparts an acidulous taste. Available in supermarkets, primarily in Jewish neighborhoods.

DOLMA (Armenian): Stuffed foods, usually vegetables, such as peppers or tomatoes stuffed with rice or meat mixtures.

FETA (Greek): A crumbly white cheese packed in brine; from ewe's milk or goat's milk.

FILO (Greek): Tissue-thin sheets of pastry, which can be purchased fresh or frozen from Middle Eastern stores or gourmet shops.

GINGER ROOT, FRESH (Chinese): Gnarled brown root sold in Oriental and Puerto Rican markets. Left whole, ginger root may be refrigerated and kept for several days. Peeled, sliced ginger may be refrigerated in a jar of dry sherry for several months.

GREBENES (Jewish): Chicken fat and onion cracklings.

KASHA (Jewish): Buckwheat groats.

KIELBASA (Polish), **KOLBÁSZ** (Hungarian): Similar garlic-flavored pork sausages.

KOSHER (Jewish): According to the Jewish dietary laws.

LEKVAR (Hungarian, Slavic): Apricot or prune butter, available in jars.

LINGÜIÇA (Portuguese): Garlic-flavored pork sausage.

LOTUS ROOT (Chinese): Long root sold fresh, canned and dried in Oriental markets.

LOX (Jewish): Smoked salmon that has been cured in a salty brine. The cut from the under part of the smoked salmon is called belly lox and is fattier, cheaper and saltier than the debrined Nova Scotia cut.

MAMALIGA. *See* Polenta

MATZO (Jewish): Flat, crisp, unleavened bread.

MATZO MEAL (Jewish): Matzo crumbs, available in boxes.

MILT: The male reproductive glands of fish; sometimes called "soft white roe."

MORTADELLA (Italian): Large smoked sausage, made from finely chopped ham and cubes of white fat and delicately spiced with garlic and anise.

MOZZARELLA (Italian): A soft, bland white cheese used in cooking; made originally from buffalo's milk but now also from cow's milk.

OYSTER SAUCE (Chinese): Thick brown sauce made from oysters, soy sauce and brine. Sold in bottles in Oriental specialty shops and gourmet shops.

PAREVE (Jewish): Neutral foods; those containing neither milk nor meat products; for example, eggs, fruit or vegetables.

PARMESAN (Italian): Fully cured Parmesan cheese is very hard and keeps indefinitely.

PASTA (Italian): A dough of flour and water; generic name for pasta products.

PASTINA (Italian): Literally, "little pasta"; used in soups.

PLANTAIN, PLÁTANO (Puerto Rican): A starchy vegetable, available in Latin American markets in its ripe (almost black) or unripe (green to yellow) stages. Never eaten raw; it is always cooked.

PLÁTANO. *See* Plantain

POLENTA (Italian): Cornmeal; also the name of the finished dish of cornmeal mush. A Romanian equivalent is *mamaliga*.

PROSCIUTTO (Italian): Thinly sliced spicy ham that has been salted, pressed and dried.

PEPERONI (Italian): Sausage of coarsely cut beef and pork, highly seasoned with pepper.

QUESO DEL PAÍS (Puerto Rican): Literally, "native cheese"; also known as Queso de la Tierra. A white pressed, semisoft cheese.

RICE FLOUR: Finely ground rice. When made from regular-milled or polished grains, it is white; when made from brown rice (which has the outer bran still intact), it is creamy in color.

RICOTTA (Italian): Soft curdlike cheese resembling cottage cheese.

SALTPETER: Potassium nitrate: a crystalline salt used in preserving meat; available through pharmacists.

SARMA (Armenian): Wrapped foods, such as grape leaves wrapped around rice or meat.

SCALOPPINE (Italian): Thinly sliced boneless veal.

SCHMALTZ (Jewish): Chicken or goose fat.

SNOW PEAS (Chinese): Flat, pale-green peas, eaten pods and all. Sold fresh in Oriental specialty stores and frozen in supermarkets.

SOUR SALT. *See* Citric salt

SUSHI (Japanese): Vinegared rice combined with raw fish or vegetables.

WASABI (Japanese): Powdered green horseradish, available canned in Oriental markets. Water is added to it to make a paste.

WATER CHESTNUTS (Chinese): Walnut-sized bulbs with brown skin and crisp white meat, sold fresh in Oriental specialty shops and canned in supermarkets.

WATER-CHESTNUT FLOUR (Chinese): Pulverized water chestnuts, available in Oriental and gourmet shops; imparts a crusty surface to foods.

YAUTÍA (Puerto Rican): Tropical root with a potatolike skin, available in yellow and white varieties.

Shopping Guide

Most of the ingredients called for in this book can be found at any grocery or supermarket. A few recipes include packaged products that are not widely available, such as poppy seeds and *lekvar*. These items can probably be ordered through your local gourmet shop, or by mail from Paprikás Weiss, 1546 Second Avenue, or H. Roth & Son, 1577 First Avenue, both in New York City. As far as the Puerto Rican vegetables (such as plantains and *yautía*) are concerned, these must be purchased fresh; therefore you will be limited by whether there is a Latin American market in your locale.

Listed below are stores that sell the equipment needed to make the red wine that appears in the Recipe Booklet.

WINE-MAKING EQUIPMENT
Milan Laboratories
57 Spring Street
New York, N.Y. 10012

Vino Corporation
Box 7885
Rochester, N.Y. 14606

WINE-ART OF AMERICA
This chain has more than 50 stores, which sell wine-making equipment. Those in major metropolitan areas are listed:

California
7357 Sunset Blvd.
Hollywood 90046

Colorado
705 East Sixth Ave.
Denver 80203

Georgia
1921 Peachtree Rd.
Atlanta 30309

Illinois
4016 Church St.
Skokie 60676

Minnesota
5308 Excelsior Blvd.
Minneapolis 55416

New Jersey
Blue Star Shopping Center
Route 22
Watchung 07060

New York
91 N. Sawmill River Rd.
Elmsford 10523

Ohio
819 West Market St.
Akron 44303

Washington
140 105th St. N.E.
Bellevue 98004

Recipe Index: English

NOTE: An R preceding a page refers to the Recipe Booklet. Size, weight and material are specified for pans in the recipes because they affect cooking results. A pan should be just large enough to hold its contents comfortably. Heavy pans heat slowly and cook food at a constant rate. Aluminum and cast iron conduct heat well but may discolor foods containing egg yolks, wine, vinegar or lemon. Enamelware is a fairly poor conductor of heat. Many recipes therefore recommend stainless steel or enameled cast iron, which do not have these faults.

Recipe Index: Foreign

General Index

Numerals in italics indicate a photograph or drawing of the subject mentioned.

Credits and Acknowledgments

The sources for the illustrations that appear in this book are shown below. Credits for pictures from left to right are separated by commas, from top to bottom by dashes.

Cover and photographs by Richard Meek except: 4—Ron D'Asaro, Walter Daran—Sal Fragliossi for SPORTS ILLUSTRATED, Mark Kauffman. 6—Lewis W. Hine courtesy the George Eastman House. 12, 13—Steven C. Wilson. 30, 31— George Haling. 34, 35—Ted Streshinsky. 38—Bob Peterson. 40—top Bob Peterson. 58—Enrico Ferorelli. 80, 81—Fred Schnell. 96, 97—Charles Harbutt from Magnum. 107—Richard Jeffery. 111—Richard Jeffery. 153, 156-159 —Costa Manos from Magnum. 163—Ted Streshinsky. 164, 165 —Fred Lyon from Rapho Guillumette. 166, 167—Ted Streshinsky. 172, 173—Ted Streshinsky. 175—Mark Kauffman. 178—Charles Harbutt from Magnum. 182, 183—Charles Harbutt from Magnum. 186, 187—George Haling. 208—Ann Meuer, Richard Meek, Robert Mason, Ben Martin for TIME.

Olga Gandara and Esther Isaacs of New York City contributed some of the recipes in this book, and assisted in testing them in the FOODS OF THE WORLD test kitchen.

For assistance and advice in the production of this book, the editors and staff extend their thanks to the following: *in California:* G. Armanino & Son, Inc.; Richard Ashton, Armenian General Benevolent Union of America; Prof. Arra Avakian, Fresno State College; H. S. Barsam, California Sun Dry Bulgur Co.; Mr. and Mrs. Edward Garry; George M. Mardikian; Robert Mondavi, Robert Mondavi Winery; Leo Pearlstein, Lee & Associates, Inc.; Mr. and Mrs. Mard Peloian; Sam Saghatelian, The Valley Bakery; Cynthia Scheer; *in Connecticut:* Mr. and Mrs. Paul Kowalsky; *in Florida:* The Rev. Fr. and Mrs. Elias Kalariotes; Louis Pappas' Riverside Café; *in Idaho:* Espe Alegria; Peggy Bleck; The Hon. Peter Cenarrusa; Clarine Villeneuve; *in Illinois:* Mr. and Mrs. Stanley P. Balzekas Jr.; Mr. Roy Berg; Edward Robert Brooks; Josephine J. Dauzvardis; Camille Jilke, *Chicago Sun-Times;* Antanas Mackevicius; Chester F. Mikolajczyk; Helen C. Pius; George Weiss, Alliance Bakery Shop; William Wright; Alfreda Zukowski, The People's Gas, Light and Coke Co.; *in Iowa:* John A. Kuba; *in Minnesota:* Josepha Contoski; *in Nebraska:* Warren Spencer, Nebraska Game Commission; Glenn Zajicek; *in Nevada:* Prof. William A. Douglass, University of Nevada; *in New Jersey:* Dorothy Esposito; The Rev. and Mrs. Andrew Hamza; The Rev. and Mrs. Joseph Kecskemethy; The B. Manischewitz Co.; Lillian Shenton; John Siranka, Slovak Catholic Sokol; Rafael Steinberg; *in New York City:* Fumie Adachi, The Japan Society; Elsa Arcelay; Carmen Gloria Baba; Mr. and Mrs. Harry Bialick; Jadwiga Daniec; Mr. and Mrs. Benjamin Finkelstein; Isaac Gellis, Inc.; Max Geltman; Greek Press and Information Service; Desa Hess; Jewish Theological Seminary Library; Joseph C. Landolt; George E. Lang; Domenick Lassandro, Park Avenue Enclosed Market Association, Inc.; Florence Lin; Fr. Juan P. Magunagoicoechea; Roman Makarenko; Meyer Mazza; Haigaz K. Mekhalian, Armenian General Benevolent Union of America; Rosetta Metes, Rumanian National Committee; Milan Laboratories; Joseph Monserrat; Manuel Otero; Mr. and Mrs. Ulf Pacher; Federico Perez; Dr. Efren Ramirez; Anna Rosenblum; Donna Schachter; Shun Lee Dynasty Restaurant; Trader Vic's Restaurant; W & B Bagels; Edward Weiss, Paprikás Weiss Importer; Zabar's Gourmet Foods; *in New York State:* The Grossinger Hotel and Country Club; *in Ohio:* The Rev. Gabor Brachna; Paula C. Constantinidis; Anne Erste; Zoltan Gombos; The Rev. Fr. and Mrs. Vasile Hategan; William Koteles; Larisa Lucaci; *in Pennsylvania:* Jean Strong; *in Texas:* Mr. and Mrs. Rodolph Smith; Mr. and Mrs. Fritz Stieler; *in Wisconsin:* Rosa Tusa, *Milwaukee Sentinel;* Mr. and Mrs. Alex Szolwinski; Kyril Vassilev; Edwin M. Wasilewski, Rams Head Inn; *in Winnipeg, Manitoba:* Dr. Simon Kalba, Ukrainian Canadian Committee; Nadya Kostyshyn; Manitoba Department of Tourism, Recreation and Cultural Affairs, W. E. Organ and Archie MacKinnon.

The following shops, firms and institutions supplied antiques, tableware and other objects used in the studio photography in this book: *in Massachusetts:* Richard Faber, Antiques, Boston; *in New York City:* Ann-Morris, Antiques; David Barrett, Antiques; Ruth Berk, Antiques; Iris Brown, Antiques; Mario Buccellati, Inc.; Connoisseur East; George Cothran, Flowers; Decorative Re-Sale, Inc.; Ginori Fifth Avenue; Globe-Trotter Antiques; Charles R. Gracie & Sons, Inc.; The House of Hite, Antiques; The Jewish Museum; H. J. Kratzer, Inc., Antiques; Mayhew, Home Furnishings; Patina Antiques; Gilbert Pelham, Antiques; Putting Antiques Corporation; Scalamandrè Silks, Inc.; The Rev. and Mrs. Joseph Sebold; 1066 A.D., Ltd.; Dorothy Thall, Antiques; John Walker, Antiques; *in Pennsylvania:* Knorrwood Antiques, Gettysburg.

Sources consulted in the production of this book include: *America's Polish Heritage,* Joseph A. Wyrtwal; *The Art of Jewish Cooking,* Jennie Grossinger; *A Basque Story Cook Book,* Ann Rogers; *Beyond the Melting Pot,* Nathan Glazer and Daniel P. Moynihan; *Chinatown, U.S.A.,* Calvin Lee; *Chinese in American Life,* by S. W. Kung; *The Cuisine of Hungary,* George E. Lang; *Everything but Money,* Sam Levenson; *Favorite Recipes of the Nebraska Czechs,* the Nebraska Czechs of Wilber; *Favorite Recipes of Z.C.B.J. Drill Team,* Cedar Rapids, Iowa; *From Many Lands,* Louis Adamic; *Guide for the Jewish Homemaker,* Shonie B. Levi and Sylvia R. Kaplan; *High Road to Promontory,* George Kraus; *Hungarian Cuisine,* Hungarian Evangelical and Reformed Church, Dayton, Ohio; *Japanese Americans,* Harry H. I. Kitano; *Leone's Italian Cookbook,* Gene Leone; *The Lower East Side,* Allon Schoener, ed.; *Nisei, the Quiet Americans,* Bill Hosokawa; *One America,* Francis J. Brown and Joseph S. Roucek, eds.; *Our Own Fare, Croatian-American Cook Book,* Sacred Heart Ladies Council, Milwaukee, Wisconsin; *The Jewish Festival Cookbook,* Fannie Engle and Gertrude Blair; *Life Is with People,* Mark Zborowski and Elizabeth Herzog; *Pigtails and Gold Dust,* Alexander McLeod; *Poftă Bună, the Romanian Way of Cooking,* St. Mary's Romanian Orthodox Church, Cleveland, Ohio; *Popular Lithuanian Recipes,* Josephine S. Dauzvardis; *Puerto Rican Dishes,* Berta Cabanillas and Carmen Ginorio; *The Romanian Cook Book,* Anisoara Stan; *Serbian Cookery,* Serbian Sisters Ravanica, Detroit, Michigan; *Spaghetti Dinner,* Giuseppe Prezzolini; *The Puerto Ricans,* Christopher Rand; *Traditional Ukrainian Cookery,* Savella Stechisin; *Treasured Armenian Recipes,* Detroit Women's Chapter, Armenian General Benevolent Union; *Treasured Polish Recipes for Americans,* Polanie Club, Minneapolis, Minnesota; *A Treasury of Jewish Folklore,* Nathan Ausubel, ed.; *The Ukrainian Canadians,* Michael H. Marunchak; *The Unprejudiced Palate,* Angelo M. Pellegrini; *The Uprooted,* Oscar Handlin; *We Who Built America,* Carl Wittke.

JAMES P. SHENTON   ANGELO M. PELLEGRINI   DALE BROWN   ISRAEL SHENKER   PETER WOOD

Six chapters of this book were written by these five authors (Dale Brown, center, wrote Chapters 3 and 4). Brief biographies appear on the opening pages of the chapters.

X Printed in U.S.A.